Travel Medicine
A Handbook for Practitioners

To my Friends and Colleagues of
the Medical Unit,
Hospital for Tropical Diseases, London
whose constant help
has made this book possible

by the same author

The Traveller's Health Guide

(Published by Tom Stacey Limited)

Travel Medicine

A Handbook for Practitioners

Anthony C. Turner
MRCS LRCP DRCOG AFRAeS
Senior Overseas Medical Officer
British Airways Medical Service
Honorary Associate Physician
and Visiting Lecturer
Hospital for Tropical Diseases, London

Foreword by
Alan Woodruff
Wellcome Professor of Clinical
Tropical Medicine in the University
of London

CHURCHILL LIVINGSTONE
EDINBURGH LONDON AND NEW YORK 1975

CHURCHILL LIVINGSTONE
Medical Division of Longman Group Limited

Distributed in the United States of America by Longman Incorporated, New York, and by associated companies, branches and representatives throughout the world.

ISBN 0 443 01164 8

Library of Congress Cataloging in Publication Data

Turner, Anthony Chalmers, 1918-

TRAVEL MEDICINE: A Handbook for Practitioners.

Bibliography: p.
Includes index.
1. Travel—Hygienic aspects. 2. Tropics—Diseases and hygiene. I. Title. [DNLM: 1. Hygiene—Popular works. 2. Travel—Popular works. 2. Travel—Popular works.
QT250 T944ta]
RA783.5.T86 616.9'88'3 75-8547

Printed in Great Britain

Foreword

One of the really important changes which has taken place in society within recent years has been the development of short term travel. As a result of this, hundreds of millions of the world's population are now travelling long distances each year whereas formerly such travellers could be numbered in thousands. Dr Turner reports that more than 400 million people now travel annually on international air routes, i.e. the number of those crossing international frontiers each year is approximately equivalent to half the earth's population. This travel on an unprecedented scale gives rise to many medical problems in addition to those within the economic and social fields. Medically, the important factor is that diseases endemic in one area may present in another area where physicians are unfamiliar with the illness confronting them. This factor is aggravated by the speed of air travel whereby those infected with diseases of short incubation period may be carried great distances during this incubation period. This leads to diseases such as malaria and dysentery making their first appearance far from their source of origin, whereas in days of sea travel those infected would either have developed their disease on board ship and been treated by the ship's doctor familiar with tropical infections, or have been put ashore at a port not far from the tropics and in which physicians were familiar with tropically acquired diseases.

All this means that physicians in the modern world must be familiar with diseases contracted in the whole of the world for otherwise the number of tragedies resulting from overlooked tropical diseases will steadily increase with the numbers of the travelling public. Already deaths from overlooked malaria, amoebic and other infections are not uncommon in temperate regions.

No one is more alive to this situation than Dr Turner who for years has been dealing with problems of travel medicine by virtue of his post with British Airways. He has realised the need for increasing the familiarity with tropical diseases on the part of doctors in temperate regions and he is to be congratulated on having the energy and foresight in putting his knowledge and experience into book form. The need for such a book is undoubted and it is certain to serve a very valuable function, and thereby to save lives. He has written in a light and attractive way which makes reading easy and into his writing he has incorporated a vast amount of common sense and great thought.

1975

A. W. Woodruff

Preface

Over 400 million people, both businessmen and holidaymakers, now travel by air every year on international routes. Thus the question of imported disease on the traveller's return has become a major issue.

Those visiting the tropics and sub tropics may contact and contract what are known as the tropical diseases. Whether they should be so called is a matter of opinion and it is important that the practitioner realises that these diseases are not confined to the tropics.

Prior to the days of air travel, these diseases usually developed on the return journey by ship. The problem of diagnosis was that of the ship's surgeon, not the GP in temperate climates, and when necessary the patient was admitted to hospital on arrival.

In the United Kingdom, National Service finished approximately 12 years ago, so the younger members of the medical profession have not had this opportunity of seeing tropical diseases. However, many of the younger practitioners in the United States and some from Australia have had experience in Vietnam. At this time modern travel makes it all the more important for every doctor to know the basic problems of imported diseases.

The purpose of this book is, therefore, twofold. Firstly to inform the GP of advice he can give his patients before they travel—the advances in preventive medicine with regard to tropical diseases have probably been greater than in any other branch of medicine. Secondly to help the GP in his differential diagnosis of these exotic diseases. It is not intended to act as a complete textbook of tropical medicine, and there is, therefore, minimal reference to pathology. This is discussed where it is essential to understand the process of the disease or the cycle of the parasite. The most important point is for the GP to recognise the problem and then pass the patient on to the specialist experienced in tropical diseases.

If the condition can be treated at home, full details of treatment are given. If hospitalisation is necessary, then only sufficient detail is given to enable the GP to keep relatives in the picture.

Travel writers and organisers of package tours are loathe to admit the occurrence of malaria in many popular sunspots, for example, most North African resorts. Even when the existence of malaria is recognised and the taking of an antimalarial advised, frequently it is not mentioned that it should be continued for 28 days after leaving the area.

In the United Kingdom there are approximately 500 notified cases of imported malaria every year. Approximately one half are of the malignant or falciparum type. Of these, 90 per cent come from Africa, and the deaths last year ran into double figures. Firstly, because these travellers were not advised adequately about the taking of antimalarials, and secondly, some deaths were due to late diagnosis leading to disastrous delay in treatment.

The commonest illnesses contracted in travel are intestinal infections. Other insect-borne illnesses are also discussed. Rarities are not mentioned other than perhaps in passing.

Simple prophylaxis against these infections is discussed, also prevention of problems caused by a change of climate. The basis for various ideas on prevention which the writer, with colleagues, has researched, is explained.

The GP must be ready to ask his patient where he has been if there is anything in his illness which cannot be immediately explained. If the patient has been abroad, the GP must consider how far to investigate prior to calling in a consultant.

It is generally considered that the most essential tests are a full blood count with thick and thin films, plus an eosinophil count and an erythrocyte sedimentation rate; preferably three stool tests and a chest X-ray.

Thick and thin films will show a malarial infection if present and an eosinophil count is usually pathologically raised in the presence of any parasitic infection in the invasive stage.

The opinions expressed in this book are those of the author and are not necessarily those of the British Airways Medical Service.

London, 1975 *A.C.T.*

Acknowledgements

My thanks are due to many helpers and supporters, in particular to Professor Alan Woodruff, Wellcome Professor of Clinical Tropical Medicine in the University of London. Without his constant support and encouragement for many years this book and other writings would not have been possible. In addition he has kindly written a foreword for which I am most grateful. Secondly, to my colleague, Doctor Roger Green, for so kindly writing the chapter on Fitness to Travel by Air. Doctor Green is a world authority on this subject, having been responsible for the selection for carriage of all invalids on British Airways for several years. He also has kindly read the proofs. Thanks are also due to Professor George Dick, one time Director of the Bland Sutton Institute, for his interest in and support of the chapter on Immunisation; Doctor Peter Oliver, Medical Director of Cunard Steamship Company, for advice on sea travel; Doctor J. Graham Taylor, Director, British Airways Medical Service, for permission to publish; my publishers, Churchill Livingstone, for their help and support, and in particular, Doctor William Thomson; Tom Stacey Limited, publishers of *The Traveller's Health Guide* from which I have taken subject matter; World Health Organisation for permission to use their maps and information from their epidemiological reviews; also all the various authors whose work I have quoted and whom, I most sincerely hope, I have acknowledged in the bibliography on every occasion (any omission is purely accidental and for which, if so, I apologise); my secretary, Miss Sandi Hobbs, and Mrs Margaret Hunter for their stoic work in typing out the entire manuscript in their free time and retyping when necessary; and last, but by no means least, to my wife for her constant support and encouragement and for enduring me when I have spent my weekends writing.

Contents

Foreword v
Preface vii
Acknowledgements ix

Part 1 Pre-Travel Advice

CHAPTER 1 Pre-Travel Immunisation 3
2 Pre-Travel and In-Travel Advice 23
3 Climate and Acclimatisation; Prevention of Heat Disorders 37
4 Diseases of Insanitation 51
5 Insect Borne Diseases 61
6 Direct Contact Problems, Bites and Stings 73

Part 2 Post-Travel Symptomatology

7 Post-Travel Problems and Heat Disorders 83
8 Fevers 93
9 Alimentary and Urinary Tract Infections 107
10 Skin Problems, Bites, Stings and Venereal Diseases 127
11 Other Infections, Both Parasitic and Non-Parasitic 143
12 Fitness to Travel by Air *by Dr Roger L. Green* 153
13 Medical Assessment for Living in Warm Climates 161

Appendices

A Vaccination Requirements for, and Climate of, Various Countries 173
B Yellow Fever Vaccination Centres 207
C Admitted Malarious Areas 221
D Overseas Medical Costs 225
E Other Useful Addresses 233
Bibliography 235
Index 241

Part 1

Pre-Travel Advice

1. Pre-Travel Immunisation

Prior to the 1939/45 war the question of immunisation before travel could well have been considered necessary by medical opinion but there were few legal regulations laid down. This presumably was due to the fact that illnesses would basically develop on the ship coming home and then, if it was smallpox, all the rest of the ship's passengers could be vaccinated on an *ad hoc* basis.

As well as this, of course, in the United Kingdom, smallpox vaccination was compulsory up to the arrival of the National Health Service in 1948. Public vaccinators were appointed for every urban and rural district and they used to offer vaccination against smallpox free of charge to all infants. Whether it was a retrogressive step to stop this with post-war travel increasing is a matter of opinion, but more about this later.

Secondly long distance travellers to the Tropics before the war were mainly service personnel, civil servants, and members of large companies, all with their families, who were vaccinated or inoculated by their organisations.

The individual long distance voyager who is very common nowadays was a rarity in those days.

All the same it was unsatisfactory when there were no standard regulations and their appearance was a good thing.

This is especially so when one looks at the state of travel nowadays. With 'jumbo jet' travel three hundred or more people can be deposited all over a country which may vary in size from Belgium to the United States of America. Within a few days of arrival one of them may develop smallpox. What if those three hundred had not been vaccinated? The spread of smallpox could be disastrous.

It was at the International Sanitary Convention under the League of Nations that in 1933 articles were first laid down to prevent spread of disease by air transport. This was replaced in 1944 by the International Sanitary Convention of Aerial Navigation. This in turn was superseded by the International Sanitary Regulations promulgated by the World Health Organisation in 1951. Certain amendments to these regulations were laid down in 1955 and 1956. In 1969 very sensibly these regulations were renamed the International Health Regulations.

Most countries in the world are signatories of these regulations although regrettably there are exceptions. The main non-signatories are Australia and Singapore. India and Pakistan have limitations over the Yellow Fever regulations.

Under these regulations, vaccination against smallpox, cholera and yellow fever is carried out. Smallpox and yellow fever vaccinations are very successful in their prevention of spread of the respective diseases. The efficacy of the cholera vaccine in this regard is a very different proposition. The Surgeon General of the United States Public Health Service, Dr Jessie Steinfeld, at the International Conference on the Application of Vaccines against Viral, Rickettsial, and Bacterial Diseases of Man, in Washington in December 1970, put to action the thoughts of many of us when he ruled that inoculation against cholera was not necessary for people entering the United States from cholera infected countries. Cholera is spread by lack of hygiene, especially in food handling, and by faecal contamination. Inoculation is of no value in preventing spread of the disease across frontiers. In the very recent outbreak of cholera in Bahrain, two passengers arrived in U.K. with positive stools and forty-three arrived in Australia. However, there were no second generation cases in the U.K. or Australia. This was in fact due to satisfactory public health services in the U.K. and Australia.

Pre-travel inoculations or vaccinations can therefore be divided into two basic groups:

1. Those which are statutorily required by the International Health Regulations and without which a passenger cannot travel to particular places. The only exception to this is if for some reason, a registered medical practitioner considers that the said vaccination or inoculation is medically contraindicated for the passenger in question. Then he can give a medical certificate on headed paper stating the reasons. This certificate must be duly authorised by the local public health authority: as such it is accepted in general by all signatories of the International Health Regulations. However, Australia, who is a non-signatory, prior to November 1974 would not accept such a certificate, and if the passenger refused to be vaccinated then he or she was put into quarantine at his or her expense, which was quite costly. Even now if the passenger has travelled from a country in which there has been smallpox in the last year they will still not accept a medical certificate. In addition the airline may be heavily fined; hence their reluctance to carry such passengers.

What has also to be remembered is that an official International Health Regulations certificate must be used when vaccination is carried out. It is quite valueless writing on headed paper that so-and-so has been vaccinated. It only causes great discomfiture to the passenger.

2. Those which are medically recommended but are not statutorily required.

And so to discuss Group 1 first:

Smallpox

It was in 1798 that Edward Jenner first published his paper on the benefits of vaccination, following the old tradition then established in

(*Map by courtesy of World Health Organisation.*)

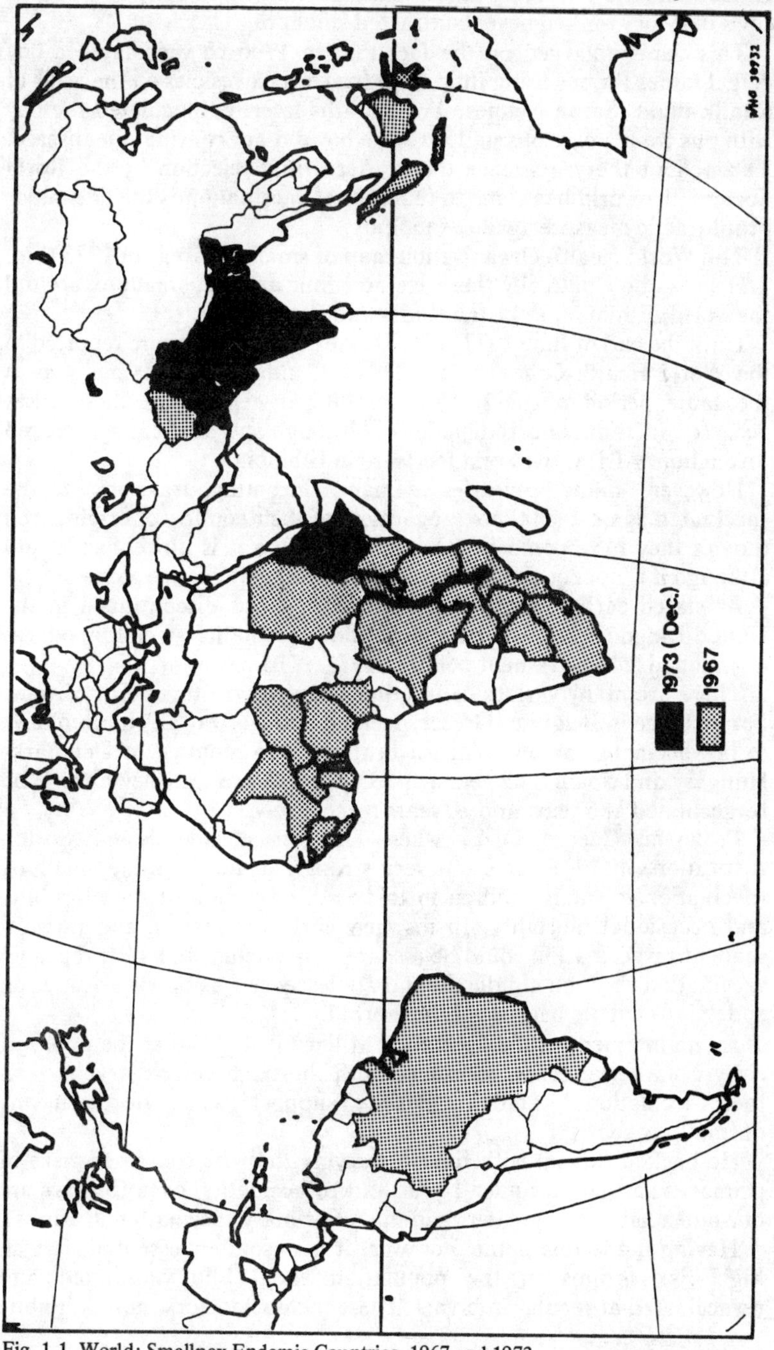

Fig. 1.1 World; Smallpox Endemic Countries, 1967 and 1973

Gloucestershire that dairy maids who had contracted cowpox from the cows that they milked never contracted smallpox.

This paper followed on the fact that in 1796 he vaccinated a boy called James Phipps using fluid from the cowpox vesicles on the arms of a milk maid, Sarah Nelmes. Two months later he inoculated the boy with pus from a case of smallpox. The boy did not contract the disease. Throughout the years since then, after initial rejection by the Royal Society, the world has come to realise that vaccination is the one major prophylactic measure against smallpox.

The World Health Organisation map of smallpox areas in 1973 (Fig. 1.1) shows how basically there are now four areas of smallpox around the world; Ethiopia, Pakistan, India and Bangladesh.

Until the end of June 1973, 78,000 cases of smallpox were reported to the World Health Organisation. This was almost twice as many as in the same period of 1972. However 88 per cent of all these cases occurred in India and Bangladesh. Although sporadic cases occurred throughout Africa, the worst foci were in Ethiopia.

However, many countries demand incoming travellers to be vaccinated against smallpox, regardless of their country of origin, even though they have come from a country where it is not endemic and although it is not endemic in the country to which they are going.

As stated earlier, compulsory vaccination was discontinued in the United Kingdom in 1948. Further routine vaccination in childhood was abandoned as Government policy in 1971.

There are many variations in other countries on this point of view. For instance in Belgium, Greece, Iceland and Norway all children have to be vaccinated by one year; in France by 15 months; in Denmark, Hungary and Spain by 2 years. In Greece and France, they have to be revaccinated at 6 years and 10 years respectively.

Professor George Dick, when Director of the Bland Sutton Institution, in 1971 came out very strongly against routine smallpox vaccination in small children in this country in view of the morbidity and occasional mortality. In his view early vaccination and no subsequent revaccination could be a snare and a delusion, whilst repeated vaccination through childhood and adolescence was only warranted in endemic countries because of the morbidity.

He maintained, as did C. Killick Millard in 1924, that the policy of early isolation of cases, combined with thorough contact tracing and their vaccination, has much evidence to support it as an effective means of smallpox control.

He backed this up with figures showing that the combined risks of primary vaccination under 1 year and revaccination over 15 years are one and a half times greater than that of primary vaccination in adults.

Having made this point, however, it is absolutely essential that all high risk groups in the population should be vaccinated and revaccinated at regular intervals. These include doctors, nurses, public health workers and other hospital staff, such as domestic workers, kitchen workers and laundry staff. As well as this one should include all airline and airport staff who come in contact in any way with passengers and passengers' fomites.

However, it is a very different problem for the traveller. Regrettably, as mentioned previously, whether the traveller has come from, or is going to, an endemic area does not necessarily matter. If the immigration authorities of the country in question demand a smallpox vaccination then the traveller has to have it.

Into the bargain most regrettably, many countries do not even lay down a lower age limit and infants have to be vaccinated from birth. There is nothing that can be done about it as many of these countries demand to see the completed vaccination certificate before they will grant an entry visa.

Professor Dick recommends that one should not be vaccinated against smallpox in Britain until one wishes to travel to a country which demands it.

Regrettably there can be administrative problems with this policy. Not everyone has a lot of notice of a need to travel. If someone is given a primary vaccination by their own doctor when he also needs a yellow fever vaccination then the special clinic which can give yellow fever vaccination cannot give it until all signs of the primary vaccination reaction have disappeared which can be up to 4 weeks. Even if yellow fever vaccination is not necessary the patient can feel far from well from about 5 days after the primary vaccination up to about two weeks.

What must be remembered is that whenever possible all vaccinations and inoculations must be given very well in advance of travel.

What are the contraindications to smallpox vaccination for medical reasons? The World Health Organisation laid them down quite clearly in their Weekly Epidemiological Review of 23 March 1973:

> 'As with the administration of any vaccine, there is a small risk of complications following smallpox vaccination. The risk may be greater among those with particular disease problems or who are receiving specific therapy. However, the risk of complications following vaccination must be carefully weighed against the risk of acquiring smallpox and thus the decision as to whether or not vaccination should be performed, must be carefully evaluated according to the epidemiological circumstances.'

In November 1971, questions in regard to possible contraindications to vaccination were carefully assessed by the W.H.O. Expert Committee on Smallpox. The following observations are taken from the report prepared by the Committee:

'1. *Contraindications in endemic regions:*

In endemic regions, the risk of acquiring smallpox far exceeds the danger of vaccination complications. Whereas the eczematous individual is at increased risk from vaccination, the risks from smallpox as well as from accidental contact inoculation with vaccinia are greater.

This eczema should not be considered as a contraindication to vaccination in endemic areas. Pregnancy also is not a contraindication: smallpox is more frequently fatal in pregnant than in non-pregnant women and the risk of complication following vaccination is small.

All travellers to endemic countries should be successfully vaccinated both to protect themselves and to prevent the transfer of smallpox from the endemic country to their own or other countries. Experience has shown that smallpox may spread from one part of an endemic country to another and may not be detected in the new location for periods of from 4 to 8 weeks or even more. Thus, if any part of a country harbours endemic smallpox, the whole of that country should be regarded as possibly infected. Travellers for whom vaccination would normally be contraindicated should, if possible, refrain from travelling to infected countries. If it is essential for them to travel they should be given vaccinia immune globulin at the time of vaccination.

2. *Contraindications in non-endemic regions*

Among the principal complications of vaccination, post-vaccinal encephalitis, generalised vaccinia and auto-inoculation are not associated with identifiable host factors and thus must be accepted as small but definite risks associated with the procedure. Other complications are substantially more frequent among persons with particular characteristics. Thus, in countries where the risk of acquiring smallpox is negligible, the hazards may be reduced if persons with certain conditions are not vaccinated. The following are the most usual contraindications to smallpox vaccination in non-endemic regions:

(a) *Eczema.* The risk of eczema vaccinatum after vaccination of eczematous subjects is unknown, but probably does not exceed 1 per cent. If this complication does arise, the case-fatality-rate is around 1 per cent and the period of disability may be considerable. The risk of severe involvement is greatest in persons with generalised eczema and in eczematous contacts of recently vaccinated persons. No member of the family should be vaccinated unless the person with eczema can be excluded from the household until the vaccination site in the person vaccinated has healed. This precaution applies to families but not to other groups such as school children and industrial workers among whom transmission is less likely to occur.

(b) *Conditions necessitating the use of immunosuppressive drugs glucocorticosteroids or radiation therapy.* The use of these drugs or procedures enhances susceptibility to many infectious agents including vaccinia virus, and progressive vaccinia may follow vaccination.

(c) *Infancy.* In non-endemic regions, vaccination is usually postponed to the second year of life as a higher incidence of complications has been observed among infants vaccinated between the sixth and twelfth months than among those vaccinated during the second year. Comparative data are not available among those vaccinated at birth or within the first few months of life, when maternal antibody is present. This situation is perhaps comparable to the administration of vaccinia immune globulin at the time of vaccination. Therefore the first few months of life may be one of the safest periods for vaccination.

(d) *Deficient immune response syndromes.* Leukaemia, lymphoma, Hodgkin's Disease and related neoplastic diseases. Conditions of these types are associated with a greatly increased susceptibility to the often fatal progressive vaccinia.

(e) *Pregnancy.* Although foetal vaccinia is rare, and other possible complications are not clearly documented, the usual practice regarding pregnant women is to avoid administering live virus vaccines and other procedures that might induce fever. Thus elective vaccination is normally postponed until after the end of pregnancy.

(f) *A history of post-vaccinial encephalitis or other vaccinial complications.* Although there is no documentary evidence to that effect, it is generally believed that persons who have previously had complications attributed to vaccination should not be vaccinated again.

(g) *Other.* Although skin diseases, infections, childhood exanthems (including chickenpox), and a variety of other conditions have been regarded by some as contraindications, none of these conditions appears to increase either the susceptibility to vaccinia virus or the likelihood of complications.'

From all the above let us summarise the problems and pros and cons for smallpox vaccination.

1. Routine smallpox vaccination of infants in non-endemic countries is contraindicated.

2. In endemic countries it should be carried out between the age of 1 and 2 years or younger but to be effective it must be repeated regularly which regrettably with medical facilities as they are in these countries, is impracticable.

3. The complications of primary vaccination in infancy followed by revaccination over the age of 15 years are greater than primary vaccination in adult life.

4. For persons who are travelling to endemic areas or areas where the authorities demand smallpox vaccination it should be carried out as long before travel as possible.

5. If yellow fever is to be given to a traveller as well as smallpox vaccination it is advisable to allow an interval of three weeks between the two procedures, irrespective of which is given first. If this is not feasible the two vaccines may be given at the same time but at different sites. If possible it is better to give the yellow fever vaccination three weeks before the smallpox vaccination.

6. People for whom smallpox vaccination is contraindicated on medical grounds should, if possible, be dissuaded from travelling to endemic areas. If, however, they have to travel, then the risks of smallpox are greater than that of vaccination and as such they must be vaccinated but it is advised that this is done in association with the giving of vaccinia immune globulin at the same time.

7. For the same people as in group 6 travelling to non-endemic areas but where smallpox vaccination is still demanded then they should be given a duly authorised medical certificate of exemption. However, this certificate may not be accepted in Australia, but their attitude is changing (see page 4).

The following conditions are contraindicative to smallpox vaccination: Pregnancy; eczema especially if generalised; leukaemia; lymphoma; Hodgkin's Disease; related neoplastic diseases; treatment with the immunosuppressive drugs and the corticosteroids; radiation therapy; history of post-vaccinial encephalitis or other vaccinial complications; failure to thrive in infancy; hypogammaglobulinaemia.

8. The problem of vaccination in infancy is dependent on the requirements of the country being visited. Many countries do not demand it before the age of one year. Others have no minimum age limit. With the latter it has to be carried out unless the medical practitioner can certify that the baby suffers from infantile eczema or it is failing to thrive.

Appendix A gives a list of the countries where a valid smallpox vaccination certificate is required. It is valid for three years. With a primary vaccination it becomes valid 8 days after the vaccination provided it has been certified that it has been successful by a registered medical practitioner. However some countries insist on 14 days. With revaccination it is valid immediately. This saves the patient having to have it rechecked but it is medically unsatisfactory because no-one knows whether there has been a reaction of immunity or whether in fact it has been a failed vaccination.

Cholera

Cholera has always been looked upon as an infective diarrhoea of India, Pakistan and China. Until recently the causative vibrio of the classical cholera was one of the three strains, Inaba, Ogawa and

Hikojima. However, during recent years the El Tor variant has spread from South East Asia through the usual areas of the classical varieties in the Indian Subcontinent to the Middle East. In 1970 it spread to Southern Russia down through the Balkans and into Saudi Arabia, where it was first isolated in 1919.

From the Arabian Peninsular it was introduced into Ethiopia through the French territory of Djibouti by smugglers crossing the strait of Bab el Mandeb by dhow and then carrying their goods by camel carriers to the interior of Ethiopia. It was spread to Ghana by crews of small fishing boats landing at coastal villages without any health control. From Ethiopia it spread North, West and South until in 1971 it was in North Africa and then briefly spread into Spain.

As such, the need for cholera vaccination for travel has been greatly increased during the last three years. Where in the past it was only necessary for travellers going to the East through Pakistan and India recently it has been necessary for many countries in the Middle East and Africa.

Travellers to Australia via the Eastern route require immunisation against cholera but if they travel through the Americas it is not necessary.

It is not necessary however to have two injections as is usually thought unless the traveller is visiting certain Middle East countries at the time of the Haj Pilgrimage. Iraq and Saudi Arabia are very particular about the two injections. Eslewhere it is only necessary to have one injection, the usual second one. One ml of the standard vaccine subcutaneously or 0.2 ml intradermally.

As mentioned previously the efficacy of cholera vaccine is regrettably open to doubt and the United States have sensibly adopted the right attitude.

At the 26th World Health Assembly held in June 1973 it was recommended that vaccination against cholera shall no longer be required as a condition of admission of any international traveller to any country. However, before this regulation could come into force, member states would have to agree and international legal ratification would have to be laid down. As such the present regulations are continuing until at least 1 January 1975 and probably later, but far fewer countries are now demanding cholera vaccination.

It has further been found that sensitivity to the vaccine may develop. This has been noticed particularly in aircrew who have been inoculated against cholera every six months for over 25 years.

Increasing local and general reaction may occur. When this happens the answer is to give maintenance doses by the intradermal method. Validity is for six months after a six day waiting period.

Yellow Fever

Inoculation against yellow fever is probably the most successful advance in preventive medicine there is. Recent inoculation against yellow fever prevents yellow fever. That is definite.

Fig. I·2 Yellow Fever Areas (shaded)

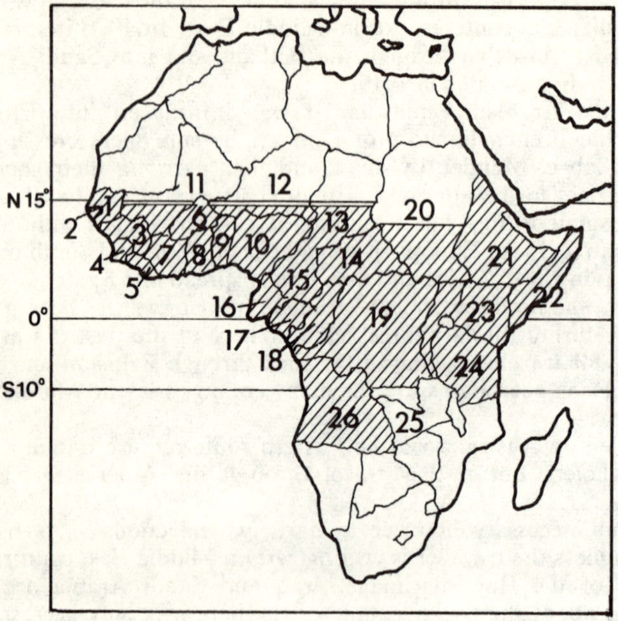

1 Senegal
2 Gambia
3 Guinea
4 Sierra Leone
5 Liberia
6 U. Volta
7 Ivory Coast
8 Ghana
9 Dahomey
10 Nigeria
11 Mali
12 Niger
13 Chad
14 Central African Republic
15 Cameroon
16 Equatorial Guinea
17 Gabon
18 Congo (Brazzaville)
19 Zaire
20 Sudan
21 Ethiopia
22 Somalia
23 Kenya
24 Tanzania
25 Zambia
26 Angola

International ports excluded from endemic area
Massawa
Asmara
Addis Ababa
Djibouti
Berbera
Hargeisha
Mombasa (air and sea)
Nairobi
Kisumu
Assab

(*Maps by courtesy of World Health Organisation.*)

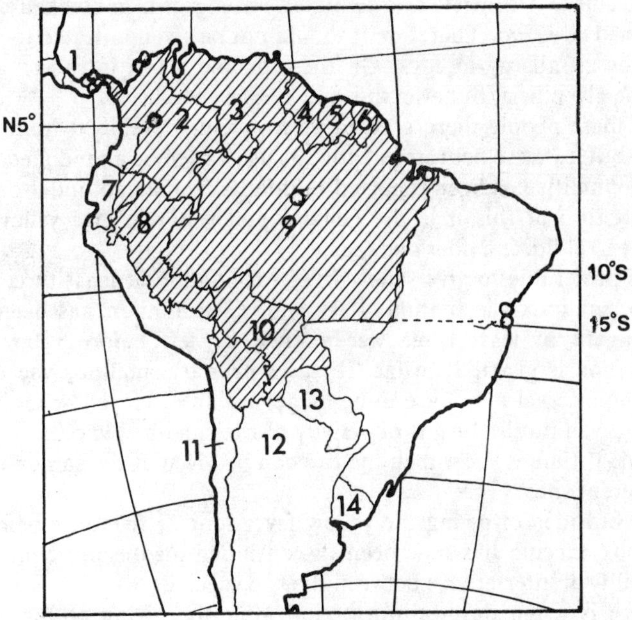

1 Panama	International ports
2 Colombia	excluded from
3 Venezuela	endemic area
4 Guyana	Canal Zone inc.
5 Surinam	Colon
6 Guyane (Fr.)	Panama
7 Ecuador	Cristabal
8 Peru	Balboa
9 Brazil	Barraquilla
10 Bolivia	Bogota
11 Chile	Manaos
12 Argentina	Ilmeus
13 Paraguay	Cartagena
14 Uruguay	Belem
	Itabuna

It is a live vaccine and as such the contraindications are as for other live vaccines. It consists of attenuated virus grown in chicken embryo and dried *in vacuo*. Therefore it should not be given untested to anyone who has an allergy to eggs. On these people a test intradermal dose must be given first, but even this may not be conclusive.

For these people there used to be a vaccine developed from mouse brain, but it was so neurotropic that its use had to be abandoned.

Encephalitis has been reported in infants inoculated under one year and because of this it is the general policy not to give yellow fever vaccine to children under one year.

It is preferable to give yellow fever vaccination at least three weeks before smallpox vaccination. If smallpox vaccination has been given first, again at least three weeks must be left before yellow fever vaccination is given. If in fact it was a primary smallpox vaccination then the interval may have to be longer because the yellow fever must not be given until all signs of activity of the smallpox vaccination have cleared. If time is short then the two can be given at the same time but at different sites.

The old idea of giving the yellow fever four or five days before the smallpox vaccine has now been discontinued on the principle of the possibility of interference between the two vaccines.

There is a ten day waiting period after the giving of the vaccine before the certificate is valid, but it lasts for ten years. As mentioned earlier it is not usually given under the age of one year. There should also be an interval of at least 21 days between yellow fever vaccination and any other vaccination with a live virus such as poliomyelitis.

The giving of yellow fever vaccination should be avoided in pregnancy and should on no account be given to anyone suffering from leukaemia, lymphoma, Hodgkin's Disease and associated neoplastic diseases.

Yellow fever vaccination is required for travellers entering or passing through the two yellow fever belts of Central Africa and Central America. It is never required for people who are purely travelling to Asia without visiting the aforementioned areas.

The actual belts are as follows:

Africa: From 15° North of the Equator to 10° South.

America: From the Northern border of the state of Panama but excluding the canal area, to 15° South of the Equator excluding certain areas of Eastern Brazil (see Fig. 1.2).

Certain ports and airports in these areas are exempted from the belt and transitting in an aircraft does not constitute staying in the yellow fever area under World Health Regulations. However, India and Pakistan do not accept these exempted ports as such and still demand vaccination for the transitting passenger. The exempted international ports excluded from the Endemic Zones are as follows:

Africa: Massawa; Asmara; Addis Ababa; Djibouti; Berberra; Hargeisha; Mombasa (air and sea); Nairobi; Kisumu; Assab.

America: Canal Zone including Colon; Panama; Cristabal; Balboa; Barraquilla; Bogota; Manaos; Ilmeus; Cartagena; Belem; Itabuna.

Yellow fever vaccination can of course only be given at special centres a list of which is included in an appendix at the end of the book.

This therefore covers the vaccinations or inoculations required by International Health Regulations (these are summarised in Table 1.1). However there are in addition several varieties which are recommended to a greater or lesser extent for medical reasons. We will go through this group in turn and assess their need.

Medically recommended immunisations:

Enteric Group of Diseases: Typhoid; Paratyphoid A; Paratyphoid B

For those of us who are old enough to remember the complaints of servicemen concerning 'TAB' in the last war, one wonders as to its usefulness. Luckily one can now dismiss a lot of these stories as ideas of the past. Advances have been made in the preparation and the giving of these vaccines such that side effects can be minimal whilst efficacy is high. Vaccines can be prepared in different ways.

1. Cultures heat killed and phenol preserved.
2. Alcohol killed and alcohol preserved.
3. Acetone inactivated.

The most commonly used vaccine is heat killed and nowadays it is given by intradermal injection. By this method constitutional side effects have been cut to a minimum. The Royal Air Force have done a lot of work on the efficacy of TAB vaccine and they have found that the heat killed variety given intradermally is far the most effective. The efficiency is probably between 70 per cent and 80 per cent. They further found that if inoculations were given on first entering the service at the age of 18 to 20 years and were given regularly from then on until the age of 35 years it was valueless to give any further inoculations because the antibody level was not raised any further. However, this policy is not effective in people who have not been inoculated regularly up to this age. If they have not been inoculated at all or even irregularly then they should be inoculated if they are travelling to enteric areas.

Recently doubt has been cast on the efficiency of the paratyphoid A and paratyphoid B portions of the triple vaccine, TAB, and a monovalent typhoid has been produced. It is fairly definite that TAB vaccine gives little immunity response against paratyphoid B. It does however give a response against paratyphoid A which is a disease occurring mainly in the Balkans and India. Paratyphoid B is common in temperate and subtropical countries rather than tropical countries. Paratyphoid C occurs in the Balkans and Guyana. The writer feels if any immunity is given it is worthwhile.

Table 1.1. Vaccinations required under International Health Regulations

Vaccination	Where required	How long before valid	Length of validity	Minimum age	Other comments
Smallpox	In general everywhere outside Western Europe, U.S.A. and Canada. Always required when arriving from an infected area	Primary vaccination 8 days. Revaccination immediate	3 years	Usually 1 year. However some countries no minimum age limit	Preferably 3 weeks apart from yellow fever. Otherwise at the same time but in different site
Cholera	Always entering and *transitting* Pakistan, India, Burma. Also some other countries in Middle and Far East and since 1970 some countries in Africa (see appendix)	6 days	6 months	Usually 1 year. However some countries no minimum age limit or less than 1 year	A few countries require 2 injections at 1 week interval (see appendix)
Yellow Fever	Central Africa 15°N to 10°S. Central America, northern border of Panama State to 15°S but including Bolivia and excluding part of eastern Brazil and Panama Canal	10 days	10 years	Usually 1 year. A few countries have have no minimum age limit or less than 1 year	Preferably 3 weeks apart from smallpox. Otherwise at the same time but in different site

The other complaint against TAB is that the side effects are far more prevalent than with the monovalent typhoid inoculation. This is so if the vaccine is given subcutaneously as of yester year but as already stated if given intradermally general reactions are very rare. Only a local reaction which is usually limited to a little irritation occurs. The writer therefore feels this argument for monovalent typhoid does not hold good.

The third reason, which is a very important one for giving TAB rather than monovalent typhoid is that TAB is put up in a combined vaccine with tetanus whilst as yet, in the United Kingdom, there is no monovalent typhoid with tetanus. This seems to be a very great pity.

It is even more important to the traveller to be inoculated against tetanus than for the resident of the U.K. The giving of TABT to the traveller who has never had a course of tetanus is therefore an excellent idea. Further, booster doses of TABT will maintain the immunity in people who have already had their TAB and tetanus separately. However some authorities consider every 3 years is too frequent for tetanus toxoid.

From this one can see that the writer's view is for TAB rather than the monovalent typhoid for the positive reasons that it gives a wide spread of immunity and it can be given with tetanus. Further the contraindication because of its side effects can be rendered invalid.

As far as its need is concerned, it should be given to everyone travelling to anywhere outside North West Europe, Canada and the North Eastern States of the U.S.A. It should certainly be given to all holidaymakers around the Mediterranean, in particular to campers.

Given intradermally either as TAB or TABT a first dose followed 4-6 weeks later with a second dose, with a third dose 6-12 months later. A booster dose should be given every three years with the limitations as discussed previously.

For people going on a two to three week holiday in a vulnerable area it is far better to give one dose before going rather than none at all. The old idea that there was a temporary decrease in immunity after one dose is now known to be nonsense. A fair immunity of fairly short duration is provided which, if given shortly before going, would cover the holiday. However, the second dose should be given on return and the course completed as usual for immune response to be maintained.

Tetanus

As mentioned in the previous section it is even more important for the traveller to be suitably inoculated against tetanus than it is for the person who never leaves the shores of the United Kingdom, the United States or Australia. Although a worldwide disease it is commoner in the subtropics and tropics. What must be further remembered is that when people are travelling they are less likely to take their minor cuts to a doctor or the local hospital for satisfactory attention. They will tend to deal with them themselves. As such it is all the more essential that they are fully up to date with complete and adequate tetanus inoculation.

Poliomyelitis

Poliomyelitis is basically a disease of warm climates. Those of us who served in the medical forces in India in the Second World War saw what a scourge it could be. Because of the excellent campaign of poliomyelitis vaccination which has been carried out in countries like the United Kingdom, the United States and Australia over the last 15 years or so, we tend to forget what a problem it is in the developing countries. As such it is absolutely essential for the general practitioner to ensure that the traveller remains adequately protected with a booster dose at least every five years.

Gregory and Spalding, writing recently in the *Lancet* from the Respiratory Unit in Oxford, quoted two cases of businessmen who had contracted poliomyelitis whilst on brief business tours to the tropics. They were both over thirty years of age and both are in artificial respirators for the rest of their lives. They further went on to say that although we look upon poliomyelitis as a disease of children and young people, as the old name of infantile paralysis infers, it can strike later in life. Further, and most important, when it does strike later in life it is more likely to be severe and so affect the respiratory system.

Hence it is very important to ensure that all travellers to warm climates whatever their age, are adequately vaccinated against poliomyelitis with booster doses at certainly no more than 5 year intervals.

Diphtheria

Diphtheria is a disease almost unknown nowadays in the developed countries because of the excellent immunisation programmes which have been been in action for over 35 years. Although it tends to attack children rather than adults the latter are not exempt. In the developing countries where there have not been satisfactory immunisation programmes the disease still exists and there can be epidemics, the occurrence of which the traveller knows nothing. Hence they may be caught up in the onrush and, if of the older age group whose childhood was prior to immunisation programmes, then he or she may be virgin soil for the Klebs Loeffler Bacillus. This type of infection can occur throughout Africa, the Middle East and the Indian subcontinent. Nepal is a country where diphtheria is particularly prevalent.

Diphtheria immunisation must therefore be seriously considered for travellers to these areas especially if a Schick test shows absence of immunity.

Plague

Inoculation against plague is not often recommended in the United Kingdom although it is frequently recommended in the United States of America. The reaction to the inoculation can be fairly severe, both generally and locally, and this is the reason why it is only recommended in the United Kingdom to people who are going to areas where plague is likely to be found. It is not recommended to people merely as a routine. It does in fact give a fairly good immune response. Two injections should be given at 10-20 days intervals, with a third one six months later. The validity is six months and it is not advised under one year of age. Because of the reaction it is inadvisable to give it at the same time as TAB and/or typhus. It is advisable for travellers to Vietnam, Laos, Khmer Republic and Ethiopia. Possibly for Pakistan and India but essential for 'overlanders' to India.

Typhus

Typhus inoculation comes very much in the same category as plague. It is far more popular with the Americans than with the British. Active immunisation affords some protection against louse-borne and flea-borne infections. Again reaction can be severe and the immune response is variable. As such it is only recommended to people going to areas of particular concern such as Vietnam, Laos, Khmer Republic and Ethiopia with again the possibility of India and Pakistan but strongly advisable for 'over-landers' to India. Two injections are required at seven to ten day intervals with a third six months later. Booster injections are required annually. Again it is recommended that it is not given at the same time as TAB and plague.

Rabies

The case of rabies in a dog in Camberley in 1969 caused, with very good reason, great concern to the community in Great Britain. There had not been a case in the United Kingdom in a dog, other than in quarantine, since quarantine had been started over 50 years ago. This shows the efficacy of six months quarantine for dogs entering this country and the absolute need to keep this quarantine at six months, despite the moves made by various people described as dog lovers who wish to cut the time to less than six months. The question of whether prophylactic vaccination against rabies should be given is a matter of great dispute. It has not in general been recommended in this country to overseas travellers. What is a definite fact is that even if a person has been subjected to the whole course of prophylactic vaccination, on being subsequently bitten by a possibly rabid animal, he has to have the antiserum followed by the full course of vaccine. As such it is very questionable whether it is wise to have a routine course of vaccine prior to travel with its possible severe side effects.

The writer thinks the fair answer to this, as suggested by the Canadians, is that any one who is in any way acting as a veterinarian or with veterinarians, should have prophylactic vaccine. With this course three doses of 1.0 ml duck embryo vaccine is given all in the same arm and at intervals of one week followed six months later by a booster dose. This course is considered to give immune bodies in the serum of 95-100 per cent of cases. Revaccination at 2 yearly intervals is recommended for people at special risk such as veterinarians.

As previously mentioned, the World Health Organisation recommends that if a vaccinated person is subsequently bitten by a possibly rabid animal they then should still have a full course of vaccine preceded by serum treatment (see page 150).

Gamma Globulin for Infective Hepatitis

This is one of the inoculations about which there remains constant discussion, if not argument, as to its efficacy and efficiency. The principal route of dissemination of viral hepatitis is by faecal contamination although the possibility of droplet infection has not been entirely excluded. In all parts of the world where standards of hygiene, including food handling and sewage disposal, are low, sporadic cases and epidemics are bound to occur. Because of this we are not surprised at its high incidence in developing countries. West Africa, Central Africa, Egypt, India and Pakistan are areas where it can be a great problem.

How effective is the giving of an injection of gamma globulin in the prevention of this unpleasantly debilitating disease which can be fatal?

Woodson and Clinton in 1969 reported a trial they had carried out in giving gamma globulin to American Peace Corps volunteers. Each patient was scheduled to be given a dose of 0.1 millilitres per kilogramme body weight on a semi-annual basis. The first injection was given just before leaving the United States for overseas service. The time of any subsequent attack of icteric hepatitis was related to the time of the injection. Ninety three persons subsequently developed infective hepatitis but sixteen were within two weeks of injection. As the incubation period for this illness is usually at least 30 days they were dismissed from the survey as probably having been half way through the incubation period before being inoculated ineffectively. Of the remaining 77 only 17 cases occurred in the first 4 months and 60 cases occurred after 4 months of which 31 were in the fifth and sixth months, whilst 29 occurred after six months in people who had failed to have their second injection after six months. The most interesting point was that the survey was divided into eight geographical regions and the incidence of the cases chronologically was the same in each area so giving strong support to any view that the findings were valid and that the protection from gamma globulin lasted only about 4 months.

Similar to Woodson and Clinton's work with the American Peace Corps, Pollock and Reid carried out a survey with the United Kingdom Voluntary Service Overseas who are a similar group of volunteers, young people of both sexes, mainly after leaving school or university, who elect to go out to the developing countries and help either with teaching or other professional or semi-professional occupations.

In this survey, 1,079 persons were each given 750 mgm of immunoglobulin to protect them against infective hepatitis whilst working abroad. Only one case of the disease developed during the first seven months after the inoculation and this case occurred in the first week and hence should be discarded as having been infected well prior to the inoculation.

Among 942 recruits who did not receive immunoglobulin infective hepatitis began to occur during their second month abroad. Ultimately the incidence of infective hepatitis was similar in inoculated and uninoculated recruits.

The findings therefore suggested that a single dose of immunoglobulin gave protection for about 6 months.

From these two trials it is obvious that immuno gamma globulin is very effective for preventing infective hepatitis for a comparatively short period of 4-6 months. If protection is to be maintained then repeat injections must be given at 4-6 month intervals. However it must not be given within two weeks of any live vaccine.

What then is the value of giving immuno gamma globulin for the prevention of infective hepatitis? The writer thinks it should be given to the comparatively short term business traveller to highly endemic areas as mentioned above. The giving of it as a routine four monthly injection to the permanent resident is very much open to question.

Table 1.2. Medically recommended immunisations

Inoculation	Where advised	Course programme	Validity	Minimum age advised	Other comments
Typhoid Paratyphoid (TAB)	Everywhere except Northern Europe	Intradermal injection. 4-6 weeks between 1st and 2nd, 6-12 months between 2nd and 3rd	Booster injection every 3 years	2 years	Can be combined with tetanus as TABT
Tetanus	Everywhere	Frequency as above but subcutaneously. Combined with TAB: frequency as above but intradermally	Booster injection every 3-5 years	NIL	Can be combined with TAB as TABT
Poliomyelitis	Everywhere	3 oral doses at monthly intervals	1 Booster dose every 5 years; if over 5 years 2 doses are recommended	NIL	Not at same time as yellow fever
Plague	Vietnam, Laos, Khmer Republic, Ethiopia. Possibly Pakistan and India. Essential for overlanders	2 injections at 10-20 day intervals, 3rd 6 months later	6 months	1 year	Preferably not at same time as TAB and typhus
Typhus	Vietnam, Laos, Khmer Republic, Ethiopia. Possibly Pakistan and India. Essential for overlanders	2 injections at 7-10 day intervals. 3rd 6 months later	1 year	1 year	Preferably not at same time as TAB and plague
Gamma Globulin for Infective Hepatitis	Countries where sanitation is poor	1 injection	4-6 months	NIL	Efficacy open to question

2. Pre-Travel and In-Travel Advice

Both to the uninitiated and to the experienced traveller a journey, whether by land, sea or air, can cause varying degrees of excitement. Dependent on the length of journey there are naturally varying degrees of fatigue. But fatigue is not only caused by the extent of the journey. It is definitely aggravated by pre-travel and in-travel excitement and anxiety; it is therefore most important for the traveller's medical adviser to persuade, whenever possible, that all pre-travel preparations such as immunisations are carried out as early as possible and so prevent a hectic rush in the last few days prior to the journey which adds to anxiety and fatigue. Because of the unavoidable fatigue that can follow long distance travel everything should be done to persuade the traveller not to overdo things in the last two or three days before embarking on their journey. For anyone who is going abroad for a long period, probably to take up a new appointment, it is obviously very attractive for them to have a final 'whale of a party', but this regrettably is physiologically very unsound as we all realise and so every persuasion must be put across to dissuade the traveller from indulging. The slightly rarefied atmosphere of the aircraft cabin is not congenial to the 'hangovers'. For a long journey then the traveller should be advised to have two good nights' sleep before setting forth.

Modern jet aircraft fly well above the bad weather and so have a far smoother flight than the old piston engined aircraft. Because of this motion sickness is far less frequent than it used to be in air travel. Stabilisers also have naturally cut down its frequency in sea travel but not all cruise liners have stabilisers. This is therefore a factor which must be considered when choosing a cruise holiday.

Motion sickness, as it should be correctly named, is indeed a rare occurrence now in air travellers. Travel sickness is a misnomer because it can occur without travelling. Swings, and to a lesser extent, roundabouts, are a major cause of this sickness.

The history of motion sickness in man dates back at least as far as the writers of Greek mythology who were familiar with sea sickness, and it seems likely that men were suffering from sea sickness well before they could make written records of it. This ancient Greek connection is brought out by the fact that the word nausea is a derivation from the Greek word *naus* meaning a ship. The same word which gave us nautical. Scattered throughout history there have been famous men who have suffered from motion sickness. Probably the first recorded great sufferer was Julius Caesar and since then there have been, amongst others, Admiral Nelson and Charles Darwin. To stress the point of motion sickness one can only add that Lawrence of Arabia is reported as having suffered from this complaint whilst riding a camel.

The condition, once established, can be a very trying and unpleasant one especially to the infrequent traveller. In general sufferers become acclimatised with further travel and the severity of the condition decreases.

Chinn, in 1963, reported that during moderate turbulence 25-30 per cent became sick to the point of vomiting within the first two to three days of an Atlantic crossing. Llano (1955) reported that the incidence among surviving aircrew in rafts on the ocean was probably 60 per cent, hence contributing to death by dehydration.

The incidence is very different in air travel, despite popular fear. Lederer and Kidera (1954) in a study of more than one million airline passengers revealed an overall incidence of roughly 0.5 per cent. However, in the study, the author went on to say that 'When motion sickness strikes in any one aeroplane, the incidence is approximately 8 per cent of those on board'. However these studies were carried out in the days of piston aircraft which had to fly through bad weather whilst nowadays the jets fly above it. The present incidence is therefore thought to be about 0.1 per cent or one in a thousand. This is borne out by figures at the College of Air Training at Hamble where during the first ten years of training pilots there, the 'throw out' rate because of motion sickness was 0.1 per cent.

Luckily infants and very young children seem, in general, to be immune to the condition. Clinically the problem, basically, is one of vomiting with the usually associated symptoms such as pallor, nausea and cold sweating. As well as the above, the concomitant findings are as follows:

1. Cardiovascular signs such as variation in pulse rate, rise or fall in blood pressure, change in arterial tone, change in peripheral blood flow.

2. Respiratory signs: increased ventilation, shallow breathing, sighing and yawning.

3. Gastrointestinal signs: inhibition of intestinal tone, duodenal spasm, inhibition of gastric motility, change in gastric secretion, salivation, loose bowels, gas or belching.

4. Blood chemistry changes: haemoconcentration, ketosis, increased pH, decreased CO_2 levels in arterial blood, decrease in eosinophils, increased concentration of 17-ketosteroids in serum, increased rate of urinary excretion of 17-ketosteroids, increased urinary secretion of catecholamines, and oliguria.

5. Fall of body, mouth and skin temperatures with cold extremities.

6. Miscellaneous signs such as ocular imbalance, small pupils, apathy and prostration.

7. Mentally there is usually depression, desire for solitude and complete indifference to their surroundings. The patient is usually inactive and may well show muscular incoordination in skilled physical work.

Aetiology of motion sickness has been controversial for many years but there are now certain established factors including the involvement of the vestibule.

In 1882 James reported that 15 deaf mutes had not been sea sick although the exposure to a rough sea was such that it would have appeared to have been a certainty. In 1903 Ruedz in Germany reported that dogs previously susceptible to motion sickness were no longer so after section of the VIIIth cranial nerve or bilateral sympathectomy. In 1945 Wang and Chinn in the U.S.A. confirmed that bilateral sympathectomy rendered dogs insensitive to swing sickness and also showed that unilateral labyrinthectomy lessened their susceptibility but did not get rid of it entirely. In 1965 Kellogg, Kennedy and Graybiel in the U.S.A. studied a group of labyrinthine defective subjects and compared them with normals. These 'LD's' all had a history of meningitis in childhood and were left with the following sequelae: partial deafness, negative caloric responses and no counter rolling of eyes in response to lateral tilt—in other words absent otolith function.

These 'LD's' and a group of normal subjects were exposed to repeated parabolic flight patterns where the forces varied from +2.5 to 0G. Symptoms of motion sickness were produced in 64 per cent of the normals, but none of the 'LD's'. The semicircular canals are sensitive to angular acceleration and the otoliths are sensitive to linear acceleration so presumably both are involved in some way.

With aetiology the eyes also play a non-essential part. In wide screen cinemas when the audience have been exposed to film taken from aircraft performing aerobatics, some observers have vomitted. Body position is also a factor and motion sickness is far less frequent in the supine position than in the sitting position.

Movement of the head is a further factor. Naturally in the supine position the head is usually immobile, but in the sitting position fixing of the head is beneficial. Unpleasant smells such as cooking and tobacco aggravate.

There is obviously a strong psychological factor: if one person vomits in an aircraft, others are likely to follow suit. Those of us who have taken children on holiday by car will recall that car sickness on the outward journey is far more frequent than on the return journey—obviously excitement is a factor.

Prevention

Mitigation of causative factors

1. Select the least bumpy postion in the aircraft, ship, or other form of transport. In the aircraft, avoid the tail and in the ship try and be midships.

General measures

1. Reassurance of the patient.
2. Diet: avoidance of fried or fatty foods, or alcohol in excess prior to the journey.
3. Attention to ventilation; body odours, engine smells, cooking smells and stale tobacco are all factors; smoke may provoke nausea even in the absence of motion.
4. Positon: if patient is lying down, symptoms are less likely to develop.
5. Habituation to a specific form of travel will render it less likely to induce nausea.
6. Improvement in the means of transport—by this one means the fitting of stabilisers and air conditioning to ships, the high altitude flying of aircraft and the avoidance of fumes and vibration in trams and cars.

Treatment

The truly successful treatment is prevention. Once a traveller has started to vomit to any extent then treatment must be by injection. This is, in practice, impossible other than for the long stay traveller by sea, provided there is a ship's doctor.

The answer is then the giving of an anti-motion sickness drug in adequate dosage early enough and for the dosage to be repeated often enough.

The two main types of drugs in use are the hyoscine group and the antihistamine group. From some antihistamines certain psychotropic drugs have been developed which can be of value in certain cases. There is no general drug of choice. The best one to use is dependant on the length of the journey and personal preference. The method of action of effective drugs remains obscure. It does not appear to be related to antihistamine properties or to a peripheral anti-acetylcholine activity. The following are the most popularly used drugs:

Hyoscine as Kwells.
Cyclizine as Marzine.
Diphenhydramine as Dramamine and Benadryl.
Meclozine as Bonamine, Postofine and Sea Legs.
Promethazine as Avomine and Phenergan.

Hyoscine (Kwells) and Cyclizine (Marzine) are fairly short acting—four to eight hours. However they are fairly quick acting and should be given about one hour before travel. Promethazine (Avomine and Phenergan) are slightly slower to act and should be given two hours before travel. However they last longer.

The severe and chronic sufferer naturally tends to develop an anxiety state over the problem and with them chlorpromazine as Largactil is usually very effective.

Most of the above have some sedative side effects which is frequently excellent for the passenger but obviously excludes the driver whether it be of car or aeroplane.

For the treatment of established vomiting Brand and Whittingham at the Institute of Aviation Medicine at Farnborough found that the intramuscular injection of L-Hyoscine hydrobromide gave markedly good results when given to 'survivors' in life rafts. A single dose of 0.2 mgm controlled vomiting within 15-30 minutes for four hours. This obviously is the treatment to consider when vomiting is established.

Wood at the American Naval Base at Pensacola, USA considered hyoscine was the best for bad risks on short journeys and promethazine hydrochloride as phenergan twice daily for longer journeys. Cyclizine as Marzine should not be given to pregnant women.

Further, in 1970, Wood and Graybiel showed that the benefits of promethazine or hyoscine were enhanced if either were given in conjunction with dextroamphetamine and ephedrine.

The writer thinks it is wrong to use dextroamphetamine for such a condition and tends to use Avomine or Phenergan for adults and Phenergan syrup for children with chlorpromazine or Largactil in reserve, whilst an injection of hyoscine is obviously the choice in an established case.

High altitude flying is clearly beneficial to the comforts of the passenger by giving a far smoother flight, but it is obviously necessary to pressurise the aircraft cabin. Because of technical reasons it is not possible to pressurize the inside of the cabin to the equivalent of sea level and in general the equivalent altitude in the cabin is usually about 5,000 or 6,000 feet. This level is found to be very satisfactory but because there is still a slight comparative rarefaction of the atmosphere intestinal gases expand tending to cause comparative distension. It is therefore advisable to eat sparingly and avoid gaseous drinks to prevent excess distension. As well as this the wearing of loose fitting clothing while in flight is beneficial.

Due to the problem of sitting in the same position for many hours on a long distance flight some venous congestion tends to occur in the legs especially if the traveller already suffers from varicose veins. With this problem some minimal oedema of the feet and even ankles occurs. It may not be clinically noticeable but it can be enough to cause tightness of the shoes. As such the popular present day elastic sided boot or shoe is not advised for air travel. A lace up shoe can be loosened and this is therefore the shoe of choice. If an overnight flight is being undertaken then it is a good thing to have loose fitting slippers in the night bag.

Another problem with clothing is the question of the rapid change of climate which occurs in present day jet air travel. The English winter one afternoon and the tropics of Africa the next morning. Besides this it must be remembered that in many parts of the tropics and subtropics there can be far greater variation in the temperature in the 24 hours than there is in a temperate climate. This is particularly so in the countries around the Arabian Gulf.

It is therefore very necessary to have something light and warm at hand for the evening.

One other point one must remember is that the modern airliner cabin has a comparatively dry atmosphere. In general, American built aircraft do not fit humidifiers whilst British aircraft do fit them. This presumably goes back to the basic principle that Americans are far keener on intense central heating or air conditioning than is the case in the United Kingdom, remembering that with both these amenities the atmosphere is far drier.

Because of this dry atmosphere and because of the fact that passengers in flight tend not to maintain their fluids a certain amount of dehydration tends to occur. This is particularly serious when people are travelling to the tropics where dehydration is the major problem in failure to acclimatise. As such, passengers should be encouraged to drink as much fluid as possible during flight. Having said this one then brings forward two contrary problems. Firstly the avoidance of gaseous drinks as already mentioned and secondly the avoidance of excess alcohol. It is known that alcohol slows down the process of acclimatisation and of course it encourages dehydration.

A further point which must be remembered is the problem of smoking in flight. Most airlines are now encouraging non-smoking and smoking areas which is an excellent idea. Carbon monoxide is one of the products of incomplete combustion of any organic matter including tobacco. Approximately 1-2.5 per cent of total volume of cigarette smoke is carbon monoxide. About half the carbon monoxide present in the inspired air is absorbed amounting to 10-15 ml^3 per cigarette. The total gas-containing capacity of the haemoglobin of an average man is about 1,000 ml^3. Thus smoking one cigarette results in the saturation of 1-1.5 per cent of the body's haemoglobin with carbon monoxide. It has been shown that an average smoker will have approximately 5.7 per cent carbon monoxide saturation of the haemoglobin and a person smoking 20-30 cigarettes a day could be as high as 10 per cent. What has been shown on top of this is that at an altitude of 6,000 feet, which is the cabin altitude, that 5.7 per cent becomes nearly 10 per cent and the 10 per cent becomes about 13 per cent which is getting in the area of early unpleasant symptoms. As such, smoking in flight should be discouraged.

One of the recent problems of high speed travel is the rapid crossing of time zones when flying East-West or West-East. For every fifteen degrees meridian of longitude that are crossed the time changes by one hour. When it is 12 noon G.M.T. in London it is 4 a.m. in San Francisco; 7 a.m. in New York; 7.30 p.m. in Singapore, and 10 p.m. in Sydney.

A mid-morning flight from London at present speeds arrives in New York shortly after lunch time which if not treated sensibly will make a particularly long day. An overnight flight to the East cuts down the period of darkness, hence in practice the period of sleeping, with increasing problems of fatigue.

These changes of time zones cause upset to several of one's physiological rhythms which are now known as our circadian or diurnal rhythms.

A lot of work has been done over the last ten years on these problems, both with long distance flying and shift workers, long-term cave dwellers and pot-holers.

In relation to normal daily living we are all aware of the standard daily rhythms of sleeping, walking, eating and elimination.

It has been found that with groups of people who are living in changed circumstances where the 24 hours cycle of lightness and darkness has been altered then there may be an alteration in their 24 hour circadian rhythm. In 1949 Kleitman showed that in submariners on long patrols they had such sleep cycle changes that definite periods of sleep had to be laid down. In 1963 and 1964 Lobban showed both with people who became totally blind and with workers in the Arctic where light and dark is seasonal rather than daily that the circadian rhythms of renal function are lost. As long as the near blind person can still differentiate light from dark desynchronisation of renal function does not occur.

Mills showed in volunteers staying for prolonged periods underground that after a lapse of sufficient time urinary rhythms of excretion of chlorides and potassium became completely disassociated.

The following are some of the various functions which show a circadian rhythm: respiratory rate and oxygen consumption; heart rate; blood pressure; body temperature; basal metabolic rate and liver function. Of the various blood and urinary levels the 17 ketosteroids, sodium, potassium, chlorides, creatinine, non-protein nitrogen, uric acid urea and amino acids have to a greater or lesser extent a circadian rhythm.

Conroy and Mills demonstrated in night shift workers a very marked diurnal rhythm in ther levels of plasma cortisol. Maximum values for plasma cortisol are usually two hours in advance of maximum urinary output of sodium, potassium and chlorides.

This plasma cortisol level appears to be an intrinsic factor whilst light and dark acts as an extrinsic factor.

Working for the Federal Aviation Agency in 1965 in the U.S.A., Hauty and Adams reported findings on healthy volunteers adapting to time zone changes after modern jet travel. They chose two groups of people for their work. Firstly young medical students and secondly middle aged laboratory workers. Various physiological and psychological tests were agreed upon which were carried out before flight, immediately after flight and for several days afterwards at the point of arrival. They were continued on the same basis after flight home to the point of original departure.

The physiological measurements studied were rectal temperature (by indwelling thermistor couplings), pulse rate, respiratory rate and palmar evaporative water loss.

The psychological tests were reaction time, decision time, subjective fatigue by a standard check list and the critical flicker fusion test. This rather complicated test is generally considered to be representative of the state of efficiency of cerebral functions. Numerical ability tests were also included.

The flights were carried out in both Easterly and Westerly directions from Oklahoma City.

Initially they flew East-West from Oklahoma City to Manila and return.

The next time they flew West-East, by flying from Oklahoma City to Rome and return. These flights were followed by a direct North-South flight from Washington DC to Santiago, Chile, and return.

All testing was done very carefully regardless of expense with all volunteers being admitted to hospital for several days prior to the departing flight, several days after the flight and a similar scheduling for the return flight. Flights were made in daylight so as to avoid any further upset due to loss of a night's sleep.

On the flight from Oklahoma to Manila, or in other words flying East-West, where there was a time displacement of ten hours, the body temperature rate was upset for four days. Prior to the flight rectal temperature throughout nine days of testing was found to be maximal at 6 p.m. First day in Manila the maximum rectal temperature was recorded at 12 noon and it was four days before it returned to 6 p.m. Heart rate was similarly upset and also took four days to return to normal. Respiratory rate did not appear to be affected. Reaction and decision time were affected for two days. With the West-East flight it was found that the heart rate and rectal temperature were upset for up to eight days. Reaction time and decision time were again increased and with the West-East flight it was again slightly longer than with the East-West flight. In both directions there was only a very slight loss of performance following the return home.

Subjective fatigue was very marked on arrival after crossing these many time zones. Again slightly greater in the West-East flights compared with the East-West. The return journeys appeared to produce little or no fatigue.

With the North-South and vice-versa flights there was no upset of circadian rhythms or psychological tests.

One further point that was quite definite was that with increasing age the subjective fatigue and the upset of circadian rhythms and all psychological tests were markedly increased.

Preston and Bateman of the British Airways Medical Service, along with Short and Wilkinson of the Medical Research Council at Cambridge University, carried out a study on the effects of flying and time changes on menstrual cycle length and on performance in airline stewardesses.

The work was carried out on 29 airline stewardesses and from this group eight were selected for further study in an isolation unit at the University of Manchester. Four subjects spent four days as a control group and were not subjected to time zone change. The second group of four were subjected to three time zone changes, of eight hours, each representing long easterly flights. Both groups were required to complete a similar battery of work load tasks during isolation. These tests included addition, reaction time, short term memory, vigilance and visual search. Only one subject of the time zoned group showed any change in menstrual cycle length, but there was a significant impairment in efficiency of this group both over the performance tasks as a whole and in particular in the ability to react quickly, memorise and search.

Colonel Adam of the British Army Medical Research team flew a group of paratroopers out to Singapore where there is a 7½ hour time change on Greenwich Mean Time. He found that for the first three days they were passing urine according to English time. Instead of the urine being passed between the approximate hours of 6.30 a.m. to 11 p.m., or therabouts, he found that decreasing over the first three days they were passing it between 2 p.m. and 6.30 a.m. In fact they were passing ⅔ of their urine during the night hours and ⅓ during the day. This naturally led to disturbed sleep, increased fatigue and lowered efficiency.

Following on the above survey Shepherd and Barlow carried out a further research programme to assess the loss of efficiency which might occur during the first three or four days after long distance flight.

They therefore designed a study to investigate the combined effects of flight fatigue including the crossing of time zones and the problem of an operation situation occurring in a group of troops recently arrived in a tropical climate.

For this they used 60 paratroopers who were initially given an intensive three day programme of tasks typical to well trained soldiers as they were. These tasks consisted of marching; digging and preparation of camouflage; carrying out a difficult assault course;

weapon handling and shooting. They were then flown to Singapore, passing through 7½ time zones. Within five hours of arrival they were called upon to carry out the tests again.

A clear loss of efficiency in the performance of marching, digging and camouflage and shooting ability was found to occur. The obstacle course was performed at the same level of efficiency in Singapore as in England but the men were more fatigued at the end of the course than in the U.K.

Weapon handling tests were carried out with equal efficiency in England and Singapore but it was noted that they were being carried out almost automatically hence the usual high standard of training in paratroops was having its effect.

In another survey paratroopers who had an enforced 24 hour rest en route to Singapore were found to have no heat casualties despite intensive field trials on arrival compared with a similar group without a 24 hour rest who had a high percentage of heat casualties with similar field trials.

From all these surveys it is obvious that there are certain physiological and psychological factors which are upset by rapid jet air travel across several time zones. This is quite definite when the number of time zones is five or more.

Probably the most important of the physiological factors is the upset of one's natural sleep cycle. As far as airline schedules will allow, travellers should try and arrive at their destination in time to be able to go to bed on the first night at the time they would have gone to bed at their point of departure.

For example, leaving London at 11 a.m. to fly to New York under present schedules one arrives there at 1.30 p.m. which is 6.30 p.m. London time. Every effort should be made to persuade that traveller to go to bed at the very latest by 9 p.m. New York (2 a.m. London) time but preferably by 7 p.m. New York. In this way the first night will be spent on nearly the same phase as before travel. The second night should be spent half way between the old phasing and the new phasing, and by the third night the new phasing can be absorbed. However it is frequently a sound practice to exhibit a mild sedative such as Nitrazepam (Mogadon) for the first two or three nights after travel both on the way out and after the return. This will certainly not encourage habituation.

Adam recorded disturbance of the night's sleep because of nocturnal frequency in an Eastward flight gradually decreasing over three nights. Prevention of fluid intake during the evening is presumably the answer to this but with travel to hot climates reduction of fluids at any time should not be encouraged.

Also important is the upset of the bowel habit. To the regular after breakfast man there can be a temporary annoying disturbance in that in flying West, the desire to defaecate as a result comes on in the early hours of the morning, while flying East it can occur in mid-afternoon. With either change it is inconvenient and the sufferer can well suppress the urge to defaecate hence causing constipation. It is therefore very sensible to advise the traveller to take a mild aperient with him for use during the first one or two days of his journey.

What, however, is far more important than the brief physiological upsets are the psychological upsets.

Hauty and Adams, and Preston and his co-workers, described definite delays in decision time and reaction time. This means it is absolutely wrong for the business tycoon to expect to fly across the Atlantic, or equivalent time change in another direction, and go straight into a meeting to discuss major business problems and make major business decisions. If they do, the wrong decision will inevitably be made and it is up to these tycoons' medical advisers to prevent them behaving this way. For many years now various politicians of every hue and colour have met their opposite numbers immediately on arrival with probable dire results. But in 1972 when President Nixon flew to China and Russia he broke his journey en route to both places for rest. In March 1973 when Premier Heath flew to the U.S.A. to see President Nixon he flew over on Saturday to rest on Sunday and see the President on the Monday. If common sense is coming even to the politicians, surely we must be able to persuade businessmen.

And what of the future of this problem with increasing speed and the arrival of Concorde? It has been put forward by some authorities that in fact with the increased speed of the supersonic aircraft we will be 'over the hump' and circadian rhythm upset will decrease with the average traveller. However this may not be so, but only time and experience will show this.

One other point that has been frequently raised about Concorde is the problem of exposure of crew and passengers to high levels of cosmic radiation.

As we go higher the shield presented by the atmosphere against galactic and solar radiation decreases.

Reviews have shown that 0.6 to 1 m-rem per hour is a representative dose for passengers at 58,000 feet and fairly high latitudes. These doses must be considered with a background dose of 120 m-rems per annum in London and about 300 m-rems per annum in Aberdeen. A person very close to a colour television set is subjected to 0.5 m-rems per hour. A mass miniature radiography chest X-ray may give 10 m-rems.

The International Commission for Radiological Protection recommends that a maximum permissible dose for the general population is 500 m-rems per year.

The aircraft is fitted with a flight warning meter which consists of a Geiger counter ionisation detector and a neutron mill-rem meter. This will display normal, alert and action ranges. The dial shows alert at 20 m-rems per hour with an amber light and action at 50 m-rems per hour with a red light. This necessitates immediate and rapid descent. In addition, the total dose rate of the flight is indicated on the dial. With the maximum permitted dose of 500 m-rems or 0.5 rems per year this would allow about 61 round trips across the Atlantic which is unlikely to be exceeded.

And so advice to give your patients prior to modern air travel is this:

1. Plan the flight well in advance. If possible a day flight and/or arrival in time to go to bed at a time equivalent to the bedtime at the point of departure.
2. Not too hectic the last 24 hours before flight.
3. Encourage the traveller to cut smoking before flight and in flight.
4. Moderate alcohol in flight.
5. Moderate food in flight.
6. Maintain fluids in flight but avoidance of sparkling drinks.
7. Loose fitting, comfortable clothes and shoes.
8. Light but warm clothing at hand.
9. 24 hour rest period on arrival after five hour time change. Never straight into a meeting or to a reception.
10. Advise a mild aperient and possibly a mild quick acting sedative.

Having fully discussed air travel we must return to the problems which may affect one's patients with sea travel.

More and more routine travel nowadays is being done by air because of the time factor. By this I mean the essential need to get from A to B.

This is so to such an extent that a large amount of passenger liners' time is taken up with cruising. Two or more weeks at sea is an excellent way to get away from it all. Because of this the 'cruise' holiday has increased greatly in popularity over the last 20 years and many elderly couples decide to take their annual holiday this way. The major shipping companies have very adequate medical departments which have shore based staff as well as ship's doctors and nursing staff aboard. These departments should be informed in advance if elderly, invalid or incapacitated people are travelling by sea. Special arrangements can then be made to help them when on board.

With regard to sunburn at sea, the movement of the ship and a cooling sea breeze with an overcast sky can be misleading and hence lead to severe burning.

As with air travel, swelling of the ankles may occur. This is probably through excessive sitting around in deck chairs especially in the tropics. This condition was, in fact, first called deck ankles or Colombo flop. Judicious exercise and the occasional use of diuretics soon clears up the problem.

It is most important that if any passengers are on regular medication then a letter should accompany the patient and enough medication to last the entire voyage.

There is frequently a major problem in the difficulty in moving between decks, especially in the smaller liners. Stairs may be steep and lifts in unsuitable places for all passengers. This excludes the recent sufferer from a coronary thrombosis or a cerebral thrombosis.

In addition, in general the larger and faster the ship the more stable she is in the water. This type is fitted with stabilisers, bow thrusters and up-to-date navigational and safety equipment.

Some of the smaller mushroom shipping companies of lesser repute who may be sailing under flags of convenience frequently provide only minimal medical facilities. For the elderly or invalid, to travel with these companies is to ask for trouble. Similarly on such liners the food is frequently of poorer quality and with the type of cooking may cause intestinal upsets which are most unpleasant when a small cabin is the only place in which to be ill. Further, with this type of cruise, remaining on board when you are meant to be going on shore trips and excursions is not encouraged, which may be very fatiguing for the elderly especially if the weather is hot. Therefore one can say if one's patients are going on a sea cruise it is well worthwhile going by a well established international shipping company. Even so this can bring problems for the elderly and infirm.

3. Climate and Acclimatisation; Prevention of Heat Disorders

In the days of sea travel the question of sudden acclimatisation to a tropical environment was not a problem. The traveller, such as the serviceman or civil servant travelling to India or Africa with or without his family took two, three or more weeks to get to his destination and all the time the weather was gradually getting warmer so the body was able to cope gradually with the changes in climate.

Now with modern air travel the whole tempo is completely changed and in 24 hours or even less someone is transferred from a temperate climate to tropical heat.

To understand how best to advise the traveller on such problems one must first discuss the basic principles of thermoregulation and the human body's capabilities of dealing with these changes.

Naturally for a body to remain stable thermally, heat lost must be equal to heat gained. This control of heat is carried out by the cardiovascular system and the sweating mechanism under the control of the thermoregulation centre in the hypothalamus. Associated with the thermoregulation centre in the hypothalamus there are other autonomic controls namely those of water balance and the preservation of homeostasis which obviously work together.

The thermoregulatory centre is divided into two anatomical divisions:

1. Heat conversion by cutaneous vasoconstriction and shivering.
2. Heat loss by cutaneous dilatation and sweating.

The circulatory system takes a lot of the strain in the sudden change to a hot climate and thus anyone who has a circulatory system whose reserves are in doubt should not go to the tropics. The involvement of this system in acclimatisation is in the following ways:

1. Vasodilatation of the peripheral blood vessels occurs at a lower temperature.
2. Heat transfer from the body core to the body surface increases so increasing heat loss by body convection.
3. Skin blood flow is higher at any body temperature above normal limits.

Regarding the changes in the sweating mechanism:

1. Sweating starts at a lower temperature.
2. The amount of sweating is greater at any given temperature.
3. The body develops an ability to maintain a high production of sweating for longer periods without the sweat glands becoming fatigued.

The interesting fact is that there is a fall in resting body temperature hence encouraging loss of sweat by convection. Heat loss by sweating is of course greatly aided by the latent heat of vaporisation.

It is quite definite that the main method the body has of dealing with heat stress is by the evaporation of sweat.

To consider the sweating mechanism in greater detail: there are two types of sweat glands:

1. Apocrine glands—these are the glands in the axillae and the groins. Kuno (1956) considered that their action was sexual. Whatever it is, it is not thermoregulatory.

2. Eccrine glands—these are the sweat glands present throughout the rest of the body and are in general thermoregulatory in action except for those present in the palms of the hands and in the soles of the feet which purely respond to psychological stimuli.

Emotional stimuli can also produce sweating from the eccrine glands, in particular from the glands of the face. It is probable that there are at least two million eccrine glands in the body and in general there are over 100 glands per square centimetre.

As mentioned earlier, with acclimatisation the amount of sweating in any period of time is greater and sweat gland fatigue does not occur so quickly as in the non-acclimatised. Ladell reported that the truly acclimatised man can sweat at a rate of up to 3 litres per hour for short periods.

The main purpose of sweating is to cause heat loss due to cooling by evaporation.

As a result of increased sweating, dehydration naturally occurs. As a result of this, anti-duretic hormone (ADH) in the urine increases (Hellman and Weiner, 1953) and this leads to reduction in the output of urine.

The above physiological changes are therefore the basis of acclimatisation to heat.

It is considered that nearly complete acclimatisation to heat occurs within 14 days but an appreciable amount takes place within five to seven days. There are, however, factors which slow down this process and these will be discussed later.

It is generally thought that with long term residents in the tropics that after they have been fully acclimatised with maximum sweating output for several months, the sweat output then tends to decline.

Regarding return to a cooler climate, it is thought that the traveller loses his acclimatisation to the heat within a month. However on returning to the heat it is thought that he reacclimatises to the heat quicker than previously. This may well be because he has learnt by previous experience how to behave and encourage acclimatisation.

What then are the factors which will either hinder or encourage acclimatisation?

Factors which hinder acclimatisation

Age

The army have claimed that men over the age of 26 years are past their prime. This is probably an overstatement but evidence shows that there is a greater physiological strain on men as they grow older when they are exposed to heat. It is quite definite that once men are over 40 their response to sudden exposure to high temperatures is far worse than in the younger man. Remembering the importance of the cardiovascular system in acclimatisation it may be that degeneration in this system in the 40's is the cause, but one must also remember the possibility of other basic disease being present by this age. Whatever the cause of this difficulty in acclimatisation in the over 40's on their first trip to the tropics, it is a very important point in their medical assessment of fitness to live in the tropics.

Fatigue

With the extra stress on the cardiovascular system which occurs during the process of acclimatisation it is most important that the new person in a hot climate does not fatigue himself unnecessarily. Accepting that an appreciable amount of acclimatisation occurs within four to seven days, it is therefore necessary that excess fatigue is avoided for at least four days. Bearing in mind also that travel East or West, particularly the former, through five or more hour time changes causes sleep disturbance and fatigue, this is even more pertinent. Nowadays cricket, athletic and football teams of both codes, travel great distances and frequently arrive in warm climates. The British Olympic team's flight to Mexico City in 1968 was a typical example of this. The writer had the pleasure of lecturing to various members of the managing staff of this venture and the advice was accepted to rest on arrival. No group of athletes will accept that they must do nothing for the first four days but they did accept that they must avoid stress for at least two days. As a result of this there was minimal disturbance in the process of acclimatisation of the team.

Of course with all athletic and other sports teams everyone is athletically fit and as such acclimatisation is accomplished far more easily than by ordinary persons.

Obesity

This is a marked deterrent to a quick and satisfactory acclimatisation. Robinson in 1942 showed that the greater ratio of body weight to surface area in a large man was detrimental. Minard, Belding and Kingston in 1957 showed in American marine recruits that in the unacclimatised heat stroke occurred more frequently in obese individuals.

Edholm *et al.* found in 1964 that among a group of unacclimatised paratroopers in which 50 per cent. became heat casualties after desert exposure the weight of those who became heat casualties was six kilogrammes (13 pounds) higher than in the non-casualties.

Sex

Work in 1963 by Hertig and Sargent showed that women do not acclimatise as well as men under equivalent circumstances. Whether this is due to the fact that testosterone is thought to be sudorific while oestradiol inhibits sweating activity is questionable.

Pyrexia

Not unnaturally if a newcomer to a tropical area develops an infective fever on arrival the process of acclimatisation is upset.

Various skin diseases

Any skin conditions which upset the sweating mechanism obviously will hinder acclimatisation.

Acne vulgaris which has been so generalised that resultant scarring has damaged the sweat glands obviously upsets acclimatisation. Along with acne there is the possibility that the sweating mechanism may be upset not only through the physical reason of scarring but also because of the androgen/oestrogen ration being upset so causing keratinisation of the sweat ducts.

Severe *seborrhoeic dermatitis* similarly can upset the normal sweating mechanism. The rare condition of *congenital ectodermal dysplasia* absolutely prevents acclimatisation because with this problem almost all sweat glands may be absent. In its milder form the efficiency of the sweat glands present can be below standard.

Factors which assist acclimatisation

Maintenance of fluids

The most important factor in the assistance of acclimatisation to the heat is the maintenance of fluids. It is essential to replace the extra fluid lost by increased sweating. It is also necessary to replace the salt lost at the same time.

In the intense heat it may be difficult to persuade anyone to drink as much as necessary to maintain hydration and even more so to rehydrate if that is necessary.

It has been found that men will drink more water if it is suitably cooled. The most acceptable temperature for drinking plenty of water is 12 to 15°C (54 to 59°F). Further, it is easier for the drinking to be done little and often. Alcohol itself causes dehydration so if alcoholic drinks are to be included in the intake then they must be dilute. Probably 'shandy' is one of the most palatable and practical forms of maintaining fluids in the person who likes some alcohol.

The basic principle to reckon on, particularly during the initial period of acclimatisation, is one pint of fluid per 10°F in every 24 hours. In other words if the temperature is in the eighties then eight pints of fluid must be consumed in the 24 hours.

For those who are metricated a similiar basis on which to work is 2 litres per day at 0°C plus 1 litre per day for every 10°C. In other words 4 litres at 20°C, 4.5 litres at 25°C and 5 litres at 30°C.

Another practical way of assessing whether enough fluid is being taken is to watch the colour of the urine. It should be kept nearly colourless or a pale yellow. If the urine becomes a strong yellow then dehydration is occurring and acclimatisation will suffer. Besides the ill effect on acclimatisation, one must remember that dehydration leads to crystalluria and ultimately the formation of renal calculi.

Maintenance of Salt

Human sweat is a hypotonic saline solution containing other solutes. Increase in sweating in order to cope with increased heat means salt depletion. The normal diet in the developed countries contains about 10 g of salt or sodium chloride in 24 hours. In a tropical climate the daily need for salt rises to between 15 and 25 g per day, dependent on the temperature and the amount of physical work carried out. From this one can say that in general an extra 5 to 15 g of salt must be taken daily—in other words it is necessary on average to double the daily salt intake. This can be taken in several ways:

1. Extra salt added in the cooking and added to the food.
2. Salt added to drinks.
3. Salt taken in the form of tablets or pills.
4. A combination of all four methods.

Work done in the Royal Air Force showed that the best way to take extra salt is by adding extra in the cooking. By this method a far greater percentage is absorbed.

The trouble in taking extra salt as a tablet or in drinks is its nauseating properties. This can be avoided by giving salt in enteric coated pills but with an active intestine these pills may be passed unabsorbed. This is particularly so if the patient is suffering from any diarrhoea with its resultant over activity of the intestines. Regrettably it is just when the patient is losing more fluids with an attack of diarrhoea that the patient needs to absorb more salt than usual. Therefore the enteric coated pill can defeat its own end when it is most needed by being passed in the stools unabsorbed. When acclimatisation has taken place, the amount of salt loss decreases so the need to take extra salt decreases.

When salt is depleted one fortunately can eat highly salted food without objection, which is very satisfactory.

One final point which must be remembered is that the salt intake should not be increased without the fluids being stepped up. It is absolutely essential to maintain the fluid balance when the salt is increased. Unless the newcomer to the tropics is carrying out heavy physical work 10 to 14 days of extra salt is usually enough.

Clothing

Accepting the principle that maintenance of adequate sweating is the most important thing in developing acclimatisation then the most important factor in clothing for a warm climate must be to facilitate the evaporation of sweat.

In some ways one could say that no clothes at all would be the best answer. However clothes protect the person against the sun, against biting by insects, against pricking by thorns or even the biting of snakes. This is of course particularly important after dark in prevention of spread of malaria by infected mosquitoes.

The basic principles needed in clothing suitable for hot weather are thus:

1. Clothes which reflect heat.
2. Clothes which absorb sweat.
3. Clothes which give a layer of air which aids evaporation.

1. All clothing for tropical climates should be light in colour as well as light in weight. McArdle in 1947, working for the Medical Research Council, reckoned the effect of every kilogram of clothing worn was the equivalent of raising the wet bulb temperature by 1°C or 1.8°F. With people working actually in the sun Hertig and Belding found that white clothing could reduce the solar heat load by about 50 per cent.

2. If clothes are being worn they must be such that they will encourage the evaporation of sweating. When the humidity is low sweat evaporates rapidly into the dry air. If the humidity is high in the 80 to 90 per cent range little evaporation of sweat can take place because the atmosphere is already nearly saturated.

As such it is generally thought that people in hot humid climates should wear as little clothing as possible so that nothing can discourage evaporation of sweat. However in hot dry climates where there is a great deal of radiant heat then white clothing light in weight should be worn to protect against heat.

The material of which the clothing is made is most important.

During the last few years, mainly with man made fibres, the very useful drip-dry materials have appeared. To the traveller, especially the businessman going round the world in two or three weeks, the arrival of drip-dry shirts was a tremendous gift. Wash out in the hand washbasin in the evening, hang over the bath overnight, and be ready to wear in the morning.

But what makes materials drip-dry? It is its inability to absorb water. This is known as its water inhibition characteristic. Microscopically the water remains on the surface and is not absorbed when drip-dry properties are great. As such these materials are not suitable for wearing when sweating is high and is to be encouraged.

Rayon and modified rayon absorb 70 to 100 per cent of their weight of water: 1 kg of rayon will absorb 700 g to 1 kg of water. However rayon is unsatisfactory for wear in the tropics, this is similarly so with wool.

Cotton is by far the best material to wear in the tropics and it absorbs 50 per cent of its weight of water.

Way down the list come many of the man made fibres, the excellent drip-dry materials. Their absorptive properties are as follows: Modacrylic (Dynel and Teklan) 15 to 20 per cent, Triacetates (Arnel, Rhonel, Tricel) 10 to 11 per cent, Acrylic (Acrilan, Courtelle, Dralon, Orlon) 8 to 11 per cent, Metallic (Lurex) 5 per cent, Nylon (Brinylon, Celon, Enkalon, Perlon, Rilson) 4 to 12 per cent, Elastofibre (Lycra, Sponzelle) 3 per cent, Polyester (Dacron, Terylene, Trevira) 3 per cent.

But then one can purchase nowadays drip-dry cotton shirts. How does this fit in? Most housewives who do their husband's washing will say that drip-dry cotton shirts are drip-dry initially but after several washings they lose their drip-dry properties. This is because they have been made drip-dry by being treated with certain resins which have removed the absorptive properties. As this resin is washed out. so absorption improves and drip-dry properties decrease. As such, a truly drip-dry cotton is not a great deal better than some man made fibres.

However it is still best to wear cotton in hot climates and the best of the man made fibres are the following: Acetates, Modacrylics, Triacetates and Acrylics.

Pure nylon should be avoided, especially the popular nylon sock. Regrettably cotton socks are becoming more and more difficult to purchase but they are necessary in the heat. Nylon socks without any power of absorption lead to sogginess of the skin and great encouragement of epidermophytosis.

However the producers of the man made fibres throughout the world are working hard on this problem and are now producing porous materials which allow the sweat to pass through these pores to the outside of the clothing.

3. The third practical point with satisfactory clothing is the necessity to maintain a layer of air under the main covering to aid evaporation. The development in Scandinavia of the string vest was a great addition to satisfactory clothing. Some people are against the wearing of underclothes in the heat but in fact a very porous layer under the top layer is good in encouraging evaporation. Further, in parts of the world where there is a great difference between midday and evening temperature porous underclothing helps to keep the resident warm in the evening: it is in this type of clothing that the latest advances in porous man made fibres can be of value.

On the subject of clothing the question of hats must be considered. At the time of the first world war the hat was considered an essential for any European in the tropics. They suffered by wearing heavy solar topees. Women in India wore similar topees or very wide brimmed hats with veils. The view at that time was that the wearing of a hat was the most important factor in preventing heat disorders. However it is now realised that the head area provides 25 per cent of the total sweat area of the body and so it should not be covered unnecessarily. However with desert climates where there is strong sun glare a hat should be worn. With the overcast humid climate when evaporation of sweat is limited hats should not be worn.

At this stage of discussion on clothing one must briefly mention the question of laundry. Obviously the best thing is one set of underclothes, shirts and socks, etc., for the working day and then one for the evening. If clothes washing facilities, or the amount of clothes, are insufficient for this then by far the best technique is to have a shower or bath after the day's work and to put on the clean clothes in the evening when the sweating is far less. These clothes are then worn again for working the next day.

Along with clothing one should mention the use of sunglasses.

Sunglasses are necessary in desert climates and where there is a clear sky. With humidity and the concomitant overcast sky they are not nearly so essential but the writer supports the use of good quality sunglasses under practically all conditions in the subtropics and tropics. This should be remembered on holidays in hot climates where strong reflection is occurring with sea and white sand. This also occurs with snow and winter sports holidays when the intensity of the sun rays aided by reflection can be very great even although the temperature is not high.

Polaroid, Crooks B Tint and Softlite No. 3 Tint are all reputable varieties. Recently new sunglasses have come on the market which become dark in bright light and then lighten as the glare gets less. These are excellent for people who have to wear spectacles all the time because of a refractive error as they are suitable in all degrees of brightness.

Two varieties of these lenses are Photosun (Goldsmith) and Umbramatic (Zeiss). The absorption varies from 35 per cent in dull weather to 75 per cent in bright weather.

Another type of spectacle for those with refractive errors is that with tinted plastic lenses and very light metal frames. These are very suitable in the tropics where the wearing of spectacles can be a nuisance, as they are much lighter in weight. The writer understands that the lenses mentioned in the previous paragraph are only available in glass and not in plastic.

And so to summarise the factors which are of help in encouraging acclimatisation and those which hinder:

To encourage satisfactory acclimatisation:

1. Maintain fluids—1 pint per 10°F per 24 hours.
2. Maintain salt—preferably extra on the food.
3. Avoid fatigue.
4. Wear loose fitting light coloured cotton clothes.

Factors which hinder acclimatisation:
1. Obesity.
2. Fatigue.
3. Age.
4. Recent feverish illness.
5. Nylon or other non-absorbent clothing.
6. Skin diseases which upset sweating mechanism.

While all the advice just given will help satisfactory and rapid acclimatisation and hence prevent the heat disorders in general they will have no effect on the unpleasant effects of sunburn. Sunburn, or to give its official name of acute solar dermatitis or acute actinic dermatitis, is a complaint to which many millions of people literally and metaphorically expose themselves every year.

It is entirely preventable by the use of commonsense and simple preparations to prevent burning.

Regrettably most 'pale skins' in the world today like to take a holiday in the hot spots and try to take on a sun tan. Presumably there must be something in the old saying 'All good looking men are slightly sunburned' because the shores of the Mediterranean every summer are covered with the bodies of the European trying to turn shades darker and the shores of the Caribbean are covered similarly with the bodies of Americans.

Almost certainly the major problem is that the vast majority of the working community, and hence their families as well, can only take a short holiday, probably about two weeks. Sometimes only one week and very rarely over three weeks. Because of this they usually expose themselves far too much initially with dire results. For the traveller from a temperate climate going to the Mediterranean, the Caribbean or similar shores, 15 minutes exposure of normally covered areas is plenty on the first day. Subsequently 30 minutes on the second day, 1 hour on the third, 2 hours and the fourth and so on until after 10 to 14 days the average person can take lying out the whole day.

One must consider briefly the actual changes which take place in the skin if one is to see whether there is anything which can be taken to help to prevent trouble. The full range of the ultraviolet rays of the solar spectrum extend from 50 nanometres to 390 nanometres in wavelength. However no rays of less than 280 nm penetrate our atmosphere. The rays that produce sunburn are in the 290 to 320 nm range. Vitamin D is synthesised in the skin in the same range. With these rays tyrosine is turned into melanin to produce the pigmentation. At the same time the pro-vitamin 7-dehydrocholesterol changes to vitamin D.

On the hypothesis that there is excess production of vitamin D in the skin associated with exposure to solar radiation and remembering that vitamin A is antagonistic to vitamin D, then one could consider the giving of vitamin A in the prevention of sunburn.

Clark and his colleagues in 1960 showed that in rats the administration of large doses of vitamin A antagonised the effects of toxic doses of vitamin D. Vedder and Rosenberg in 1938 showed that the toxic effect of large doses of vitamin A could be reduced by simultaneous administration of vitamin D.

Further the anti-keratinising effect of vitamin A has been assumed on the basis that deficiency causes drying, scaling and hyperkeratosis. These latter changes can be reversed by giving vitamin A. It has been shown that excess vitamin A produces hyperplasia, parakeratosis and increased mitosis of the epidermis in animals. In humans oral vitamin A was shown by Pinkus and Hunter to increase epidermal thickness. In addition Johnston and Zakon showed that the oral administration of vitamin A was beneficial with oral lesions of lichen planus, and perhaps more interesting, Fitzpatrick and Mathews-Roth noted a marked reduction in the photosensitivity of patients with erythropoietic protoporphyria after being given B carotene—a precursor of vitamin A. In addition Cluver and Politzer in 1965 showed serum vitamin A levels drop soon after intensive ultraviolet radiation and can be restored with oral vitamin A.

The excess vitamin D, which is laid down in the skin with sunburn, has calcium retaining effects although probably much of this calcium is fixed other than in the skin.

It is on the above hypotheses and also facts mentioned that the idea was raised to give vitamin A and calcium carbonate in the form of os sepia as a prophylactic against sunburn.

Since about 1955 a preparation called Sylvasun has been on sale in South Africa. It became available in the United Kingdom in 1968. Each pill consists of 25,000 units of vitamin A and calcium carbonate 120 mgm. These pills had a great reputation in South Africa and were in fact used with great success by the British Olympic teams both at Rome in 1960 and at Mexico in 1968. On the latter occasion they were put to the real test by the sailing team at Acapulco where with sea and sun the ultraviolet must have been excessive. None of the British team had any problems but it must be remembered that the games came fairly late in the season for British sailors so they probably had a basic tan already.

In summer 1970 the writer, in association with two colleagues in the British Airways Medical Service, Dr R. M. Barnes and Dr R. L. Green, carried out an extensive trial to assess the effectiveness of Sylvasun pills.

Sylvasun pills were issued to nearly 3,000 BOAC and BEA staff and their families. Due to the fact that airline staff and their families have 'cheap fare' facilities available subject to the seats being unsold to the general public immediately prior to take off the greater majority of them travelled to warm climates on a worldwide basis. In fact 68 per cent of all participants travelled to the Mediterranean area, 7 per cent to subtropical areas and 15 per cent to tropical areas. In other words 90 per cent went where the sun was hot and strong so ensuring that the survey was a fair test.

Regrettably it had to be accepted that a placebo could not be used for people on holiday abroad and therefore away from any control. However it was thought that with the large numbers involved plus the above average experience as travellers to sun spots that a fair assessment would be obtained against previous sunburn experience.

Prior to the issue of the pills everyone had to complete an initial questionnaire under the supervision of one of the three authors. Everyone participating was placed in one of four categories on previous sunburn experience.

1. *Severe:* needed to see a doctor or skin blistered.

2. *Moderate:* visited a chemist or first aider. Gave up sunbathing for two days or had two or more disturbed nights.

3. *Mild:* soreness but insufficient to stop sunbathing or had disturbed night.

4. *Nil:* no unpleasant side effects.

In addition to the question on previous burning history there were questions on age; sex; complexion colour; natural hair colour; eye colour; and any drug therapy being taken at the time of the holiday.

A further questionnaire had to be completed after the holiday in which they had to give their sunburn experience and the place they went to on the holiday.

In all 1,688 returned and completed the questionnaire. Of the remainder a random 20 per cent or 230 were taken. Their previous histories were found to be statistically the same as the 1,688 completed. Their past holiday characteristics were again found to be statistically similar to the 1,688.

Thus it could be clearly accepted that the results of those who had not completed the questionnaire were the same as those who had.

One further point in assessment, the questionnaires were computer analysed after every 250 were received. At no survey did the parameters between each group vary by more than 2 per cent which was remarkably constant.

The participants were instructed to take one pill twice daily starting two days before sun exposure, with the possibility of increasing the dose to four tablets on any one day if they felt they had had too much sun, for not more than 14 days.

This is a standard dose of 50,000 units of vitamin A per day. It is not suggested that these pills should be taken for longer than 14 days because satisfactory tanning should have occurred well before two weeks have elapsed and so there is no further need.

As far as any possible vitamin A toxicity is concerned Bergen and Roels in 1965 showed that the smallest dose of vitamin to cause toxicity was 41,000 units daily for a minimum of eight years. Shaw and Nicolai showed that a dose of 200,000 to 275,000 units daily had to be taken for two months to cause symptoms of hypervitaminosis A. From this it can be seen that 50,000 units daily used for only two weeks is well below any toxic limits.

In the survey improvement was defined as movement from a more severe to a less severe sunburn category. Of the 1,688 participants, 1,103 or 66.1 per cent moved to a more favourable category, 431 or 25.8 per cent remained in the same category and 134 or 8 per cent moved to a worse category. Perhaps of the greater interest and more importance were the findings in the categories of people who on previous history were in the severe and moderate groups. These indeed are the people who require help in preventing the trouble of a painful and toxic response to sunbathing.

Out of the total 1,688 there were 630 people in these two categories: 163 or 9.8 per cent of the total in the severe category and 467 or 28 per cent in the moderate.

Thinking only of these 630 of which 25.9 per cent were severe and 74.1 per cent were moderate before using Sylvasun.

After using Sylvasun there were only 15 or 2.4 per cent in the severe group, 44 or 7 per cent in the moderate, 246 or 39 per cent in the mild and 325 or 51.6 per cent in the nil category.

In other words out of the 630 severe and moderate burners 90 per cent moved into mild or nil categories after taking a vitamin A—calcium carbonate preparation.

One should add that all participants were told to continue to use a moisturising lotion or cream as before while sunbathing, and naturally were also told to use the same care and circumspection as they had always used previously. The writer and his colleagues felt, not unreasonably, that anyone given a pill reputed to help them against sunburn would certainly not take more care; they might well tend to take less care. Hence the figures obtained might well be pessimistic and certainly not optimistic.

Of other points found in this survey, subjects with fair complexion, blue, green/hazel eyes and auburn, blonde or light brown hair had, as was to be expected, a much greater tendency to burn than other subjects. It was found that the subjects in these categories were helped more than people in other categories. It was noted that subjects with blonde hair benefited to a greater extent than any others, while auburn haired with green eyes were helped less and should therefore take even greater care with exposure.

There was no difference between male and female. Further, there was no difference between a group of 216 women who were menstruating at the time of their holidays and those who were not. There was no difference between women taking a contraceptive pill or in people taking aspirin regularly.

In two small groups of 63 taking antibiotics and 65 taking antihistamines the effect was marginally less beneficial to Sylvasun, but this may not have been significant.

Although further trials with a placebo could well be of value, the writer considers it is well worthwhile recommending the vitamin A-calcium carbonate preparation mentioned.

What must be mentioned is that this oral preparation in no way affects the tanning, unlike a barrier cream.

Some of the participants claimed that their tanning was greater and the skin peeling was less but at no time is this claimed. The only property claimed is the diminution of the pain of sunburn.

As previously mentioned, throughout the above trial participants were advised to use a moisturing application, whether it be a lotion, cream or oil.

Furman in 1972 in two surveys of 44 subjects taking Sylvasun and 33 subjects taking a placebo reported that Sylvasun did not reduce solar erythema and further the subsequent taking of increased dosage did not reduce the pain from sunburn. In fairness to the preparation the writer feels it should be recorded that :

1. Sylvasun is not reported to cut down erythema. This is a stage in tanning.
2. The subjects did not use a moisturising cream as recommended.
3. The subjects were exposed on the first day to one hour of midday sun in Johannesburg which is greater than anyone would recommend.
4. Following the writer's and colleagues' work, it is not suggested that the preparation will be beneficial therapeutically, only prophylactically.

Kraft, Hoch, Newcomb and Quisna in 1972 carried out a survey of suntan preparations in the U.S.A.They came to the conclusion that oil based vehicles provided better protection than oil and water vehicles. However oil and water vehicles were superior in promoting tanning. In their survey they used three oil based vehicles, three oil and water based vehicles and two controls. In each vehicle the same screening agent, dipropylene glycol salicylate, was used. Tests were done under both sunlight and artificial light. They said that the best protection against sunburn under either light was gained through the oil based formulations, but with the emulsions there was less blistering and peeling, and improved tanning.

The writer with his own experience with patients in the tropical sun supports lotions and creams in that they appear to be better absorbed and therefore are better moisturisers which is the most important factor. Excess of oil in intense heat can in itself cause burning.

To the truly sun sensitive a barrier cream must be used. The most usual and effective bases of these creams are the benzophenones. One of these is mexenone, which is 2-hydroxy-4-methoxy-4′-methyl benzophenone. This is sold as a 4 per cent cream in an oil and water base under the name of Uvistat. It is non-irritating and non-sensitising. If applied heavily it is truly a sun barrier which as such will prevent tanning but obviously if the application is gradually reduced in amount increasing amounts of sun rays in the 290-320 nanometre range will filter through so giving a resultant satisfactory but far slower tan.

And to summarise, the writer considers that as far as advice to prospective sun worshippers is concerned, besides telling them to be sensible in their gradual exposure to the sun and use of moisturising applications, that they should take a vitamin A-calcium carbonate preparation.

4. Diseases of Insanitation

'There shall ye eat of all that are in the waters: whatsoever hath fins and scales in the waters, in the seas and in the rivers, them shall ye eat. And all that have not fins and scales in the seas and in the rivers, of all that move in the waters, and of any living thing which is in the waters, they shall be an abomination unto you: They shall be even an abomination unto you: ye shall not eat of their flesh, but ye shall have their carcases in abomination. Whatsoever hath no fins nor scales in the waters, that shall be an abomination unto you.'

Leviticus 11, 9-12

'I am poured out like water, and all my bones are out of joint my heart is like wax; it is melted in the midst of my bowels my strength is dried up like a potsherd.'

Psalm 22

By far the commonest problem that affects the traveller is the onset of diarrhoea. It is interesting that reference was made even in the Old Testament to it and to its common cause, the shellfish.

In the past, the average holidaymaker who set forth in search of the sun travelled with intense optimism and seldom thought that they would suffer sickness. However, nowadays, with increased public education in medical matters, they are beginning to realise that very frequently they may be assaulted by diarrhoea.

By far the commonest cause of this diarrhoea is the ailment which we now officially call travellers diarrhoea. It has many other names: in general associated with the part of the world where the traveller is suffering from it.

Probably the commonest and oldest name associated with this problem is Gippy Tummy. This is the name by which it was known by men of all services, whether of the then British Empire forces or those of the United States of America throughout the Second World War. In fact it was the British Army who first generated this name when they were serving in Egypt even before the First World War. Since then, as mentioned already, various geographical names have been given such as Basra Belly, Delhi Belly, Rangoon Runs, Hong Kong Dog, Ho Chi Minhs, Tokyo Trots, Montezuma's Revenge, Aztec Two Step or, in Mexico, Turista. This is probably the one really sensible name because it is the tourist who suffers so frequently from it.

Gordon, the eminent public health authority in the United States of America in the book *Control of Communicable Diseases in Man,* which he edited in 1965, described it as 'a notorious worldwide illness lasting one to three days, declaring itself often with a precipitous onset of loose stools and variable other symptoms including nausea, vomiting and abdominal cramps. It often occurs sporadically as isolated cases, though epidemics do occur within families or groups of travellers of all ages'.

Professor Kean of Cornell University was the first man seriously to research into the problem of travellers diarrhoea but other work had been done before him and this should be mentioned first.

In 1941 to 1943, Bulmer, in charge of a large medical division of a military hospital in Egypt found that with all cases of diarrhoea, including the mild ones labelled as Gippy Tummy, the incidence decreased dramatically in any particular person with increasing length of service, so inferring development of some immunity.

This was confirmed by work carried out with the United States forces in the Middle East also in the Second World War. They found out that the incidence of diarrhoea decreased every year a soldier served abroad: the annual rate per thousand decreasing each year from 196 to 170, 115 and 79. They also found interesting that Negro troops in the Mediterranean area in the war showed consistently lower infection rates for intestinal diseases than white troops.

Bulmer went so far to say that British troops were attacked in such a way that a military campaign could not successfully be conducted during the first weeks after arrival in the area. Probably every soldier of the British Army on the Middle Eastern front had at least one attack of acute diarrhoea, usually soon after arrival.

In 1946 McGregor, in another survey in the Middle East, found that there was no increased incidence of diarrhoea at the time of the hot dry wind called the Khamsin, nor, perhaps more surprisingly, was there an increase during the time of the sandstorms.

In 1947 Kershaw renewed the idea that in H.M. ships where ventilation was draughty, acute chilling of the abdomen could cause enteritis.

In 1954 Kean started his extensive research. Initially with Smillie he searched for the incidence of intestinal protozoa in American students visiting Europe from the U.S.A.They obtained 804 stool specimens from 582 students; 222 were examined on the way there and on the return. With the remaining 360, half, or 180, were examined on the way out and the other 180 on the return. Although over 50 per cent had diarrhoea in Europe, there was no statistical increase of protozoa in returning students than in the outgoing. This precludes any suggestion that travellers diarrhoea is protozoal in origin, particularly as over 50 per cent of the students had diarrhoea during their visit. The main point of interest was that the incidence was far higher in those visiting the Mediterranean area compared with Northern Europe. One point of interest was that 4 per cent of American students on leaving the U.S.A. were found to be infected with *Entamoeba histolytica*. The incidence was the same in returning students.

Kean then changed his studies to Mexico and Hawaii. Two areas with similar climates. 1265 tourists from Mexico and 210 tourists from Hawii were interviewed at Los Angeles Airport. Of those that had been away for more than seven days the incidence of diarrhoea among those from Mexico was 33 per cent while among those from Hawaii the incidence was 7.6 per cent. This therefore is against a straight climatic cause.

Kean also looked into the time and the length of the attack. He found that 63 per cent of people suffered within the first week and a further 32 per cent in the second week, making a total of 95 per cent of cases within two weeks.

In 57 per cent the attack lasted one day and in a further 32 per cent two or three days, hence 89 per cent conformed to Gordon's description of one to three days.

As well as this he divided the sufferers into age groups and here he found that the incidence was up to 43 per cent in people of 24 years of age or less, 36 per cent in the 25-40 years group, 29 per cent in 41-55 and only 18 per cent in people over 55 years. He considered that this could have been due to one of two reasons. Firstly the older group had travelled more and developed a certain immunity or secondly they may have been more sensible in where and what they ate. This the writer thinks is the more likely.

In the third survey he carried out with colleagues he tried to find out something on the bacteriological aspects of travellers diarrhoea. They looked for Salmonella species, Shigella species, Klebsiella species, Paracolobacterium species, Proteus species and *Escherichia coli.* They found the incidence of pathogenic *Escherichia coli* to be far higher in those with diarrhoea than without. This was particularly so in the cases with more severe diarrhoea. No cases showed the presence of Salmonella or Shigella.

In 1958, at the time of the political troubles in the Lebanon, the United Nations sent in political observers of various nationalities. G. T. Haneveld of the Royal Netherlands Navy carried out a very extensive survey of the diarrhoea which occurred amongst these observers. They were all healthy males between the ages of 20 years and 50 years. He found the incidence of diarrhoea was far commoner in the men from Europe than in the observers from Asia and South America. In the former group the incidence was 41 per cent, or 166 out of 416, while in the latter group the incidence was 10 per cent, or 16 out of 160. The lowest rates of diarrhoea definitely occurred in representatives from countries where the sanitation facilities were least satisfactory.

In 1966 the author carried out an extensive survey on the incidence of travellers diarrhoea in BOAC staff and families travelling overseas on a worldwide basis using the cheap staff fares which are available if the seats have not been sold by the time of departure of the aircraft.

Nearly 1400 people took part in this trial. The incidence of diarrhoea was nearly 30 per cent among those visiting the African continent; 25 per cent the Middle East; 17 per cent Southern Europe; and just over 20 per cent around the entire Mediterranean littoral. The author further found that 35 per cent of the attacks lasted one day and 80 per cent lasted no more than three days. This, along with Kean's work, fits in with Gordon's description.

More recently the main work on the aetiology of the problem has been done by Rowe, Taylor and Bettelheim from the Colindale Reference Laboratory in association with the British Army.

The incidence of travellers diarrhoea can be a severe problem in the army with the need to have a strategic force based in the U.K. which is flown out suddenly to trouble spots for immediate service. The incidence of travellers diarrhoea in 30 per cent of men in a battalion due for action could be extremely serious.

A very careful study was therefore carried out by Rowe and his fellow workers on a group of 540 British soldiers who had travelled by air from England to Aden. Thirty-eight of them had an attack of diarrhoea within 14 days of arrival. Faecal specimens were investigated from 35 of them. Salmonellae were isolated from two cases but in the remaining 33 cases neither Salmonellae or Shigellae were isolated. A new serotype of *Escherichia coli* with antigenic structure 0148K ? H28 was isolated in the acute phase from 19 or 54.3 per cent. In the remaining 14 cases or 40 per cent, a number of different *E. coli* serotypes were isolated including serotypes which cause infantile diarrhoea; these were not related to travellers diarrhoea.

Most cases of travellers diarrhoea are said to occur within the first two weeks in a new area. In this survey the peak incidence of the occurrence of diarrhoea was at the tenth day and this was the peak time for the finding of *E. coli* 0148K ? H28. Further, this serotype was not isolated from healthy subjects, nor has it been found in Great Britain except in one case of laboratory infection associated with this work. The case of the laboratory infection was most interesting and it is quoted verbatim from Rowe, Taylor and Bettelheim's paper:

'A laboratory assistant in Great Britain working with *E. coli* 0148K ? H28 complained of colicky abdominal pain starting in the early morning of 21 December 1966, and a few hours later developed severe diarrhoea. From 21 December to 24 December the abdominal colic continued with passage of profuse watery faeces up to 12 times a day. During this time he complained of general malaise and weakness but was apyrexial. Faeces were examined on a number of occasions; blood and mucus were absent and Salmonellae and Shigellae were not isolated. On 21 and 22 December specimens yielded *E. coli* 0148K ? H28 in pure culture on McConkey's Agar. On the morning of 24 December treatment was started with oral colistin sulphate 250,000 units six hourly, diarrhoea ceased within 24 hours, but treatment was continued for a further three days. Stool cultures taken on the fourth day after treatment ceased and on subsequent days failed to show *E. coli* 0148K ? H28.'

The most interesting thing is that it would be difficult to have a more classic description of travellers diarrhoea.

A further survey was carried out with another group of troops in Sharjah and this produced basically the same result.

One further interesting point found was that while infantile, *Escherichia coli* are enterotoxic and adult organisms are invasive, *E. coli* 0148K ? H28 was enterotoxic.

Sakazaki and his colleagues reported that other serotypes (0124, 0136, 044 and 0144) were commonly found in cases of diarrhoea in older children and adults in Japan.

All the above work is very positive evidence that the majority of cases of travellers diarrhoea are infective in origin and almost certainly due to pathogenic *Escherichia coli,* whose serotype varies around the world.

There is obviously a small percentage of cases of travellers diarrhoea which may not be infective in origin. Such dietetic problems as a sudden increase in consumption of cheap wine, also cooking in olive oil, can act as laxatives.

How are we therefore to prevent this annoying complaint which can upset a family holiday if one or two are laid low with it. More important to the businessman carrying out an intensive sales tour to the Middle or Far East, or even further, the sudden interference of two days of diarrhoea in a tight schedule of visits may be disastrous.

Prevention is dependent on two basic disciplines:

1. General preventive methods by standards of food hygiene.
2. Providing anti-infective agents.

Although the first is certainly the most important, especially as it is by these methods that one avoids all the other forms of food poisoning, let us deal with the second first because this is a direct follow on to the surveys carried out by Kean and his workers, and by the author.

Kean carried out two separate surveys with a placebo and with iodochlorhydroxyquinoline or clioquinol sold usually as Enterovioform but also as Entosan. Combined with antispasmodics it is sold as Sedacol (zyma), Enterosan and Entroquin.

In his first trial 33 per cent taking a placebo had diarrhoea while 38 per cent taking clioquinol suffered. In the second trial 33 per cent with both the placebo and with clioquinol had diarrhoea. From this he naturally assumed that clioquinol was valueless in preventing diarrhoea.

With the prolonged taking of clioquinol one must also consider the possible connection with subacute myelo-optico-neuropathy. In the work of Nakae, Yamamoto, Shigematsu and Kono, out of 1839 cases of S.M.O.N. 1381 or 75 per cent had received clioquinol. Spillane reported a probable case from Cardiff where the patient had taken two tablets of clioquinol four times a day for five days.

In a further double blind trial Kean and his co-workers found that phthalylsulphathiazole was far more effective than Neomycin, but surprisingly in clinically severe cases this was reversed.

In the 1960 Olympic Games in Rome, D. J. Cussen, medical officer to the British Olympic team, in conjunction with Professor May, decided to give the entire team one tablet twice daily of Streptotriad, which is a May and Baker preparation containing Streptomycin 65 mgm, sulphadimidine 100 mgm, sulphathiazole 100 mgm and sulphadiazine 100 mgm.

Although other teams in Rome had an appreciable amount of diarrhoea the British team had none.

In the survey the author carried out on BOAC staff and families the 1400 participants were divided into three approximately equal groups who were given: (1) an inert control; (2) neomycin/sulphatriad (neomycin sulphate 200 mgm, sulphadimidine 100 mgm, sulphadiazine 100 mgm and sulphathiazole 100 mgm); (3) streptotriad (streptomycin/sulphatriad).

In this way the difference in the active groups was only between neomycin and streptomycin.

The incidence of diarrhoea was slightly higher in those taking neomycin/sulphatriad than those taking the placebo but not statistically so. The incidence of diarrhoea in the streptomycin/sulphatriad group was appreciably less than in the other two groups.

If in fact travellers diarrhoea is usually infective in origin and caused by an *Escherichia coli,* it is not surprising that a streptomycin/sulphatriad tablet is effective.

Based on Cussen's original work and the author's work, Raymond Owen, medical adviser to the British Olympics team in Mexico City in 1968, gave the entire team and camp followers Streprotriad prophylactically. Out of 300 athletes and camp followers there were six cases of athletes who had to cease training for two days each. No one was confined to bed. Considering Kean's figures of 33 per cent, a figure of 2 per cent was very dramatic.

Further, since 1966 all BOAC staff going on overseas duty for periods of up to three weeks have been offered Streptotriad prophylactically. The incidence of travellers diarrhoea has been cut drastically and in seven years this has not changed. This absence of loss of effectiveness indicates that resistance to the drug has not developed.

It is therefore suggested that the taking of Streptotriad, one tablet twice daily, for the time someone is away plus two days after return to cover late infection for up to a maximum of three to four weeks is beneficial.

To turn next to the general preventive methods.

These points are commonsense along with principles of public health.

When any medical practitioner is given the opportunity he should press the points home to his travelling patients.

Of these factors the first to be considered are water and milk. When one considers the enormous population explosions which have been occurring in the holiday resorts of the Mediterranean littoral over the past few years, one must realise what a stress can be put on the public health services of these places. Just over 12 years ago there was not a holiday resort on the Costa Brava, just a few primitive fishing villages. The Costa Blanca and the Costa del Sol are of even more recent development.

It is only necessary for the sewage system, the swimming pool purification systems or the personal habits of the food handlers to be other than above reproach and severe trouble is bound to occur. If any of the above three points fail, then many of the intestinal infections which are discussed in Chapter 9 may occur. This includes all the Salmonellae infections, both forms of dysentery and other water or milk borne infections.

The only really satisfactory answer is to boil all drinking water and milk. This can be difficult for anyone staying in a hotel. Regrettably, however, the hygiene of some hotels of even the leading worldwide groups are not necessarily satisfactory. However, it is essential with all camping holidays.

There are three other measures which can be used instead of boiling. They are not as satisfactory but they are better than nothing. The first is drinking only mineral waters produced by a reputable firm.

It is a practical point to find out who has the local agency for either Coca Cola or Pepsi Cola. Both these minerals are made under strict licence from the United States of America throughout the world. As such, the 'factories' are regularly inspected by public health inspectors out from the States who are employed by the parent companies. High standards of hygiene are maintained in the factories and this indirectly maintains the standard of the other products, besides 'Coke' and 'Pepsi'.

The second answer is the use of chloramination tablets such as Sterotabs, which can be obtained from most chemists.

The third one is for those staying in hotels where boiling of the water would be difficult and where the buying of mineral waters may be expensive. It is dependent on a satisfactory hot water system in the hotel. The principle is basically the same as that of pasteurisation of milk—the maintenance of a high temperature, but one below boiling, for a prolonged period. If the hot water system is maintaining the water at 140°-160° Fahrenheit or more then it is most likely that most of the organisms are killed. On this basis the answer is to use water from the hot water tap as drinking water. Fill a container from the hot water tap and keep until it is cool for drinking but *making sure the container is covered.*

An extra point that must be remembered is that ice cubes should be made from boiled water. It is no good drinking only boiled water and then adding ice cubes which are made from unboiled water but which dissolve in the drink in a matter of minutes.

One of the delicacies of many tropical, semi-tropical and Mediterranean hot spots which pull in the ever-increasing holidaymakers is shellfish. These as we all know can be of very doubtful purity. They can cause the common attack of travellers diarrhoea, the slightly less common bacillary dysentery, the serious typhoid or the rare paragonimus Westermanii infection. Even when Leviticus was written the problems of the shellfish were recognised. Wherever you go you are usually told that the local prawns are satisfactory. It is the prawns of another area which cause trouble. This, of course, is nonsense. The purity depends initially on the purity of the water in which they are breeding and secondly the treatment which they are given after they are caught.

For the campers who are doing their own food purchasing, it is sensible to insist on all shellfish being alive when they are bought. This is obviously not possible in a hotel but at least in these surroundings it is worthwhile for the visitor to see that the fish have been well cleaned and all the non-edible parts have been removed.

The habit of eating underdone steaks is bad. Some countries prefer to call them rare steaks. Whatever we call them, they are an unsatisfactory way of eating meat. Tape worms are killed by satisfactory thorough cooking but not by cooking if the steak is served up 'red'.

Steak tartare is a dish which must be rigorously avoided in the Middle East. Not only should all meat be well cooked, but it should be recently cooked and only once cooked. This principle goes for all cooked food and not just meat.

Uncooked food is another problem. All fruit which can be peeled should be peeled and this includes tomatoes. Fruit which cannot be peeled, such as strawberries, or salad such as lettuce, must be washed in a chloraminated solution, such as a weak solution of Milton or Roccal. Watercress should be avoided unless its purity of origin is well known.

The large Middle Eastern water melon with the pips scattered throughout the red flesh can create a problem. In some of the markets of the Middle East where it is sold by weight it is not unknown for the local merchants to pump in water—which may be dirty—with an instrument like an ear syringe to increase the weight.

Great care must be taken with cold buffets which are frequently known as the 'Chef's special table'. If this refers to a specially high incidence of infection, it may be a good name. Regrettably, even in presumed high quality hotels, one can see dishes of cold meats, joints, various salads, and cold sweets laid out uncovered on a table with flies abounding and dive bombing the food. This is particularly so in warm holiday spots where the dining area is on the hotel terrace and hence open to the outside and the insects. Where feeding is indoors in an air conditioned area, the insect count is far lower. But this is not the only reason for avoiding salads.

Similarly, cocktail parties and receptions for the visiting businessman can also be a problem with canapes and other cold cooked 'goodies', left out to the open air and the flies.

Ice creams are naturally very popular among holidaymakers, especially in Italy, where they are so delicious. However, standards of production vary and it must be remembered that *Salmonella typhi* is not killed by freezing. Travellers should be advised to buy only ice creams made by the large reputable firms. *On no account should they buy them, or other forms of food, from street hawkers.*

Finally the avoidance of fly infested restaurants is an essential. If the actual restaurant is fly infested, the kitchen will almost certainly be even more so.

If one has any doubt as to the possible lack of cleanliness in a restaurant, it is a good thing to have a quick look in the lavatory before entering the restaurant. If the lavatory is dirty then it is more than likely that the kitchen will be dirty as well.

In addition to the problems of food and drink there are the results of ill advised bathing and swimming. Infective hepatitis is accepted in general as faecal spread and as such any place where there is sewage effluent must be avoided. As such, in and around harbours or places where ships are lying offshore must be taboo for swimming.

As well as this there is the problem of schistosomiasis (see Chap. 9). This is spread by either drinking or washing, paddling or swimming in infected water. Geographically, schistosomiasis occurs in Africa all the way down the Nile Valley, right across Central Africa from West to East, and South into Rhodesia and South Africa. It is present in the islands of Zanzibar, Madagascar, Réunion and Mauritius. There are scattered areas throughout the Middle East. Further East a variety occurs in Laos, Khmer Republic, China, Southern Japan and the Philippines. In the New World the waters of Venezuela. North Eastern Brazil and the island of St Lucia are infected. Wherever there is schistosomiasis there should be no fresh water sailing or bathing. Also drinking water must be boiled.

And so one gives ten commandments for the avoidance of travellers diarrhoea and all of the more serious intestinal infections.

1. Boil all drinking water and milk.
2. Be very careful of shellfish—perferably see them alive before eating.
3. All cooked food should be well cooked and recently cooked.
4. All fruit including tomatoes should be peeled.

5. Lettuce and unpeeled fruit sterilised by chlorination—no watercress.
6. No left-overs or food on display.
7. Avoid local ice creams— only large firms.
8. Large firm mineral waters.
9. Avoid fly infested restaurants.
10. Take one tablet of Streptotriad twice daily.

5. Insect Borne Diseases

Many of the diseases of insanitation are in themselves indirectly spread by insects such as flies.

However, other than these diseases, by far the most important and largest group of diseases occurring in the tropics and subtropics are those directly spread by the biting of humans by insects.

To classify the diseases by the incriminating insects let us consider the mosquito borne diseases. Malaria is spread by the anopheline mosquito. Yellow fever, and Rift Valley fever of Kenya, are spread by the aedes group and the *Wucheria bancrofti* form of filaria or elephantiasis is spread by the culecine group.

Varieties of sandfly spread the leishmanial infections (including kala azar), dengue fever and phlebotomus or sandfly fever.

The tsetse fly spreads trypanosomiasis or sleeping sickness. The chrysops fly spreads the loiasis variety of filaria and the small black fly spreads onchocerciasis, another variety of filaria.

In addition to the above there are the Rickettsial group of diseases which are spread by a variety of insects. Louse borne typhus and trench fever are spread by the human louse. Rocky Mountain fever, fièvre boutonneuse, fièvre nautique de Toulon. Q fever and tick typhus are spread by ticks frequently from dogs. Scrub typhus or tsutsugamuchi disease is spread by a mite usually from rats. Endemic or murine typhus is spread by the rat flea, as also is bubonic plague.

However, by far the most important disease to consider here, especially in regard to methods in its prevention, is malaria.

There are two points which must be remembered about malaria.

1. In its more serious form it can be fairly rapidly fatal, especially in the non-immune traveller.

2. It is preventable. If there is a breakthrough despite adequate prophlaxis it is a treatable disease with a happy outcome.

It is caused by various species of Plasmodia which are spread to man by the bite of the anopheline mosquito.

There are four varieties of Plasmodium: *P. falciparum, P. vivax, P. malariae and P. ovale.*

There are three basic principles in the prevention of malaria:

1. The prevention of the breeding of anopheline mosquitoes.

2. If there are mosquitoes, to prevent them from biting human beings.

3. If they bite human beings, to prevent malaria developing.

To discuss each principle in turn.

1. The prevention of the breeding of anopheline mosquitoes is naturally the responsibility of the local government, and the visitor to a malarious, or one time malarious, area must rely on their efficiency. Regrettably, in some of the developing countries in areas where previously there had been adequate malaria control, there has been a relaxation of standards. As a result malaria has either returned to these places or the incidence has increased in amount.

The prevention of breeding depends on several factors of which briefly the following are the major controlling forces.

(a) The drainage of all areas of stagnant water, particularly shallow pools. To the new visitor to a malarious area it is wise to remind them not to leave outside empty tins, cans or other receptacles which can fill with water after rain, else they will encourage the breeding of mosquitoes.

(b) The treating of pools, shallow streams and banks with oil. D.D.T. or other insectisides to destroy the mosquitoes in the larval stage.

(c) The spraying of houses with an insecticide to kill the adult mosquito. Of these insecticides there are two basic types:

(i) Those which are applied to a wall or other surface, like a paint, and remain toxic to the mosquito for months, so that by alighting on the wall that has been treated it absorbs a toxic dose of the insecticide. This type of spraying is usually carried out by the local authority. 'Residual insecticides' are used. The main residual insecticides are the chlorinated hydrocarbons, and where resistance has occurred to these, organophosporus compounds may be used. In the first group there are D.D.T., B.M.C., Dieldrin and Aldrin. In the second group there are Diazinon, Malathion, Fenthion and Dichlorvos.

(ii) Those which are sprayed around the rooms of a house usually at sunset. They act by killing the mosquito and are therefore known as 'immediate or knock down' insecticides. The mosquito may die rapidly or after several hours. These immediate insecticides are now usually sold in aerosol cans and it is advisable for the visitor to a malarious area to take one with him. He should spray his room at sunset and on going to bed. The main ingredients of the immediate insecticides are pyrethrum and allethrin but a number of substances which act synergistically are usually added and hence reduce the dose of pyrethrum. Of these the main ones in use are Piperonyl Butoxide, Sesame Oil, Pine Oil and D.D.T.

2. The most important thing to remember in the prevention of the spread of malaria by avoiding being bitten by an anopheline is that the anopheline mosquito only bites from dusk to dawn. This is not so with the culecine and other mosquitoes, but they do not spread malaria. Hence every precaution must be taken to prevent being bitten during this time.

Firstly clothing must be such that as much of the body as possible is covered after dark: for men, long-sleeved shirts buttoned or linked at the wrists and long trousers: with the ladies they should be encouraged to wear long sleeves and long skirts. Anyone who prefers to do otherwise should apply an insect repellant cream to exposed areas.

On the exposed parts, an insect repellent should always be used. There are several insect repellents which are used in sticks or creams. Probably the most effective is Diethyl Toluamide, which is contained in Flypel and Skeet-o-Stik. The next best are probably Dimethylphthalate and Indalone. Oil of Citronella was one that was used in the past. In general their action lasts for up to four hours, but when sweating the activity can be cut down to three or even two hours. Care must be taken to avoid the eyes and lips, also spectacle frames and rayon clothing.

The other principle, besides clothing and repellents, is to avoid mosquitoes getting into the bedroom.

Mosquito netting is therefore an essential in all malarious areas if the bedroom is not fully air conditioned.

Netting may be of two varieties. Either the tightly fitting frame in the open half of the window or the old fashioned mosquito net over the bed. The net must be carefully tucked in all round and under the mattress after getting into bed. It does not matter which type of netting is used although the former is pleasanter. What is important is that it is well fitting with no gaps and in good condition, with no holes. If a patient is visiting a malarious area he must be advised on these points.

However, nowadays most hotels and more and more private houses in malarious areas quite rightly have air conditioning. Provided this is used sensibly, the air conditioner is well fitting, and the bedroom is shut at sundown when the air conditioner is turned on, the netting is not required. However, it does no harm to have an aerosol and spray the bedroom as previously mentioned, at sundown and on going to bed. However, there may be gaps around the air conditioner.

3. The third point, the prevention of malaria developing in the anopheline bitten person, is the most important factor for the visitor to malarious areas. It is not possible to avoid completely being bitten by mosquitoes, but as already mentioned a serious illness can be prevented by adequate prophlaxis by this method.

To discuss the efficacy of the various prophylactic drugs one must consider briefly the life cycle of the malarial parasite as it passes through man, the mosquito and man.

When the anopheline mosquito bites man, and it is always a female, the male and female gametocytes are ingested in the human blood into the mosquito stomach. Here fertilisation takes place. The fertilised female gametocyte then penetrates the stomach wall to develop into a cyst below the lining membrane. Inside this cyst the sporozoites develop and when suitably mature the cyst ruptures and the sporozoites are freed into the insect's body cavity. They migrate into the salivary gland of the mosquito from where they are injected into the human when the mosquito bites again.

It is necessary for this part of the life cycle to occur before a mosquito can infect a human being.

With *P. vivax* infections it is usually about 11 days; with *P. falciparum* about 12 days, but with *P. malariae* as much as 18-20 days.

Once the sporozoites have developed and the mosquito has become able to pass on malaria as above, the sporozoites remain viable and infectious in the mosquito for many weeks.

When man is bitten the sporozoites leave the blood stream, entering the polygonal cells of the liver where for approximately the next seven days they develop into merozoites. This is known as the pre-erythrocytic or P.E. phase. After the merozoites have developed, the liver cells rupture and the merozoites are thrown into the blood stream, entering the erythrocytes to start the asexual life cycle or erythrocytic or E. phase. These parasites grow and then divide to form more merozoites and the erythrocyte ruptures to spread more parasites into the blood stream. This is the cycle as it occurs with *P. falciparum* infections and prophylactic drug therapy is dependent on this cycle.

However, with *P. vivax, P. malariae* and *P. ovale* there is a further phase in the human life cycle which calls for additional prophylaxis.

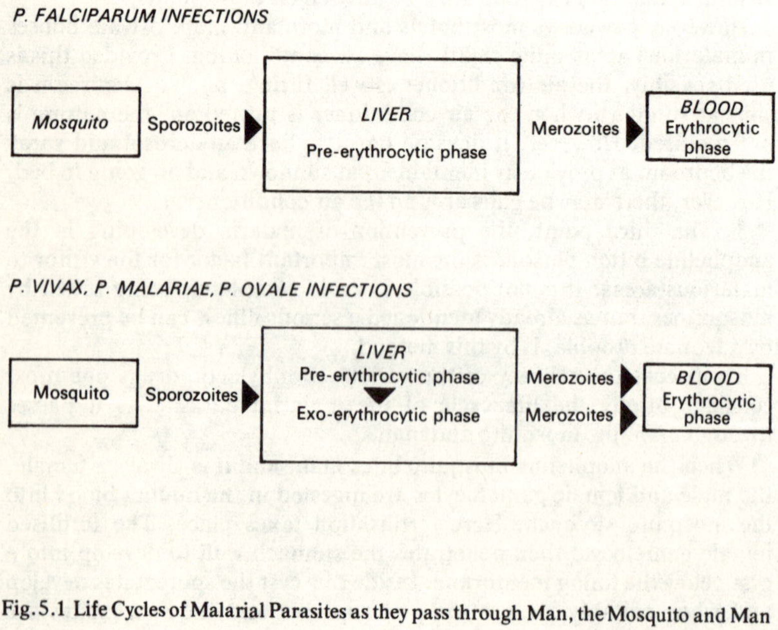

Fig. 5.1 Life Cycles of Malarial Parasites as they pass through Man, the Mosquito and Man

This is the exoerythrocytic or E.E. phase and this is what causes the relapses. With these infections more than one cycle occurs in the liver. These cycles start with the pre-erythrocytic phase but continue to produce merozoites which are periodically sent out into the blood stream to enter the erythrocytes—hence the relapses.

These phases have to be considered in the assessment of the most suitable drug to use.

The specific antimalarial drugs can be divided into several groups:

1. Cinchona alkaloids: Quinine.
2. 9-Aminoacridin compounds: Mepacrine (Atebrine, Quinacrine).
3. 4-Aminoquinoline compounds: Chloroquine (Aralen, Resochin, Nivaquine), Amodiaquin (Camoquinet).
4. 8-Aminoquinoline compounds: Pamaquin; Primaquine; Pentaquine.
5. Biguanide compounds: Proguanil (Paludrine), Chlorproguanil (Lapudrine).
6. Diaminopyrimidines: Pyrimethamine (Daraprim).

The stage of the life cycle at which these drugs are effective varies.

Let these stages be considered next.

Sporozoites—No drug is effective.

Pre-erythrocytic phase in the liver—Proguanil and Pyrimethamine in *P. falciparum* infections.

Exo-erythrocytic phase—Pamaquin; Primaquine and Pentaquine.

Asexual parasites in erythrocytic phase—All groups except Pamaquin; Primaquine and Pentaquine.

Thus any drug that acts on the pre-erythrocytic phase or the erythrocytic phase can be used as a suppressive in *P. Falciparum* infections. Drugs that act on the exo-erythrocytic phase must be used to prevent relapses in vivax, malariae and ovale infections.

Chloroquine is the most rapidly acting schizonticide known and is the drug of choice for treatment. As such, in general, it should be kept for treatment although it is a valuable suppressive. Resistant strains have been shown in South East Asia and South America. Amodiaquine has action very similar to chloroquine.

With both these drugs, if used for prophylaxis, they are taken once or preferably twice a week.

Mepacrine is little used nowadays. It is less effective than the above drugs and more toxic. It causes yellow staining of the skin. Further, it has to be taken for two weeks prior to entering a malarious area.

Quinine is not a good drug for use in prophylaxis, as it is unsuitable and if prolonged is toxic. Further, there is the risk of blackwater fever with prolonged use, and it is not as effective as synthetics.

Proguanil is an active schizonticidal acting more slowly than chloroquine. As such, it is not nearly as effective as the latter for treatment, but as it is the least toxic of all antimalarial drugs it is of great value in prophylaxis in falciparum infections. Resistance has developed in certain areas which regrettably are in general the same areas where chloroquine resistance has developed.

It must be taken daily as a prophylactic but it is a known fact that it is far easier to remember to take a tablet on a daily basis than on a twice weekly basis.

Chlorproguanil has similar action but is longer acting and as such is taken only once weekly. It is Proguanil with one chlorine element added.

Pyrimethamine. This drug is used only prophylactically. Its action is like that of proguanil. Toxicity is low if taken in correct dosage, but it can cause a megaloblastic anaemia if taken in excess. One of its great benefits, but also one of its problems, is that it is practically tasteless and as such can be taken by small children. Proguanil is very bitter. However, great care must be taken in storage because of its tastelessness so as to prevent children taking it to excess.

What are the other factors which must be considered in the choice of the best prophylactic against malaria?

Falciparum malaria can be a killer and as such it must at all costs be prevented.

With the exception of Mepacrine, which is now rarely used, it is necessary to start taking an antimalarial on the day of departure for a malarious area. What is most important is that they must be taken for at least four weeks after the traveller leaves the malarious area.

There are two definite schools of thought as to which is the best prophylactic to take to prevent falciparum malaria.

There is the Proguanil school of thought, which is the general one in Britain, Canada and the Netherlands.

Then there is the chloroquine group, who are in the United States, France and Germany.

The writer is very much a member of the first school for three main reasons:

1. It is an established fact that it is far easier to remember to take a tablet every day rather than to take one twice a week or once a week.

2. If you do forget to take a daily tablet once, you go 48 hours, but if you completely forget to take a weekly tablet you go 14 days without one, while the incubation period of malaria is 10-12 days. This could be disastrous. Even with forgetting a twice weekly tablet once a week can be critical.

3. Chloroquine is established as by far the best drug for treatment and should be kept for treatment so preventing the development of disastrous resistance.

However, whichever drug is used, the essential points are starting 24 hours before entering a malarious area, taking the drug regularly throughout the time in the malarious area and for 28 days after leaving the area. It must be remembered that while passing through a malarious area a traveller may be bitten by an infected mosquito during a transit stop at an airport. Although everything is done at international airports to keep down the mosquito population this can occur and so everyone travelling at night in a malarious area should be taking prophylactic antimalarials for the requisite time.

The other prophylactic against falciparum malaria which must be mentioned is Pyrimethamine, especially because of its great value with children because of its absence of taste. The dosage for prophylaxis of these drugs is as follows:

Proguanil: 100 mgm daily for an adult. In holoendemic areas, in men of over 200 lb, 200 mgm daily may be taken. Children: birth to 1 year, 25 mgm daily; 2 to 10 years, 50 mgm daily.

Chloroquine: 2 tablets (300 mgm base) weekly. Children: birth to year, ¼ tablet; 1-3 years, ½ tablet; 3-6 years, ⅓ tablet; 6-10 years, 1 tablet; over 10 years, 2 tablets.

Pyrimethamine: Adult, 25-50 mgm (1-2 tablets) weekly. Children: birth-1 year, ¼ tablet; 2-12 years, ½ tablet weekly.

N.B. With all drugs continue to take for 28 days after leaving the malarious area.

However, in general, the above drugs have no effect on the destruction of the *P. vivax, P. malariae* and *P. ovale* in the exo-erythrocytic phases in the liver which cause the relapses in the infections.

In order to prevent these relapses it is essential to give a course of pamaquine for 10 days or primaquine for a fortnight after the completion of the 28 days of the usual prophylactics after leaving the malarious areas.

If this is not done then a vivax, malariae or ovale infection may well occur after the 28 days are completed. These infections will not break out while the usual prophylactics are being taken but these latter only act as suppressants.

However, pamaquine and primaquine are both toxic, especially the former. There is very little difference between the therapeutic doses and the toxic doses.

Intravascular haemolysis occurs in people who are deficient in glucose-6-phosphate dehydrogenase. This deficiency can occur in people of Caucasian origin, but it is commoner in people of Mediterranean origin.

If there is a deficiency of G6PD then acute haemolysis occurs, usually after about three days of administration of the drug. Along with this haemolysis, methaemoglobinuria occurs. The haemolysis usually lasts for about one week, during which time severe anaemia may result. It then stops spontaneously but will recur if the drug is re-introduced.

Because of these complications pamaquine or primaquine should only be given in hospital. Anyway for the first four or five days to well cover the period during which haemolysis would start. Dosage with pamaquine is 10 mgm of the base three times a day for ten days, and with primaquine 15 mgm of the base for 14 days.

Fig. 5·2 EPIDEMIOLOGICAL ASSESSMENT OF STATUS OF MALARIA, JULY 1974.

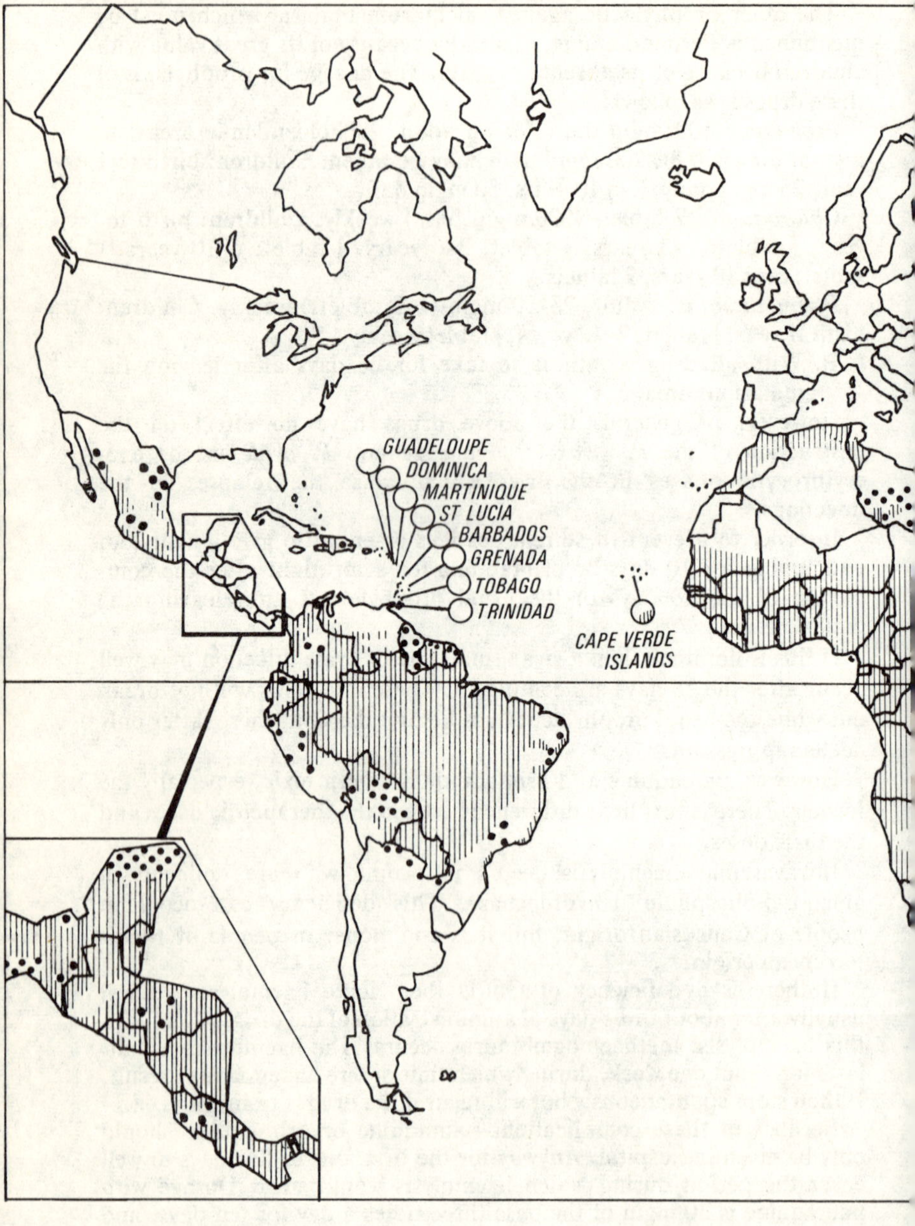

(Map by courtesy of the World Health Organisation)

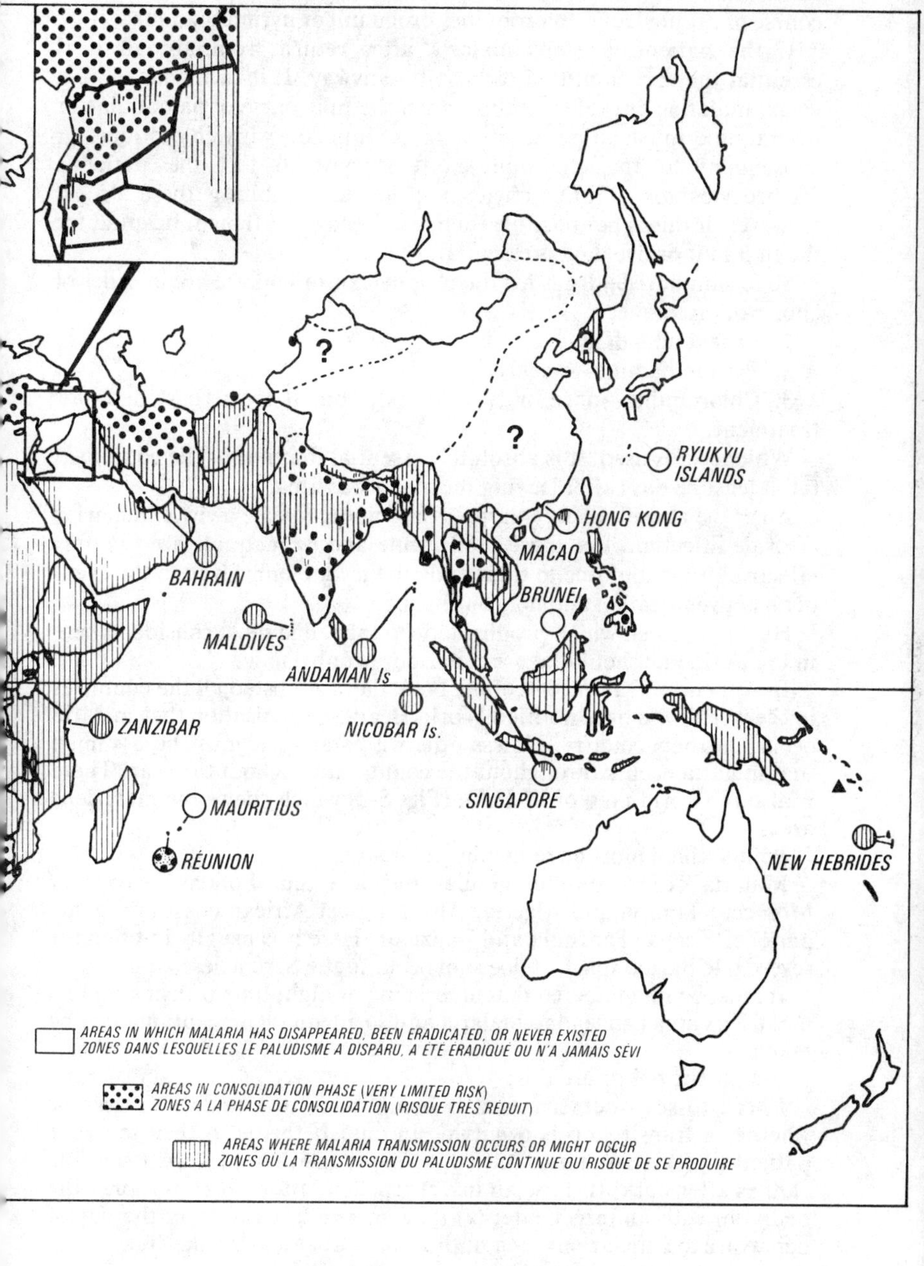

Remembering that vivax, malariae and ovale infections are rarely fatal, it is generally considered that the wisest policy is not to give pamaquine or primaquine prophylactically after finishing the full course of prophylactic chloroquine, proguanil or pyrimethamine.

If the patient develops malaria after return from abroad it is essential they are admitted to hospital anyway. If it turns out to be a vivax, malariae or ovale infection, then the full course of pamaquine or primaquine must be given either in conjunction with chloroquine or subsequent to the chloroquine. It is best to test the patient's erythrocytes for G6PD deficiency prior to exhibiting these drugs. However, if this is not possible then, as already mentioned, hospital for the first four or five days is essential.

So to summarise, drugs for the prophylaxis of malaria are in order of choice of preference:

1. Proguanil—daily.
2. Pyrimethamine—weekly.
3. Chloroquine—once or twice weekly, but it is the best drug for treatment.

Whichever is used, it is absolutely essential that it must be continued for at least 28 days after leaving the malarious area.

All of the above will only suppress and not eradicate a vivax, malariae or ovale infection. For these pamaquine and primaquine are the only effective drugs, but due to their toxicity they are only given in the event of an active infection and not routinely.

Having decided which prophylactic to take, one must consider where in the world one should take a malarious prophylactic.

In Appendix C at the end of the book there are listed all the countries in the world who have notified World Health Organisation that malaria occurs in their country. Unless otherwise stated, it must be assumed that malaria occurs throughout the country throughout the year. There is also the world map of W..H.O. (Fig. 5-2) which shows the malarious areas.

Points which must be remembered are this:

Malaria occurs in the popular package tour holiday centres of Morocco, Tunisia and Algeria. Also the East African coast and game parks of Kenya, Tanzania and Zanzibar. Here it is usually in the most severe falciparum form. It does not occur in the Seychelles.

It must be remembered that an evening or night time transit stop in a malarious area can lead to malaria and so adequate precaution must be taken.

Finally the points are this:

Check to see whether a visit is being made to a malarious area or whether a transit stop is occurring in one. If this is so then tell your patient to: (i) see that mosquito proofing is adequate; (ii) wear sensible clothes after dark; (iii) use an insect repellent after dark; (iv) spray the bedroom with an insecticide; (v) take an antimalarial from the day of departure to a malarious area until 28 days after leaving the area.

Remember malaria can kill, and can kill quickly.

With the other mosquito borne infections the use of an insect repellent throughout the day is essential because although the anopheline keeps its biting of the human being until after dark, other varieties are not so selective.

With sandfly spread infections the human being again is entirely dependent on insect repellents in the open air and insecticidal sprays indoors because no mosquito proof netting will keep out the sandfly due to its very small size. Any mesh which kept out the sandfly would prevent satisfactory breathing.

Holidaymakers who are going on safari and visiting the game parks must be reminded very strongly about using their mosquito nettings: especially if their first night or two on arrival in Africa is spent in an air conditioned hotel they may well forget the need of netting. They must be told of the problems of sleeping sickness spread by the tsetse fly. Regrettably more than one holidaymaker has returned from a game park to develop trypanosomiasis, sometimes with fatal results.

Filarial infections spread by mosquitoes or flies, dependent on the variety of infection, are most likely to occur in agricultural workers and those working in dam and bridge construction, particularly where swamps abound.

In East, Central and South Africa where tick typhus occurs, visitors should be warned not to wear sandals and have their lower legs uncovered while walking in the long grasses because this is where the tick tends to live and hence bites the legs of the human.

6. Direct Contact Problems, Bites and Stings

Although this is the last chapter in the portion of the book devoted to prevention, the problems of treatment will be discussed at the same time. An effort will be made to try and cover the majority of reptiles, insects and coral derivatives which cause toxic reactions in the human. In general all forms of worms have been discussed in the chapters on intestinal infections and parasitic diseases.

Snakes

Although it is reported that 15 drops of viper venom are necessary to kill a man, only three drops of cobra venom to do the same while one drop of sea snake would be more than sufficient, the results are luckily not so dramatic.

H. Alistair Reid of the Liverpool School of Tropical Medicine, who is a leading authority on snakebite, in an excellent article in the *British Medical Journal* in August 1968 described the problem very succinctly as follows. 'Fortunately, however, biting human beings is a defensive reaction which rarely results in much venom being injected. *The paramount fact about bites of man by poisonous snakes is that more than one half of the victims will have minimal or no poisoning. Only about one quarter will develop systemic poisoning. Hence poisonous snakebite is not synonymous with snakebite poisoning.*'

The principle to remember is that in general snakes do not attack for the pleasure of it. They attack in self-defence when they are disturbed. They tend to hunt at night and slide around in dark places objecting to the light. They therefore usually bite when disturbed and are trodden on.

Hence in snake infested areas people are advised to shine a torch in front of them when they go out at night. When snakes enter houses here again they tend to live in dark corners. Small snakes often hide in shoes. It is therefore sensible to shake shoes upside down before putting them on the feet.

There are five main groups of poisonous snakes including sea snakes.

The Viperidae or True Vipers

Found in Europe, Asia and Africa. Short stumpy. snakes with a triangular head. Venom is cytotoxic and haemolytic.

The Crotalidae or Pit Vipers

Found in the Americas and Asia. So called because there is a small pit between the eye and the nostrils which is thermosensitive and used for hunting warm blooded animals. Venom is cytotoxic, haemolytic and neurotoxic.

With both these groups there is early oedema around the puncture marks and subcutaneous haemorrhage with oozing. Blisters and necrosis follow. In general nausea, vomiting, pallor, dyspnoea with a feeble pulse and dilated pupils. Haemoptysis, haematemesis, melaena and haematuria may follow. Without treatment death may occur from heart failure in a few days.

The Elapidae including kraits, mambas and cobras

Found in all continents except Europe. Long with a pointed tail and a small head. Venom is mainly neurotoxic.

Locally usually there is tingling or numbness. With cobras there is usually local necrosis. Of the systemic changes ptosis is probably the most important diagnostically. Dyspnoea, painful joints and unsteady gait follow. Sometimes severe abdominal pain. Initially the pupils are contracted but subsequently become dilated. Death may occur within 12-24 hours. If there are no systemic symptoms within 24 hours death is unlikely.

The Colubridae

Found only in Africa. Wide jawed in their bites. Venom is mainly neurotoxic.

There are few local changes. After a few hours petechiae appear with some haemolysis. Systematically ptosis, dysphonia, dyspnoea and finally respiratory arrest.

The Hydrophinae or Sea Snakes

Found in the coastal waters of the Indian and Pacific Oceans especially around Malaysia. They are also present off the northern coast of Australia. They tend to be caught in the nets of the off-shore fishermen and do not inhabit the shallow waters of the bathers and majority of swimmers.

Short fanged with flat rudder-like tail. Swim sluggishly. Sea snakes with the round tapering tails are harmless.

They rarely bite but are very toxic if they do. Little to see locally and only minimal pain in bite area. However within half an hour generalised stiffness and aching, and within about four hours myoglobinuria occurs followed by ptosis and, if a severe bite, respiratory failure within a few hours. Leucocytosis is rapid rising to the neighbourhood of 20,000 per mm^3.

For travellers to snake infected areas advice on first aid treatment should be given to them prior to travel.

The first thing to remember is that when anyone is bitten by a snake the major symptom is one of acute fear and impending doom which is not factual. Reassurance is therefore the most important part and every effort should be made to get the patient to a local hospital, if possible, and if this is not possible to a local doctor.

The site of the bite should be wiped with a clean handkerchief or equivalent, so wiping away any excess venom. After wiping, it should be covered with a clean dressing. On no account should it be incised as first aid treatment. If the bite is on one of the limbs then a firm but not tight ligature should be applied proximally to cut down spread of venom but on no account should the arterial supply be cut off. Further, the limb should be immobilised to reduce the spread of venom.

Analgesics and/or alcohol can be given to relieve pain.

If the snake has been killed it should be taken by the tail along to the hospital for identification and hence assistance in the giving of antivenom but on no account should any effort be made to catch and kill the snake.

The patient should be admitted to hospital and a sedative given. If there are any signs of toxicity then, if possible, the specific antivenom given by intravenous drip if the specific snake is known. If the latter is not known the polyvalent serum should be given. However care must be taken to carry out sensitivity tests to the antivenom serum prior to giving it as an intravenous drip. Broad spectrum antibiotics should be given as well to prevent infection. If there is local necrosis tetanus antitoxin is essential. If respiratory failure ensues then a tracheostomy is necessary.

Lizards

In general lizards are non-venomous and travellers can be fully reassured on this. The only venomous lizards are the Heloderma species which occur in the Mexican and Arizona deserts. Symptoms of poisoning by these heavy stout lizards are dyspnoea, paralysis and convulsions.

Poisonous Fish

There are three main groups of venomous fishes which mainly live in tropical water.

The group of *scorpion fish* are found in tropical and temperate seas but are particularly prevalent in the seas around India, Sri Lanka and Mauritius.

The *stingray* group are found in tropical and subtropical estuaries. They tend to lie just under the surface in the sand and inject poison when the sufferer steps on them.

The *weaver fish* group is found in the Mediterranean and the Atlantic shores. As such they can be found on the south western shores of England. Again they lie buried in mud and sand and stepping on them once again causes the trouble.

Toad fish inhabit the shores of the Caribbean.

Stonefish are found on the shores of the islands of the Indian Ocean such as the Seychelles, around the Malaysian coasts and further east to Indonesia and New Guinea. Looking like a stone, as their name suggests, bathers around a coral reef walk on them and a toxin is injected from dorsal spines into the feet.

Symptoms. In general with stings from all the above fishes the wounds are usually on the feet and lower half of the lower leg. There is usually severe and immediate pain. Local oedema and sometimes necrosis follows. Regrettably, as well there is usually severe shock and sometimes diarrhoea.

Treatment initially consists of removing any spines which may be left in the skin. Hot soaking of the foot in water or magnesium sulphate solution as hot as the patient can bear without blistering is beneficial. This should be carried out repeatedly. Procaine may be injected locally to relieve pain. With the stonefish local injection of a solution of emetine hydrochloride 30-60 mgm is of value. Morphia is often necessary for relief of pain and shock. Cardiovascular and respiratory stimulants may also be needed.

Other fishes can cause poisoning by being eaten. Of these fishes the barracuda is one. It is generally eaten in South America. If eaten at spawning time it can cause severe gastrointestinal symptoms. Paraesthesiae and muscular weakness amounting to paralysis also occur. Snappers, graupers and many eels can cause this trouble as well as the barracuda.

Neostigmine, hydrocortisone and intravenous fluids are necessary. However stomach wash out and/or purgation is essential.

Coelenterates

This group includes all hydroids, jelly fish, corals and sea anemones.

Jelly fish are found in the cold waters of the Atlantic, also in the warmer waters of the Mediterranean, Indian Ocean, Pacific Ocean and Caribbean. The hydroid in the form of the far more toxic Portuguese man-of-war is a problem. Like a large jelly fish with blue or purple colouration plus a long tentacle or trigger hair. On touching the trigger hair minute barbs sting the part of the anatomy touching it.

With all forms of hydroids and jelly fish pain may be intense with local swelling. Toxic symptoms are variable but can be severe with pyrexia, vomiting, dyspnoea and muscular cramps.There is frequently an accompanying urticaria. In fact the active poison of the Portuguese man-of-war is the same as with the wasp. As it causes a release of histamine, antihistamine creams are effective.

What must be remembered with the Portuguese man-of-war is that the trigger hair may be as long as 10 feet so they must be given a very wide berth by swimmers.

The Cyanaea group of jelly fish are found off the Australian shores but remain in deep water and therefore are less troublesome. They are about the size of a dinner plate and slimy with a 'mop' underneath due to hundreds of tentacles. Severe pain, blistering and urticaria ensues. Shock may be intense.

The Gymnothorax variety occurs in the Red Sea, Indian Ocean and the seas of Indonesia. Within 20 minutes there is numbness, laryngeal spasm and loss of speech. Paraldehyde by intramuscular injection is an answer.

Sea anemones can cause a severe contact dermatitis. This is known as sponge fishers' disease or Skevos Zervos disease. Locally there is severe irritation and presence of vesicles. Nearly always the vesicles become pustular. General symptoms are of nausea and vomiting. Local application of vinegar and olive oil is best.

Many of the pleasant tropical holiday resorts have coral reefs. Coral dermatitis is very common after contact with the coral. Care must be taken not to walk on coral with bare feet else abrasions will occur which will turn into indolent ulcers. The lesions are red, oedematous and highly irritating. They are extremely slow to heal. Lesions on the feet can be avoided by swimming with light weight shoes, but it must be remembered that the sport of 'goggling' is very popular on and near coral reefs. It is here that the beautiful tropical fish are found so care must be taken not to get abrasions of the shin and elsewhere by swimming over coral which is only just below the surface of the sea. Another problem with coral is coral induced external otitis caused by a few fine granules of coral getting into the external meatus. Careful cleaning of the wound with a simple antiseptic to try and get rid of the coral granules is the only answer. Antibiotics as well if secondary infection, which is common, occurs.

Sea urchins are another common problem on tropical beaches especially in the Caribbean. When walking on or touching sea urchins the spines break off from the urchin and remain in the skin. The lesions they cause soon become septic and there may be generalised allergic reaction.

These spines are very difficult to remove without breaking. Because of this there are many 'housewives' tales' as to treatment. Probably the best two remedies are either soaking with olive oil such that they soften and lose their brittleness: thus they do not break when an effort is made to extract them. The other system which is probably best but not always available is the use of paraffin wax as for removing superfluous hair from ladies. Melted paraffin wax is applied and when it has cooled and gone solid it is stripped off the skin taking the sea urchin spike with it.

However antibiotics and antihistamines may have to be given for sepsis and general symptoms.

Scorpions are found throughout the tropics and in many areas of the subtropics. They occur around the Mediterranean and in the

Caribbean as far as the holidaymaker is concerned. The scorpion is like a beetle and about two inches in length with its tail slightly longer. The scorpion is nocturnal in habit and spends the day hiding under stones. Like the small snake it will, not infrequently, hide in shoes. Again it only attacks when molested. Hence it is a good thing to shake shoes before putting them on. The sting is in the tail, but the scorpion has claws in the front which grip the patient first and then the tail is swung over the head to bite near the claws and inject the poison.

Scorpion stings are very painful but can not be considered dangerous other than in small children when the dose of toxin may be overwhelming. Geographically, Southern Europe including the Mediterranean littoral, throughout Africa, the Caribbean, Mexico and the Far East. Intense pain at the time with varying degrees of profuse perspiration, pyrexia, vomiting, and even convulsion in children.

However subsequently there may be glycosuria, hyperglycaemia and pancreatitis due to the toxic absorption. Myocarditis with inversion of the T-wave has also been described. These symptoms may develop after the sufferer has returned home and the scorpion may not be associated.

With *spiders* the genus of Latrodectus is poisonous. The classical Latrodectus mactans, or Black Widow spider of California, is the best known. They tend to hide in dark corners of barns, outbuildings and privies so should not affect the normal traveller. Clinically the actual bite may not be noticed but severe radiating pain develops. Muscular spasm of the intercostal and abdominal muscles follow with resultant dyspnoea. The pain may go on increasing for two to three hours and then take two to three days to disappear. Nausea, sweating and abdominal pain also occur which may mislead the attendant helpers to think it is an abdominal emergency.

However their toxicity is in general over-rated and, like a scorpion, death normally only occurs in small children.

The Loxosceles group are found throughout North and South America, in Australia and certain parts of Africa. These are the vesicant group and include the well known Cantharides spiders of which the bright green Spanish Fly is one. Care must be taken not to kill the spider by squashing it on the person else the resultant blisters are increased.

Clinically severe pain lasts two to six hours and a blister forms. There is localised erythema and marked oedema which may spread throughout an entire limb. The erythema changes to a blister which turns black, sloughs and ulcerates taking several weeks to heal. Haemolysis may also occur with haemoglobinuria and jaundice.

The Phoneutria group are found in South America and definitely cause fatalities in children due to their neurotoxic properties which lead to respiratory and cardiac collapse.

The Atrax group are found in Australia and New Zealand. They are purely neurotoxic without local pain.

Treatment

Rest is the main thing. Antiseptic dressings to the local bite. Antihistamines by mouth if there is a severe local reaction also corticosteroids. Chlorpromazine for pain is effective. I.V. calcium gluconate 10 per cent is helpful for muscle spasms.

Antivenoms have been prepared and should be given intravenously if available.

The *leech* is found only in damp, mainly forest, areas so in general only causes trouble to the constructional worker. The bites are painless so when the leech becomes attached they may not be noticed for some time and loss of blood may occur. When noticed, any of the old stories of applying salt, vinegar or the lighted end of a cigarette to its tail are very effective. The wounds nearly always turn septic so should be treated with iodine or a similar strong antiseptic and antibiotics exhibited.

However all insect repellents act for a longer time against leeches than against mosquitoes so it is most important for workers in this type of area to maintain their repellent.

With *centipedes* the two front claws contain some poison. With small centipedes there is only minor inflammation resulting, but with larger ones there may be marked pain but no toxicity. Application of ammonia is the best answer.

Visitors to the developing countries should be warned against handling stray dogs because of the possible incidence of rabies but also because of the far more likely chance of picking up a toxocaral infection.

Part 2

Post-Travel Symptomatology

7. Post-Travel Problems and Heat Disorders

The main immediate post-travel problems are those of the heat disorders which may occur by the traveller failing to behave sensibly on arrival in warm climates. The whole problem of heat acclimatisation has been fully discussed in Chapter Three. If the advice given is carried out then most of the heat disorders can be prevented. If they occur at all they should be mild.

Before discussing the heat disorders a brief mention of the few upsets which may occur after air travel.

As referred to in Chapter Two, because of the upset of circadian or diurnal rhythms, travellers may complain of sleeplessness for the first few days. The answer here is a non-habit-forming hypnotic such as nitrazepam (Mogadon) in decreasing dosage over about four nights.

As well as sleeplessness constipation may occur for a few days initially. This should be treated again on a very short term policy by the laxative or aperient of the attending practitioner's choice.

One rare complication of air travel which must be remembered is venous thrombosis in the lower limbs.

This will only occur in the traveller who has already a poor venous drainage system in the lower legs and who has probably already had thrombotic episodes. Besides the presence of a poor venous drainage it is necessary for the traveller to have been a very great distance and failed to take any excercise on the journey. The periodic walking up and down the cabin and getting off at the transit stops is sufficient to prevent this problem.

To turn to the heat disorders, it is probably best to give the World Health Organisation International Classification of Disease. If the traveller suffers from any of these diseases, it is more than likely they will occur while he is away, but with the rapid travel that is now available it is always possible that some may occur immediately after return, so the practitioners in the temperate climates must be ready for them.

Heat disorders: International Classification

Modified by the Medical Research Council (Weiner and Horne, 1958).

A. Heat stroke: N.9810
B. Heat hyperpyrexia: N.981.5a
C. Heat cramps: N.981.2

D. Heat exhaustion
   Type 1. Salt deficiency: N.981.3a
   Type 2. Anhidrotic: N.981.3b
   Type 3. Water deficiency: N.981.3c
E. Sunburn: N.981.4
F. Prickly heat: 714.O.A
G. Heat oedema
H. Heat syncope

A & B. Heat Stroke and Heat Hyperpyrexia

These are basically the same condition. In both cases following exposure to intense heat there is a thermoregulatory failure and as a result body temperature rises to above 105°F. With heat hyperpyrexia the mind on the whole remains clear and there may be some sweating. With heat stroke there is clouding of the senses which may pass into coma and subsequently there may be a fatal result.

Long continued exposure to intense heat is essential. By this is meant at least several hours per day, usually aided by physical effort. On top of this the wrong clothing, alcoholism and a recent, if not present, toxic pyrexia. The latter three points are the most important factors with the short term traveller overseas. If the holidaymaker has had a dysenteric infection which has aided dehydration, given him a toxic pyrexia and then having recovered he decides to make up for lost time in the heat, heat hyperpyrexia or even sunstroke may ensue. It is naturally encouraged if the atmosphere is humid and there is no breeze so preventing evaporation of sweat: it is obviously far more likely to occur prior to full acclimatisation occurring. This again may well precipitate it in the holidaymaker or business traveller.

Age and excess weight are bad prognostic factors.

Symptomatology. The onset may be gradual or rapid. In the cases with gradual onset there are usually symptoms such as headache, giddiness, nausea, vomiting, and general weakness plus lack of energy. A clouding of the senses, speech difficulties and sometimes delirium ensue prior to coma. Tachycardia is present and there may be cyanosis of the extremities. By this time all or nearly all sweating has ceased. In some cases coma may occur without any apparent previous symptoms. The temperature rises rapidly. Convulsions and Jacksonian epilepsy with muscular twitchings are not infrequent.

Subarachmoid haemorrhages and cardiac failure may occur.

Prognosis is always bad as the mortality can be high.

Diagnosis is made by the three classical signs: (1) high temperature; (2) dry skin and (3) central nervous system signs.

But it is absolutely essential to exclude any other toxic cause of pyrexia. In particular it is most important to exclude falciparum malaria in an endemic area and, just as important, in someone who has recently been in an endemic area. If this is not excluded by blood slide, death may occur from malaria.

Treatment. This is by cooling the body down and lowering the body temperature. The best way is by laying the patient on a bed and sprinkling the body with tepid water and then using a fan of some form to aid evaporation. The other method is to immerse the patient in a cool bath or wrap in a damp sheet. However by the former method heat is lost by convection and evaporation: with the latter method it is by convection only. On no account should the body temperature be lowered below 39°C (102.2°F). It must be remembered that a temperature of 42.2°C (108°F) is not uncommon with heat stroke and temperatures of 45°C (113°F) have been recorded. The temperature should be recorded at least every 10-15 minutes so that excess cooling does not occur.

Having reached a temperature of 39°C (102.2°F) cooling usually continues despite the cessation of active treatment. If it does not occur then active cooling should be recommenced but it is a bad prognostic sign.

Chlororamazine as an intravenous injection in the dosage of up to 50 mgm at the start of active cooling is frequently beneficial as it cuts down restlessness and aids peripheral vasodilatation.

If the hyperpyrexia has been present for more than four hours then the prognosis is made worse especially in respect of sequelae if a fatality does not occur. There may be resultant personality changes or hemiplegia.

C. Heat Cramps

Synonyms: Stoker's cramp; Miner's cramp; Fireman's cramp; Cane Cutter's cramps.

Aetiology. Generally thought to be due to either salt depletion or water intoxication. In other words it occurs in people taking violent exercise at work or in play and failing to increase their intake of salt although increasing their intake of water. In fact the failure to increase the intake of salt is by far the most important.

In some ways heat cramps could be put down purely as a symptom of heat exhaustion caused by salt depletion because muscular cramps occur in this condition. However in the latter condition other symptoms occur as well and heat cramps may occur entirely on their own.

Clinically the cramps occur always after several hours of manual labour or exercise. Therefore usually in the afternoon.

The pain can be intense and last for two or three minutes associated with acute spasm and 'knotting' of the muscles. The arms and legs are the most affected in particular the calves. Cramps of the recti abdominis can occur. If they persist, as they can, for several hours, shock may ensue.

Rest for 24 hours is advisable. However adequate salt in the normal diet as a preventive measure is best.

D. Heat Exhaustion

Type 1. Salt deficiency

Aetiology. Failure to replace salt following excessive sweating during intense heat. Usually associated with marked physical labour and the patient has replaced the lost fluids but not the salt. Severity is increased if there has been associated diarrhoea and particularly vomiting. Occurs particularly frequently in the unacclimatised who fails to replace the salt. Hence it is not infrequent in the short term traveller.

Symptoms. Usually insidious in origin starting with lassitude, anorexia, headaches, giddiness, nausea and vomiting. Fainting frequently occurs later on, and muscle cramps occur in about 50 per cent of the cases.

Signs. Typically the skin remains moist, there is no cessation of sweating. Tachycardia and fall in blood pressure are usual.

Pathology. Urinary chlorides are low. Plasma sodium falls. Blood urea rises and haemoconcentration occurs.

Treatment. If the symptoms are severe, especially if there is vomiting, then intravenous therapy is essential. Even with the milder cases the taking of salt may cause vomiting and some authorities believe intravenous therapy with isotonic saline is essential in all cases. If shock is present an initial 500 ml of plasma is effective. With the severe cases the first litre should be given rapidly in about half an hour and up to five litres in the 24 hours. Continuation of intravenous fluids should be controlled by testing for urinary chlorides quantitatively (Fantus test) and plasma sodium. With disappearance of symptoms especially, treatment can be continued with oral intake of salt. Potassium should be added at this stage. Bed rest is essential during treatment even if treatment is purely oral and not intravenous.

However as written in the chapter on acclimatisation the preventive treatment is the best for this problem.

Salt intake should be increased from the usual 10 g daily to 15-25 g daily. In practice doubling the salt intake is a satisfactory policy. But salt intake must not be increased unless fluid intake is increased at the same time. This increase in salt need not be maintained after acclimatisation unless vomiting or diarrhoea occurs.

Type 2. Anhidrotic

This is a condition which in general has been mainly found in servicemen in war time after about four to seven months' service in the tropics. Hence it is unlikely to occur in the short term visitor and will only be dealt with briefly. It was first described late in the second world war by Australian, American and British authorities almost simultaneously from areas scattered as far apart as Northern Australia and New Guinea, the American deserts, The South Pacific, Iraq and Karachi.

Aetiology. The most important factor in its aetiology is that it nearly always follows prickly heat. It is presumably because of this that it does not occur until four to seven months in a hot climate usually, but not always, humid.

Symptoms. Gradual in onset. Exhaustion, giddiness, headache, dyspnoea, anorexia and insomnia. Other than the last symptom they tend to occur in the heat of the day.

Initially periods of rest after the activity which has brought on the symptoms will bring relief but after a while rest will not help.

A mild pyrexia in the 37.2-38°C (99-100.4°F) range is usual but it may rise to 39°C (102.2°F). Tachycardia is present. The important factor is that sweating practically ceases on the trunks and limbs. Sweating continues on the face, neck, palms, soles, axillae and groins. There may even be small areas of sweating in the dry areas.

Classically however, a skin eruption of mammillaria occurs. This eruption consists of small grey papules like rice grains often with fluid vesicles on the trunk and limbs. They can be differentiated from prickly heat in that they have no surrounding erythema and do not itch.

Prognosis. Excellent with treatment.

Treatment. Rest in a cool area.

Correction of any salt/water unbalance is essential.

Although recovery is rapid it tends to recur and it is therefore a sound indication for transfer from a tropical climate.

Type 3. Water Deficiency

This can be divided into two groups. Involuntary water depletion which is the severe condition which occurs in people shipwrecked or others who may be cut off in the desert when their motor vehicle has broken down. The voluntary group is when dehydration occurs in a person who has foolishly failed to drink enough even although fluids are available.

Aetiology is simple. Failure to replace the fluid which has been lost by increased sweating.

Symptoms. The most important symptom is thirst which gradually increases to such an extent that it becomes an obsession. There are mild headaches and possibly a little giddiness but far less than with salt depletion. There may be a slight rise in temperature. Muscle cramps do not occur. The mouth becomes dry and as the water depletion increases sweating decreases as also does the output of urine. Initially the urine becomes concentrated and dark in colour and as depletion increases it greatly decreases in amount. Delirium, coma and death ensues. The whole process of water depletion heat exhaustion is far more rapid than salt depletion exhaustion.

Pathology. Urine amount decreased but urinary chlorides remain normal. Plasma sodium is raised and haemoconcentration is late and mild.

Treatment. Rest in bed in a cool atmosphere. If mild, rehydration can usually be by mouth as vomiting is rare. Up to 6-8 litres (10-14 pints) of fluid with normal salt intake in the 24 hours is the amount necessary to rehydrate. If severe, and certainly if unconscious, intravenous therapy of 4-5 litres (7-9 pints) in the first 24 hours is necessary. Litres of isotonic saline alternated with 5 per cent glucose is the best treatment. If there is pyrexia then tepid cooling may be necessary.

E. Sunburn

For many years sunburn has been considered as a self inflicted injury in the services and as such is a chargeable offence. There is a lot of truth in this outlook. If commonsense is used aided by suitable lotions and creams plus the use of a vitamin A-calcium carbonate compound sunburn should not occur. Initially erythema occurs within a matter of two to six hours. Without further exposure this erythema will soon fade. If exposure is sensible and controlled then erythema will gradually change to browning with the deposition of melanin.

If exposure is excessive then the skin becomes oedematous and tense. The edge of the erythema, which is usually the edge of the exposure, is raised. If continued excess exposure occurs then capillaries and small arterioles become prominent. Subsequent to the oedema blisters may form indicating advanced burning of the skin. Along with these latter skin changes there may be toxic reactions with nausea, vomiting, headache and pyrexia associated with the very definite pain associated with a true burn. Heat hyperpyrexia and heat stroke may follow excessive exposure. If the blister formation is very excessive the toxic state may be severe and death has been reported.

Treatment. Prevention has been fully discussed in Chapter Three. If this advice has not been taken then the treatment is fairly simple.

Calamine lotion is still the best treatment for the mild erythema. For the skin that shows oedema and thickening a corticosteroid ointment is advised. Antihistamine ointments should not be used because of the danger of allergic sensitisation. However antihistamines by mouth can be most helpful with the fairly severe cases. Antibiotic ointments may be necessary if blisters become infected. With the very severe cases corticosteroids and antibiotics by mouth with intravenous rehydration may well have to be considered.

F. Prickly Heat

Synonyms. Miliaria rubra; lichen tropicis; heat rash. An erythematous papulovesicular rash which is irritating and prickling. Common in the tropics and subtropics. Secondary infection both pyogenic and fungal frequently occurs. Basically caused by prolonged wetting of the skin with sweat and without evaporation. Hence worse with humid climate. Infants and the obese are especially affected. In general commoner in new arrivals to the tropics prior to acclimatisation. Males suffer more frequently than females. Permeability of the clothing is a most important factor with prickly heat and non-absorbent drip dry man made fibres are frequently basic factors in the development of prickly heat. The advent of air conditioning or even air cooling has decreased the incidence of this complaint greatly. The principle of an eight hour relief from sweating afforded by bedroom air conditioning has been a tremendous factor in the decrease in incidence of prickly heat.

Loewenthal in 1961 produced the theory that sweat duct obstruction and the periductal oedema may be due to the sodium chloride from the evaporated sweat continuing to lie on the skin.

Clinically. Initially numerous scattered papules which soon become vesicular. These lesions are surrounded by an erythematous area. This erythema may even be generalised. Where there is generalised erythema it is quickly replaced by papules and then vesicles. These vesicles contain a slightly milky fluid. Because they are so irritating both with itching and prickling it is very difficult for the sufferer not to scratch them. As a result they become broken and frequently secondarily infected with pus formation. The commonest areas affected are the concavities of the body surface namely where sweat collects and fails to evaporate; also areas where clothes are in close approximation such as under the belt, or with ladies under the brassiere straps (especially if nylon). Hence the anterior surface of the elbows; the posterior surface of the knees; over the sternum and clavicle; around the waist and in the axillae. The palms and soles are not affected although the dorsum of the hands can be affected. The face is rarely affected. The irritation may be so severe that sleeplessness ensues with deterioration in the general condition. With improvement the irritation disappears and is then followed by white powdery desquamation with disappearance of the papules and vesicles. With infants the condition can be serious as the whole body can be affected and secondary infection is commoner.

Diagnosis. This is mainly from the skin manifestations of anhidrotic heat exhaustion. However with prickly heat there is sweating and erythema as well as the papules and vesicles. With anhidrosis there is no sweating and no erythema.

Treatment. This can be difficult. The treatment guaranteed to cure the condition is to remove the sufferer from the climatic surroundings but this is usually not practical. Thus the only effective treatment is the application of astringent lotions after washing with an antiseptic soap and careful drying.

Of the lotions one in 2,000 mercuric chloride in 95 per cent alcohol or 2 per cent salicylic in 95 per cent alcohol are probably the best.

Calamine lotion can be very helpful. If secondary infection occurs then an oral antibiotic such as penicillin should be used. Ointments in general should be avoided.

The important problem is that with people who have once suffered from prickly heat they are very likely to have recurrences under similar climatic conditions.

Intense heat should be avoided. Loose fitting clothing with absorptive properties should be worn. Tepid baths twice daily with careful drying.

G. Heat Oedema

Heat oedema is also known as deck ankles and Colombo flop. In the days of travel to India by sea to take up an appointment one of the major ways of passing the time by day was walking the decks. Hence as they reached the tropics the feet and ankles began to swell due to vasodilation in the increasing heat.

Women are more commonly affected than men and it usually only occurs in the unacclimatised.

Aetiology is not generally known but it is probably due to upset of the salt/water balance in the unacclimatised with the additional factor of increased vasodilation in the skin.

Clinically there is usually only mild oedema over the feet and ankles. Rarely it extends to the lower calves. Pitting of the oedema is not always present unless the condition is severe.

Diagnosis is by excluding general disease such as cardiac and renal oedema. Hence the urine must be tested.

Treatment. Rest and avoidance of excess exercise for one week plus advice on salt and water intake.

H. Heat Syncope

Heat syncope is also known as heat collapse and exercise induced heat exhaustion. The latter name being of importance as to its aetiology. The other main point is that it happens in the apparent absence of either water or salt depletion.

Aetiology. The one factor which is always present is change. Usually in the form of a new arrival in a hot climate. The vast majority of cases occur in the unacclimatised. However it can occur in the acclimatised if they suddenly increase their amount of physical work or exertion or on the other hand the weather becomes suddenly humid. Leithead in 1960 described how several cases of heat syncope occurred amongst Arab road workers in Kuwait when there was a sudden change from intense dry heat to humid heat.

Pathology. Intense peripheral vasodilation occurs leading to peripheral pooling and hypotension. Hence any excess stress can lead to syncope.

Symptoms. During the first few days of exposure the patient complains of giddiness and light headiness to such an extent that when standing or doing any physical work he feels he will faint. Along with the above symptoms others frequently present are yawning; nausea; epigastric discomfort; urgency to defaecate and blurring of vision. Associated with the above symptoms there is hypotension and tachycardia.

If the patient does not lie down with the onset of the above symptoms syncope will occur. Pallor is present and the pulse rate slows to below normal. The temperature may be raised.

The syncopal attack is usually very brief and full recovery occurs after a few hours rest in cool surroundings.

8. Fevers

The two commonest forms of presentation of exotic diseases are either as a fever or as a gastroenteritis.

Firstly let us consider the various causes of fever of which quite definitely by far the most important is malaria.

Malaria

As it has already been stressed in Chapter Five, malaria can be a killer. One can only quote again the figures for England and Wales for 1971 when out of 269 notified cases of malaria 138 were due to *P. falciparum* and of these there were eight deaths or 5.8 per cent. It is generally considered that this high mortality rate is due to delay or even missed diagnosis and hence delay in treatment. In 1973 there were 540 cases in the United Kingdom.

Malaria is extremely protean in its facies and hence this makes diagnosis even more difficult. So frequently it can initially be diagnosed as an influenzal type infection or it may even start with diarrhoea and be labelled as a gastroenteritis. However the patient gets worse and within three or five days the central nervous system is involved; there is hyperpyrexia; or there may be renal failure. By this time treatment may be too late.

This brings up the old point that it is essential to ask a patient whether he has been abroad and if so where and when. In the appendices there is a list of all the countries where malaria occurs. To be strictly accurate this list refers to countries who have notified the World Health Organisation that malaria was occurring in their country as of July 1972. Obviously one can assume that it is definitely present in these countries but of course there is a possibility that a few cases may occur elsewhere but they have not been notified. This list does not differentiate the type but in general *P. falciparum* or malignant malaria occurs in hot and humid climates. Benign tertian caused by *P. vivax* is widespread involving temperate zones as well as the subtropics and tropics. Quartan due to *P. malariae* is also widespread but far less frequent. However it is an infection which is difficult to eradicate and may relapse for years. Ovale malaria is caused by *P. ovale* and only occurs in East, Central and West Africa especially the latter.

Classically the symptoms are fever, anaemia and an enlarged spleen occurring 10 to 15 days after being bitten by the infected mosquito. Only with the less frequent *P. malariae* infection is the incubation period up to one month. This incubation period is when the parasites are developing in the liver prior to their appearance in the blood. However it must be remembered that the incubation period may be lengthened if the patient has been taking prophylactic drugs. This is particularly so if they have been taking them whilst in the malarious area and then ceased immediately after they have returned home. On these occasions the illness may well develop two weeks after their arrival home when in fact they were bitten by the infected mosquito well before they left the malarious area. This of course makes early diagnosis all the harder.

Initially prior to fever there may be two or three days of general malaise, headaches and vague pains. If the patient sees the unsuspecting doctor at this stage the diagnosis of 'flu' can easily be made and the patient goes away happily reassured. By the time he realises he is getting worse rather than better it may be too late.

The average holidaymaker or businessman visiting a malarious area is non-immune and as such he or she is likely to suffer a far more severe infection, especially if he or she has not been taking an antimalarial.

Classically in such people an attack consists of regularly recurrent paroxysms of fever which have three distinct stages: (1) cold stage; (2) hot stage; (3) sweating stage.

The cold stage starts with lassitude, headache and often nausea. A rigor ensues and the patient feels cold and shivery; the skin is blue. The headache is severe and there is frequently abdominal pain and vomiting. The temperature rises rapidly to 102°-106°F and it is at this stage that division of the parasites by schizogony occurs and the erythrocyte ruptures. The pulse may be weak. This stage usually lasts for 30 minutes to two hours. Following on the cold stage there is *the hot stage* when the patient becomes very hot and the face and skin are congested. Headache is intense and the patient complains of intense fever. Nausea disappears and thirst ensues. The pulse is full and respiration rapid. The duration is usually longer than in the cold stage, being up to four or six hours. Subsequent to this there is *the sweating stage* when perspiration is intense and with this the patient starts to feel far better as the temperature falls.

This is the classical picture but it may well not occur thus; especially in the serious falciparum infections.

With *P. vivax* infections these attacks occur on alternate days while with the *P. malariae* infections they occur every third day. With both varieties usually in the afternoon or early evening. Both these forms of malaria can be very unpleasant but they are rarely fatal. With *P. ovale* the attacks are always mild and are usually self-limiting.

Along with the typical paroxysms other likely symptoms and signs are an enlarged, soft and tender spleen and *herpes labialis*. The liver may also be enlarged. It is not essential for a rigor to occur in the cold stage. If, of course, there is a mixed infection then the typical periodicity may be lost.

Having dealt with the typical clinical picture which usually occurs with *P. vivax, P. ovale* and *P. malariae* infections one must pass on to the regrettably usually atypical picture of the far more serious and severe infection of *P.falciparum* which one must stress so frequently occurs in the traveller from Africa, especially East, Central and West.

With these infections prodromal symptoms may be severe and last for the last few days of the incubation period. The patient may be generally unwell and feeling depressed. Usually any or all of the following symptoms occur: severe headache; nausea and vomiting; diarrhoea; generalised aches and pains; and feelings of being cold. How like a description of influenza this could be. How easy for someone back from Africa in January or February to mistake or be mistaken for influenza.

When the initial febrile attack occurs the cold stage is usually short in duration and the hot stage far longer than with the other infections. All the prodromal symptoms continue as the temperature rises. The patient is generally far more toxic and the duration of the attack may last for 24-36 hours. Although it is referred to as malignant tertian it frequently does not assume a periodicity for a few days by which time it could be too late for successful treatment. On the other hand the temperature may fall between attacks but not right down to normal. In the more severe infections one attack passes straight into another and the patient becomes increasingly toxic. Headache, nausea and vomiting continue. There is increasing weakness and the spleen enlarges. Haemolytic anaemia occurs due to the break down of the erythrocytes by the plasmodia. There is usually a leucopenia with reduction of granulocytes.

The blood pressure falls and with increasing complications shock will ensue.

If untreated, various complications will occur unless it is only a very mild infection.

The most important of these complications is of course *cerebral malaria.* This may occur with a sudden onset of coma but it is usually preceded by intense headache along with quiet delirium, acute mania or hyperpyrexia. There may be convulsions or the patient may lapse into coma and then recover to lapse again. Once the illness has got to the stage of coma the fatality rate is very high however intensive the treatment.

With *hyperpyrexia* the skin is hot and dry due to failure of sweating. This condition usually leads to cerebral malaria.

As well as the above there may be *congestive cardiac failure* or *renal failure* leading first to oliguria with albuminuria and finally anuria.

Complications of the *gastrointestinal system* may also occur simulating acute bacillary dysentery or even cholera.

Haemolytic jaundice is another complication due to excessive blood destruction.

There is the *algid* form in which acute shock ensues with the patient frequently lapsing into coma. Regrettably it may occur in what appears to be otherwise a mild attack of falciparum malaria.

Finally there is *blackwater fever* which is due to great haemolysis of red cells. As it is almost always associated with irregular long-term giving of quinine it is unlikely to occur in the short-term visitor to malarious areas.

Diagnosis of malaria should be made on clinical findings associated with a good history, finding out in particular where and when the patient was in a malarious area. However there is only one certain proof and that is the finding of the malaria parasite in the peripheral blood. Thick and thin films must always be taken if malaria is queried. Malaria should always be queried in anyone with a fever of unknown origin who has been in a malarious area. It is at this stage that it is so essential to take a geographical history of the patient's movements and if he has been in a malarious area to find out what preventive drugs he has been taking.

Treatment should not be instituted until blood slides have been taken. General practitioners should be ready and prepared to take blood slides and transfer them direct to the local laboratory because they are likely to be called to see the patient during a febrile attack when it is most likely that a positive film will be obtained. If the patient's temperature has fallen by the time they reach hospital then the blood may be temporarily negative and a positive diagnosis is not obtained until the next bout of fever. A thick film and a thin film should be taken on *clean, dry* slides. If malaria is suspected it is essential that the patient is transferred to hospital, preferably to a tropical diseases unit if there is one near at hand.

However early treatment is most important if a falciparum infection is a possibility and this should be instituted *after* the taking of the blood films.

For treatment of malaria in the visitor to a malarious area who would come in the non-immune category chloroquine is the drug of choice. Chloroquine is a 4-amino-quinoline. Worry over side effects can be dismissed for two reasons. Firstly if you do not treat the patient he may not live to know about side effects and secondly side effects occur only after prolonged treatment.

It can be given as chloroquine phosphate (Avlochlor and Resochin) or as chloroquine sulphate (Nivaquine and Plaquenil). In each case the initial dose is four tablets equivalent to 600 mg of the base. A second dose of two tablets or 300 mg of the base six hours later and then followed by two tablets daily for two or three days. If it is a vivax, malariae or ovale infection the chloroquine must be accompanied by or followed up by a course of primaquine, the problems of which have been discussed in the section on prophylaxis in Chapter Five.

If the general practitioner is first called when the patient is comatose or near comatose it may be necessary to give an intravenous or intramuscular injection of 200 mg base of chloroquine. However if given intravenously it must be given very slowly in 20 ml of water as it can increase the shock. If malaria occurs in the relatively immune then one dose of four tablets is enough. Further dosage will upset the immunity.

Kala-azar

Kala-azar or visceral leishmaniasis is an infection which occurs around the Mediterranean and therefore it is a fever which must be considered in the returned holidaymaker especially with the numerous inclusive tour holidays which are now taking place in this area. Like malaria it is a protozoal infection. The other forms of leishmaniasis will be mentioned in the chapter dealing with the skin problems. The kala-azar parasite is the *Leishmania donovani.*

It is an infection of the reticuloendothelial system and is spread from man to man by the bites of the sandfly *(Phlebotomus).* Dependent on the area where the infection occurs so the particular type of sandfly varies.

It is divided into four main geographical areas although the most important as far as United Kingdom practice is concerned is the Mediterranean area.

With the other three types there is the Indian infection occurring in the Eastern side of India, Burma and Assam. It mainly occurs in older children.

In the African variety it occurs in the semi-arid area south of the Sahara right across the width of Africa.

The third type occurs in Central and South America.

However the important Mediterranean type occurs sporadically around the Mediterranean littoral, in particular in Southern Greece and the Greek Islands; parts of the coast of Yugoslavia; the toe of Italy; Sicily; Corsica; the western end of the French Riviera; parts of the western and southern coastline of Spain; and the southern tip of Portugal — all ever-popular resorts. The Mediterranean variety appears to have a predilection for children.

Clinically the incubation period is usually about three weeks to three months, but it can be as long as ten years and it is reported even far longer. This of course makes it difficult to associate the fever with travel but an unexplained fever occurring within three to four months of a visit to these places which does not settle can well be kala-azar. The pyrexia is irregular but much sweating occurs with the paroxysms. If not seen or diagnosed in the first few weeks, bouts of pyrexia occur interspersed with periods of apyrexia. Because of its insidiousness and lack of severe toxicity the patient may not even report for some time. By then he has usually a grossly enlarged spleen and to a lesser extent an enlarged liver. Because of this the abdomen may become prominent. In particular there is a general feeling of debility and lassitude associated with sweating to excess. Loss of weight occurs so making the abdomen appear more prominent. Despite this the appetite usually remains good. Oedema of the ankles, bronchitis and bronchopneumonia are frequent complications. Skin pigmentation occurs even in the coloured races particularly over the cheek bones and around the mouth. This is why it is called kala-azar, meaning black fever. Diarrhoea may occur at a fairly late stage. Leucopenia occurs in a severe form; even agranulocytosis. Once kala-azar is suspected the patient should be admitted to hospital for full investigation and treatment (preferably a tropical diseases unit).

Diagnosis is confirmed by the finding of the parasites in the liver, spleen, bone marrow or blood, either by direct examination or by culture.

The Leishman skin test or Montenegro test is not positive during active kala-azar. It only becomes positive after successful treatment and is therefore only of value in surveys of endemicity.

Mortality used to be very high, even up to 80 per cent, but now by treatment with antimony derivatives it is quite low. Pentavalent antimony is given in the form of urea stibamine intravenously. Initially 5 mg per kg body weight increasing to 10 and 15 mg per kg body weight to a total of ten injections. Another treatment is the diamidines as pentamidine 3-4 mg per kg body weight for ten days; two or three courses may be necessary.

The problem of course is intercurrent infection occurring prior to diagnosis.

Trypanosomiasis

Trypanosomiasis or sleeping sickness is the third protozoal disease which must be considered as a cause of a fever in someone returning from the tropics. This is even more important with the now very popular 'safari' trips to the game parks of Africa. The tsetse fly carrier of trypanosomiasis has not been eradicated from the game parks. Two varieties of trypanosomiasis occur scattered throughout Africa between 20° North and 20° South. There is also a third or South American variety called Chagas' disease which will be discussed later.

The magnitude of the problem of trypanosomiasis can be gauged when one realises that the tsetse fly inhabits 280,000 square miles out of the total of 640,000 square miles of East Africa. During 25 years of preventive measures there was only a net gain of 3 per cent in land permanently cleared of the fly.

Trypanosoma gambiense occurs in high endemicity in Guinea, Ghana, Nigeria, Gambia, Sierra Leone, Congo and into Uganda. *Trypanosoma rhodesiense* occurs in Rhodesia, Zambia, Uganda and Tanzania.

The two varieties differ clinically mainly in that with *T. gambiense* or the West African variety there are basically two phases with a gradual transition while with *T. rhodesiense,* the East African variety, there is one main acute phase.

With *T. gambiense* the incubation period is usually two to three weeks but may be shorter. Initially at the site of bite a nodule appears with brown induration. There may be a surrounding area looking just like a bruise. This area may ulcerate and become infected. If fluid is aspirated trypanosomes are found. Treatment at this stage will cure the infection but this is rare.

Following this local reaction stage 1 or the stage of trypanosome fever ensues. This may follow in a matter of a few weeks but it may be a great deal longer, even months or even two to three years. Fever is irregular, frequently with apyrexial intervals. The pulse and respiration are both rapid. The lymph glands are enlarged, at first painlessly but later they become painful. The posterior cervical triangle is particularly affected (Winterbottom's sign). This glandular enlargement may in fact be the first sign. The liver and spleen are usually enlarged, the latter sometimes to a very great extent.

A transient pink rash may appear mainly on the chest and back soon after onset of the fever. Less frequently it appears on the face and arms. It is described as being a circinate erythema, the rings being variable in size. It only lasts a few hours so is frequently missed especially as there is no subsequent desquamation.

At this stage there is usually a mild microcytic anaemia. Trypanosomes are usually scantily distributed in the blood and are most likely to be found in fluid from the lymphatic glands. As yet there are no trypanosomes in the cerebrospinal fluid. Slowly the scene changes and the next stage of central nervous system involvement develops, in particular involvement of cerebration. Thus we move into stage 2. It is usually at least six months before this change occurs and it may well be up to a year or more. When this happens trypansosomes have invaded the cerebrospinal fluid. The picture is truly one of a slowing down of cerebration in all forms. A vacant sad expression; apathy and a loss of desire to work; a slowing of the thought processes: all leading to drowsiness. Along with these symptoms are severe headache; tremors of the tongue; tremors of the limbs; shuffling gait; emaciation; frequently a confusional state.

Sensory and motor changes also occur. Kerandel's sign is significant. If pressure is put on deep tissue and then removed pain follows. Tingling sensations in the extremities occur. In the end the patient becomes semi-comatose and finally comatose lying with their limbs flexed. Without treatment death will ensue.

With *T. rhodesiense* the whole process is far more acute taking sometimes a matter of weeks. The pyrexia is greater, the glandular involvement less. In fact cerebral involvement may occur before glandular involvement.

It is also far more resistant to treatment. Confirmatory diagnosis is finding the trypanosomes. In the early stages in *T. gambiense* in lymph fluid and in *T. rhodesiense* in the blood. In the later stages in the CSF in both infections. Treatment for the gambiense infection is pentamidine or Suramin plus tryparsamide. For the rhodesiense infection Suramin or Mel B. The South American variety *trypanosoma cruzi* or Chagas' disease usually only affects infants. It is therefore rarely seen amongst travellers.

Toxoplasmosis

A fourth protozoal disease which must be considered is toxoplasmosis. Becoming perhaps an increasing problem amongst residents of temperate climates, it has been an established problem in warmer climates for some time. It is an infection caused by the intracellular protozoal parasite the *Toxoplasma gondii*. Although known to occur as a parasite in animals for approximately 60 years it was only found in man about 30 years ago. It is known to occur in domestic cats, dogs, cattle, sheep, as well as wild animals. Mode of spread is not truly known but it may be by faecal spread. The parasites occur chiefly in the cells of the reticuloendothelial system and in mononuclear leucocytes in particular. A noteworthy point in this illness is that it can be congenital as well as acquired hence any chance of it occurring in early pregnancy must be very carefully followed up.

Geographically it is a worldwide infection but in particular it occurs in the Middle East, Far East, Australia and the Americas. Incubation period in the acquired form is thought to be two to three weeks.

In the acquired form it can take on several pictures of which the commonest is enlargement of the lymph glands. All the lypmh glands may be involved but cervical, axillary and inguinal group are nearly always affected. They remain discrete and are not tender. They may remain enlarged for weeks or months or on the other hand they may settle down in a matter of days. There is an intermittent fever associated with the adenitis but usually starting before the adenitis.

Another more serious form which occurs, usually in children but not always so, is like an acute meningoencephalitis, frequently with deafness or choroidoretinitis. This type in children is frequently fatal while in adults it may go on for many months in phases of activity and quiescence but frequently leading to mental disturbance or choroidoretinitis.

In the third type, after a few days of fever a maculopapular rash appears all over the body except for the palms of the hands and the soles of the feet (compare tick typhus). However in a majority of infected subjects there may be no history of any clinical illness. This of course can be a serious problem especially with the incidence of the congenital variety which follows on the mother being infected in the first trimester of pregnancy.

The characteristic triad of symptoms in the congenital variety are hydrocephalus, choroidoretinitis and calcification in the brain. Frequently the infant is stillborn but if it survives there may be blindness or mental deficiency. Microcephaly also occurs. There are toxoplasma antibodies in the blood.

Diagnosis may be by biopsy of a gland but it is usually by specific complement fixation test or the Toxoplasma Dye Test. The Toxoplasma Dye Test is qualitative and quantitative and is the best test especially on repetition to find a rising or falling titre. However it has to be done in special laboratories which causes delay in obtaining a result. Recently there has been developed the simple Toxoplasma Slide Test which is a complement fixation test and can be carried out in a matter of minutes. It will not give an accurate titre but it can give graded results of severe, moderate and mild. Treatment in the past has been a two week course of full dosage sulphadiazine or sulphatriad with pyrimethamine 50 mg initially followed by 25 mg in six hours and 50 mg daily for the rest of the 14 days.

With the arrival of trimethoprim sulphamethoxazole (Septrin) this is now being used.

Typhoid

Amongst the possible fevers from abroad one must consider typhoid, paratyphoid A and paratyphoid B along with acute bacillary dysentery. However these will be discussed fully in the Chapter on Intestinal infections.

Acute Infective Hepatitis

This is a fever which must always be considered in the traveller returning from the subtropics or tropics. As it is accepted it is faecal spread it is naturally far commoner in the lands of doubtful sanitation. It is common throughout the Indian subcontinent and in many of the developing countries of Africa. The 'overlanders' who travel by bus or hitchhike from Western Europe to India frequently develop hepatitis. This can be due to two causes. One, when they develop the acute viral infective hepatitis living it rough in unhygienic circumstances. The second way however is more sinister. A percentage of these overlanders are on drugs of one type or another and then they may well develop homologous serum hepatitis. With the first variety the incubation period is 15-40 days while with the latter it is probably two to six months. The former is caused by virus A, the latter by virus B. There is no need to describe in detail the symptoms and signs of acute viral infective hepatitis, but one important point is with this form of jaundice as soon as the jaundice appears the patient starts to feel better and the temperature goes down. Tests for Australian antigen are negative with infective hepatitis but are usually positive in the acute phase of the serum type although they return to negative later.

To reiterate, a fever occurring soon after the return of an overlander can well be an infective or serum hepatitis.

Leptospirosis

Having just discussed hepatitis, previously known as catarrhal jaundice, this is probably the place to look at leptospirosis, previously known as spirochaetosis icterohaemorrhagica or Weil's disease. In fact it is now accepted that there are many variations in form of leptospiral infections. They can vary from a severe illness with fever, jaundice and haemorrhage to a quite mild infection. Geographically the distribution is worldwide but as the other host is a rodent, usually a rat, it is far commoner where rats abound. Spread is via the urine of the rat. Infection occurs through wet or damaged skin.

Incubation period is usually about 10-14 days. The onset is sudden with shivering, rigor and severe prostration — more than one would expect for the clinical signs. Joint and muscle pains are present and the muscles are frequently very tender. There is usually a very severe conjunctivitis which should be suggestive. Pyrexia may be to 105°F but the pulse may be comparatively slow. Jaundice appears about the fifth day but the temperature continues for a few days more. Haemorrhages occur in the form of petechiae, purpuric spots and sometimes bleeding from various mucosae such as haematemesis, epistaxis and bleeding gums. Leucocytosis and liver enlargement are present. The pyrexia usually settles after about ten days and the patient appears to improve. However a second bout of fever may occur about the second to third week and at this time meningeal irritation or meningitis may complicate matters. After this second fever the condition settles down. Diagnosis is by a compound screening antigen (CSA) for use in a complement fixation test prepared in and distributed by the Reference Laboratory. This is available in the Public Health Laboratory Service.

Treatment is by large doses of penicillin.

Yellow Fever

This is the remaining febrile jaundice of note but as inoculation against yellow fever is one hundred per cent effective and the control of yellow fever inoculation and certification is internationally tight there is no fear of cases being transferred to a non-endemic country by travel.

Dengue Fever

This is another Group B arbovirus disease like yellow fever. It is an acute non-fatal disease transmitted by the Aedes mosquito usually the aegypti variety. It is also known as breakbone fever or seven day fever, both of which are suitably descriptive names as it causes intense influenzal backache and limbsache.

Geographically it occurs only in the tropics and subtropics but it is extensive in these areas occurring in the Caribbean and the South American continent, around Africa, the Mediterranean littoral, through the Middle East and Arabian Gulf area, around the Indian subcontinent and into Singapore and coastal Thailand. Also in many Pacific Islands and the northern coast of Australia.

The incubation period is usually from 5 to 14 days so it is easy for the holidaymaker or business traveller to any one of these many coastal areas to develop it on return to his homeland.

Clinically it has a sudden onset with severe headache and aching eyeballs frequently with photophobia. Pyrexia may be up to 106°F. There are always intense pains in the joints, long bones and back. These are severe enough to prevent sleep. Suffusion of the face occurs with some erythema. There is usually anorexia and nausea and sometimes vomiting.

The fever usually settles about the third or fourth day but then after two or three days it frequently returns with also a return of the pains although they are less severe. A further eruption may also occur initially on the hands and feet and later on the arms, legs and trunk. It is erythematous in nature and tends to coalesce. It is very irritating and fine desquamation occurs.

At this stage there is a bradycardia.

The whole illness settles after about a week and there is no mortality although subsequent depression may be prolonged. No specific treatment. Convalescence is slow. Adequate prevention of mosquito bites will prevent this illness.

Sandfly Fever or Phlebotomus Fever

Another viral infection but spread by the sandfly which will get through any mosquito netting.

Geographically all round the Mediterranean littoral both on the north and south shores. Also India, Burma, China and South America.

Incubation period is only four to six days so is more likely to occur overseas than dengue.

Clinically pyrexia to 104°F; rigor; severe headache; aching eyeballs and photophobia; and general pains. It usually only lasts four or five days and there is no eruption. Otherwise it is very like the initial phase of dengue. Never fatal. Difficult to differentiate from dengue or influenza.

Acute Viral Encephalomyelitis

This forms a group of acute fevers which again, although they occur in temperate climates, are far commoner in warm climates where they may break out in circumscribed epidemics which of course the visitor does not know about with the result that he may return home and develop it, not knowing he had been a contact.

Geographically they occur all over the world and frequently have different names in the different places but in general are very similar illnesses.

Incubation period about one week and is followed by an acute onset. Headache, fever and signs of meningism with muscle spasticity occurring. Mental disorientation, delirium, epileptiform attacks or even coma may ensue. In fact the onset may be with an epileptiform fit in someone who has never suffered from this previously. However there is pyrexia at the same time. If the cord is involved paralysis may ensue. Onset may be fulminating and death occur within three days but usually the acute symptoms last for one to two weeks but the mental disturbance is usually slower to disappear. A lack of alertness may last for several weeks.

Diagnosis is more difficult in the returning traveller as a local epidemic where he or she has been is probably not realised.

Lumbar puncture will probably show raised pressure, raised protein with an increase in cells.

There is no specific treatment.

Typhus Fevers

The typhus group of fevers are caused by the Rickettsiae and can be divided into two groups.

1. The epidemic group of typhus fevers of which the louse borne disease is the classic type. In general this is of course a disease of war and filth and need not be considered in the ordinary traveller. In fact it occurs in the colder regions of the world but outbreaks have occurred recently in Ethiopia.

2. The endemic group of typhus fevers. The most important of this group is tickborne typhus and this is a fever which must always be borne in mind in people who have been to South and East Africa. Other forms are Rocky Mountain fever, fièvre boutonneuse and Q fever but it is the first that is most important.

Tick typhus is spread by cattle ticks and dog ticks. It occurs in East, Central and Southern Africa. Fièvre boutonneuse or Marseilles fever is similar and occurs around the Mediterranean. It also is spread by the dog tick. Initially there is a black eschar at the site of the original bite sometimes with local lymphangitis. there is then an incubation period usually of one to two weeks when a marked fever occurs which is remittant and rises into the second week. On about the fourth day of fever a rash like an early measles rash occurs. This disappears and a roseate rash then appears starting at the extremities and spreading centrally. They may become confluent and even necrotic. Classically the rash is on the palms of the hands and the soles of the feet. Diagnosis is confirmed by the Weil Felix Test. Treatment is by chloramphenicol or tetracyclines.

Care must be taken in convalescence as myocardial infarction is a known late complication.

Brucellosis

Although this fever regrettably occurs in Great Britain it is commoner in the warmer climates. The causal organism of Malta fever was discovered by Bruce in 1887. At first called *Micrococcus melitensis* it was subsequently named *Brucella melitensis.* It occurs throughout the world in goat rearing areas of the tropics and subtropics. *Brucella abortus* infects cattle and *Brucella suis* pigs. Man becomes infected by drinking infected milk other than with farmers who become infected by handling the products of parturition. Incubation period is about 7 to 21 days. Initially the symptoms are malaise, muscular pains and gastric disturbance. Then follows a period of usually up to three weeks of undulating pyrexia. Associated symptoms are headaches, profuse sweats and muscular pains. The spleen is enlarged and tender. Following these three weeks a period of apyrexia follows and then a relapse which is shorter than the first pyrexia. From then on the pyrexial attacks get shorter and the apyrexial attacks longer. However with the fever continuing arthritis, oesteomyelitis, epididymoorchitis, endocarditis and anaemia occur.

Diagnosis may be confirmed by blood or urine culture; also agglutinations as with Widal testing agglutinations.

Smallpox

This fever must always be remembered if a vesicular type rash occurs in someone who has returned from India, Pakistan and Bangladesh in particular. Certain areas of East, Central and West Africa and parts of South America are also involved. In particular in Brazil alastrim or variola minor is a problem.

Incubation period is 10 to 15 days. the prodromal symptoms are severe and the patient is very toxic. The rash starts on the face and hands and spreads on to the trunk reaching the legs and feet last. It can take on the discrete, confluent or haemorrhagic forms. The severity of the illness increases in the type as mentioned. The haemorrhagic variety is nearly always fatal.

Other Fevers

Other fevers which occur more commonly in the warmer climates but also occur in the U.K. are glandular fever and poliomyelitis.

Glandular fever which originates in Africa appears to have a greater tendency for bouts of recurrent fever. Regarding poliomyelitis one must remember that although it is primarily a disease of children and young adult life, when it strikes later in life its symptoms are frequently very severe, particularly involving the respiratory system.

9. Alimentary and Urinary Tract Infections

The acceptance by travellers of intestinal infections when they travel to warm climates is practically universal.

The crux of the matter is these infections can be very mild and short-lasting such as travellers diarrhoea or they can be a very serious and perhaps fatal illness such as typhoid. Equally they can cause prolonged ill health as in amoebiasis which has been untreated and amoebic hepatitis has ensued.

To start with what is obviously the most frequent problem—*travellers diarrhoea.* This has been fully discussed in Chapter 4 when its frequency, its cause and its prevention were looked at. The most important thing to remember about travellers diarrhoea, or under whatever local name it is known, is that it is a self limiting illness lasting for probably not more than three days. A diarrhoea following overseas travel which lasts for longer than this time or which is recurring must be fully investigated because it could well be some infection of a far more serious nature. The other point for the doctor at home to remember is that travellers diarrhoea is an illness of very short incubation and is correctly titled. As such, any diarrhoea which occurs more than two or three days after the traveller has returned home, is not travellers diarrhoea.

When someone does suffer from diarrhoea following an overseas journey, probably the first thing that should come to one's mind is that the patient could be suffering from a *shigella infection.* The two varieties which cause the acute attacks are *S.shiga* and *S.flexner. S.sonne* causes a mild attack and is frequently a persistent cause of trouble in old people's homes and day nurseries.

Bacillary dysentery clinically presents with the passage of frequent small stools. There is almost always blood and mucus present. Colicky abdominal pain and tenesmus are severe. Here again the incubation period is short. It may be a few hours: usually two to four days: maximum about one week. If therefore diarrhoea starts more than one week after return and it is the first attack, it is unlikely to be a bacillary dysentery contracted abroad. However, the patient may well have had a first attack on his holiday or trip and this is a recurrence having not been satisfactorily treated.

It can either be insidious in onset, or very acute and sudden. With the severe cases which are usually Shiga, all faeces may be passed within the first few motions and subsequently there is only severe abdominal colic associated with intense tenesmus and the passage of only bloodstained mucus. This can be very exhausting. Headaches and vomiting are frequent. Pyrexia may be absent but usually initially fairly high. With the very severe infections death can ensue rapidly: these are luckily rare.

Usually symptoms settle in about five days but if untreated recurrences will occur and a chronic bacillary dysentery may develop. The chronic infection is associated with arthritis, iritis, stenosis and haemorrhoids.

Confirmatory diagnosis is best by stool culture; treatment by fluids plus antibiotics to which the organisms are sensitive.

Prior to passing on to amoebic dysentery one should at this stage mention *staphylococcal food poisoning*. This is far more common than was previously thought. Spread by food handlers who are chronic staphylococcal carriers: frequently in their nose. Usually uncooked or cold foods predominate, particularly dairy products. However, the enterotoxin that the staphylocci produce is heat resistant and is not destroyed by cooking.

Incubation period is very short, usually two to four hours: nausea, vomiting and diarrhoea ensue but usually clear with 12 hours. *Salmonella food poisoning* is a greater problem. Although of the same genus as *salmonella typhi* the causative organisms of these forms of food poisoning are antigenically different. There are hundreds of variants but the commonest are probably *salmonella typhimurium* and *salmonella enteritidis*. Usually several people eating the same food will be affected.

Incubation period is usually about 24 hours but may be more or less. Clinically in symptoms, severity and length of illness it is very similar to a shigella infection. Diagnosis is by stool culture.

Treatment as for shigella, namely fluids and an antibiotic to which the organism is sensitive.

Amoebic dysentery must next be considered. It is caused by an infection with the protozoa *Entamoeba histolytica*. It is far more insidious and chronic than bacillary dysentery. There are other Entamoeba, such as *Entamoeba hartmanni, Entamoeba coli, Entamoeba nana,* and *Iodamoeba butschlii*. These are all now considered to be non-pathogenic and their presence in the stool is of no concern.

Geographically, it is a disease of warm climates and lack of sanitation combined. To be more specific, in Europe the coasts of Portugal and Spain; the lower half of Italy and the Balkans. In Asia all round the Middle East, India, Pakistan, Burma, Thailand, Indonesia and areas of China. Scattered areas in Australia. Most of Africa, other than the desert lands. Scattered areas in the U.S.A., Mexico, Central America, the Northern part of South America and scattered areas of Brazil. However, because of the nature of the disease, chronic carriers are common and as such the disease can be spread with ease.

The *Entamoeba histolytica* exists in two forms. The vegetative form is present in fresh stools in the acute stages only. It soon dies even in faeces. The second form is the cystic form which lives a long time as long as there is moisture. It dies however if dry. As such amoebic dysentery thrives with humidity. This cystic form is the cause of spread. The presence of cysts in food handlers can be a disaster. It is difficult to assess the percentage of amoebic cyst carriers in a community. Obviously high in warm countries with poor sanitation. Approximately 0.5 per cent in Britain. Kean and Smillie (1954) found it to be 4 per cent in American students travelling to Europe.

Incubation period is very variable but is probably from about two weeks to three months but can be longer.

Starting insidiously with the bowels getting looser and the stools becoming offensive. They are frequently spotted with mucus and blood. There is no fever. If untreated, this condition becomes chronic with recurring diarrhoea interspersed with constipation and associated with generalised lassitude, anorexia and loss of weight. A feeling of distension and gurgling is common; also the appetite is frequently satisfactory until the sight of food when nausea ensues. There is a more acute form but this is rare. The diarrhoea is more intense but there is still no pyrexia and little toxaemia. As well as this there is the apparently well cyst passer who is in fact a far greater trouble to his fellows than to himself.

Diagnosis is by stool examination and sigmoidoscopy when scrapings from the colonic ulceration will produce vegetative and cystic amoebae.

The classic complication if untreated is of course amoebic hepatitis and liver abscess. As well as this there is the amoeboma of the colon which, on more than one occasion, has been mistaken for a carcinoma. Amoebic infestation of the appendix can cause acute appendicitis; localised peritonitis and skin ulceration and amoebic abscesses elsewhere (brain) are rare complications.

Treatment. While one form of treatment may be best for the vegetative form another is better for the cystic form.

When the infection is purely confined to the bowel lumen, such as an acute dysentery or symptom free cyst carrier state, diloxanide furoate (furamide) is very effective in the dosage 200 mg per kg body weight, daily for ten days. It is reckoned to be 95 per cent effective with chronic cyst carriers.

Metronidazole (Flagyl) has become very popular recently in the dosage of 800 mg orally thrice daily for five to seven days. It is also effective with amoebic hepatitis.

As well as the above two more recent additions, the old faithful emetine as dehydroemetine hydrochloride is guaranteed effective against the vegetative tissue invading forms. It is valueless with cysts. However, emetine bismuth iodide eradicates cysts. It is often good to give a course of one of the tetracyclines at the same time to kill off symbiotic organisms. It must be remembered that all forms of emetine are cardiotoxic therefore, bed rest is essential during treatment.

With amoebic hepatitis or even small abscesses, metronidazole or emetine are effective. With large abscesses aspiration is necessary as well.

A further protozoa which must be very seriously considered in intestinal infections nowadays is the *Giardia lamblia* (or *Lamblia intestinalis*) which causes giardiasis. It used to be considered to be entirely non-pathogenic. This is definitely not so. Maybe there are no symptoms if the infection is mild but it certainly can cause symptoms presumably with a heavy infection. It is a flagellate protozoa and inhabits the duodenum or jejunum.

Geographically, it occurs in very similar areas to amoebiasis liking moisture, warmth and insanitation. It is very common in the Eastern Mediterranean. With a heavy infection, it causes bulky fatty loose yellowish stools which tend to float in the lavatory pan. Abdominal discomfort and distension plus nausea are the usual accompanying symptoms. It seems to be becoming more common in the traveller. Diagnosis is by finding the protozoa in the stool. Treatment is simple, cheap and effective—Mepacrine Hydrochloride 100 mg three times a day for seven days. Metronidazole (Flagyl) is also very effective but is far more expensive and should be kept in reserve in case the Mepacrine fails.

At this stage *balantidiasis* or infection with *Balantidium coli* should just be mentioned. Spread by cysts from the stools of pigs it is worldwide in distribution but comparatively rare. Clinically, it is almost exactly like amoebiasis but infects lymph glands and never the liver. It can only be distinguished from amoebiasis by finding in a fresh stool or by scraping from the colonic ulcers by sigmoidoscopy. Treatment is by one of the tetracyclines.

The next problem which must be considered is *typhoid fever*. Firstly because of its seriousness and secondly because with increasing travel it is becoming more common in developed countries as sporadic rather than epidemic cases.

One can only recall, when in 1969, 38 cases were known to have occurred amongst holidaymakers who stayed at the same hotel in Tunisia: eight from Britain, 16 from Germany, 13 from Switzerland and one from Holland. One British and one German patient died. How many of these patients may subsequently have become carriers? Since then other holidaymakers and business travellers have returned to the U.K. and developed typhoid. The subcontinent of India, the north coast of Africa and the whole of the Mediterranean littoral are particularly suspect. Along with typhoid we must consider paratyphoid A and paratyphoid B and the rare paratyphoid C. Typhoid is an acute fever caused by the specific organism *Salmonella typhi*. Geographically, typhoid is a worldwide fever unaffected by climate but encouraged by poor public health conditions. Hence it occurs where sanitation is poor. One must remember that in rapidly expanding communities due to the enormous holiday boom, sudden stresses must be put on the public health facilities hence the possibility of a breakdown in efficiency.

In general however, typhoid is unusual in endemic or epidemic form in Northern Europe. Paratyphoid A is rare in America and Europe, other than the Balkans. It occurs extensively in India. Paratyphoid B has the same distribution as typhoid. Paratyphoid C occurs primarily in the Balkans and Guyana. Typhoid is generally spread by faecal contamination of water and milk, shellfish, uncooked food and flies. Shellfish are particularly suspect. The Croydon epidemic in the late 1930's was caused by a building labourer who was a carrier micturating into a drinking water supply. The Aberdeen epidemic of 1964 was put down to infected corned beef. The paratyphoid group are spread more frequently by milk, milk products and meat, less frequently by water.

What must be remembered is that the typhoid bacillus survives in ice so wherever the water is suspect, water for ice for drinks must be boiled first before being frozen.

Incubation period is usually about ten days to two weeks, but unlike many infections the incubation period appears to be dependent on the heaviness of the infection. With a severe infection, incubation may be cut to three to five days, while with a light infection, it may be as long as three to four weeks.

Clinically the onset is typically insidious with general malaise; headache, usually severe; easy fatigue; anorexia and generally constipation. Initial diarrhoea is rare. There are also frequently the suggestions of an early bronchitis especially in children. Nose bleeds are not infrequent. On examination the tongue is furred with general signs of increasing toxaemia. The patient is flushed, lying still and has a general attitude of lassitude. The temperature should rise classically in a staircase fashion but this does not occur with previous inoculation, although it gradually rises through the week. Most prominent however, is the definite bradycardia comparative to the pyrexia. As the week progresses the patient becomes more toxic and by the end of the week a soft spleen is usually felt. At the same time the classical rose spots appear on the trunk. They fade easily on pressure. The lips are dry and sordes frequently appear around the mouth. The patient is now very toxic and his whole mental process seems to slow down very definitely such that he may almost be stuporose. Constipation may continue or diarrhoea ensue with pea soup stools. This is a bad prognostic sign and may be a warning of ensuing haemorrhage or perforation at the end of the second week. At the same time abdominal distension and tenderness on pressure occur. With increasing toxaemia the previously slow pulse may become rapid.

By the third week, with the mild cases, the pyrexia starts to fall and the patient although very exhausted begins to improve. With these cases gradual improvement occurs through the ensuing two or three weeks although relapses can occur.

However, with severe cases, in the third week the typhoid state may set in. This is well described by Christie in the following words:

> 'The patient is now completely out of touch, dull, disorientated and stunned with toxaemia, stupid and unanimated, torpid yet sleepless, confused and muttering, not unconscious but conscious of nothing . . . His face reflects the profound toxaemia sunken, sallow, but with a flush over the cheekbones that tends to spread as the illness worsens, his eyes glistening and perhaps injected, but expressive of nothing but inexpressible insensibility'.

It is also towards the end of the second week or in the third that intestinal haemorrhage and/or perforation may occur.

Haemorrhage may be very severe. The temperature falls and the pulse rises. The signs of acute shock in an already very toxic patient. Death may ensue rapidly. With perforation there is immediate shock which is followed, as with a perforated appendix, by a deceptive silent period prior to the onset of signs of acute peritonitis, once again with the signs of acute toxaemia superimposed.

Luckily with the arrival of chloramphenicol these complications have become less frequent.

Other complications or sequelae of typhoid are pneumonia, parotitis, peripheral neuritis, temporary deafness (very frequent), bacilluria and transient nephritis, myocardial involvement and thrombophlebitis. Late complications may be chronic cholecystitis, leading to a chronic carrier, and periostitis with bone abscesses.

Diagnosis is usually confirmed by the pathological tests but toxaemia, staircase temperature and comparative bradycardia are classic. If the diagnosis has not already been made the enlarged spleen and rose coloured spots should confirm. Geddes found in his series of 74 cases in Birmingham that early diarrhoea was far more common in children.

Confirmatory pathological tests are as follows:

White count. Leucopenia with relative lymphocytosis early. Subsequently with intestinal lesions becoming infected a leucocytosis with excess polymorphs occurs.

Blood culture. Positive in at least 90 per cent of cases during the first week. Percentage drops in second week. This is the earliest conclusive test. 5-10 ml of blood must be taken before antibiotics are instituted especially chloramphenicol else the blood may become sterile in a matter of hours.

Faecal culture. Positive stools are later in the illness. The earliest is at the end of the first week, increasing in the second week and 75 per cent positive in the third week. The stools may remain positive for many months and of course a remaining positive stool is an absolute bar to the patient being a food handler.

Urine culture. 25 per cent positive in third and fourth week from culture of centrifuged urine. Bacilluria is intermittent and morning specimens should be examined every day for a week.

Widal test. The Widal test depends on the presence of H agglutinins (flagellar) and O agglutinins (somatic) in the blood.

The H agglutinins, not normally present in serum, are practically specific for each organism in the enteric group. They are however, affected by TAB or typhoid inoculation. The O agglutinins are present in normal serum to a dilution of about one in 20, they are not specific for each organism in the enteric group, but they are not affected by inoculation. Hence a raised O titre will show an enteric group infection. The H titre is valueless if previously inoculated but if not previously inoculated it can be of assistance in defining the specific type of infection.

Either way, the most important part is a rising titre occurring with two successive Widal tests.

It is not positive until the end of the first week but with an infection, rises during the second week to a maximum late in the third week. It is positive in over 90 per cent of patients. Usually titres against *Brucella abortus* infections are considered in the same test.

N.B. The clinician should tell the laboratory of any history of TAB vaccination.

Specific treatment is by chloramphenicol, ampicillin or trimethoprim sulphamethoxazole (septrin).

Chloramphenicol is probably the best treatment but Anderson and Smith and Butler, with his co-workers, have regrettably, recently reported resistance of *S.typhi* to chloramphenicol in Mexico. and Vietnam respectively. Ampicillin has not proved to be any more effective and reports on trimethoprim sulphamethoxazole are mixed. Corticosteroids may be necessary in association with the antibiotic in severely toxic states.

Ampicillin however, is probably more effective with the carrier state but cholecystectomy must be seriously considered.

The *paratyphoid* infections are clinically very similar although they tend to be milder infections. However, the onset appears to be more rapid and diarrhoea is more frequent early on. In other words, more like the other salmonella infections. The spleen tends to be larger and the rash more prominent.

Toxaemia and complications are less frequent, except meningism and even meningitis can occur.

Treatment is the same as for typhoid.

Cholera is an acute self limiting infective disease caused by the *Vibrio cholerae.* The vibrio multiplies in the intestine but does not invade the tissues or bloodstream. It is characterised by intense watery diarrhoea with abdominal cramps and collapse. It is spread by faecal infection of water and so its spread is limited to areas of bad sanitation. Basically a disease of Asia it has, however, recently spread elsewhere. For many years it was recognised that there were three strains of vibrios namely the Inawa, Ogawa and Hikojima strains, but comparatively recently the spread of cholera throughout South East Asia and into the Middle East and Africa has been by the El Tor variant.

The whole subject of the spread of cholera has been discussed in the chapter on necessary immunisations but it obviously must be considered in the diagnosis in a patient from a choleraic area.

Geographically then it occurs throughout South East Asia, especially where humidity is high. Recently it has spread through the Middle East into Iran, the countries around the Arabian Gulf and Red Sea and thus into East, Central and West Africa. From there it spread to North Africa and even into Spain and Italy.

Incubation period is usually up to four days, but may be as long as a week. Hence it can be excluded if the patient has left the area for more than one week.

Clinically, there is intense diarrhoea with a very watery stool; acute abdominal cramps and collapse. The patient can rapidly become extremely dehydrated. The onset is very sudden and there may be intense vomiting as well so increasing the dehydration. Thirst is severe and the stools become only water and mucus—the classical rice water stools.

Collapse usually occurs within 12 hours. Diagnosis is by culturing the vibrio from the stools. Treatment is of course in hospital with intense intravenous rehydration. This is the major factor in saving life although tetracyclines should be given for the infection.

Having considered the bacterial and protozoal infections before passing on to the metazoal infections, one should briefly consider a problem that, it is accepted, may follow on some of the previously mentioned infections.

This problem is the one sometimes called *tropical sprue* and sometimes *the malabsorption syndrome of the tropics.* The aetiological picture of the malabsorption is very mixed. All that is clear is that there is a decrease in intestinal absorption mainly fat but also of certain carbohydrates. There seem to be two major points of note, one nutritional and one infective.

Before the second world war it was considered to be mainly an illness of middle aged Europeans in India, which certainly did not suggest nutritional! In the second world war it occurred at the same time as outbreaks of intestinal infections. It can occur quite a long time after someone has returned from the tropics. Possibly there is a disturbance of intestinal flora which could follow intensive antibiotic therapy for an intestinal infection. Geographically, it occurs throughout the subcontinent of India but more in the coastal areas, Burma, Vietnam,

China and Indonesia. In the Western hemisphere in the southern states of the U.S.A., Central America and Puerto Rico. It is practically unknown in Africa. It is of interest that in Africa saturated fats such as palm oil and coconut oil are in use and there is no sprue but in India where there is sprue unsaturated fats predominate.

The term incubation period can strictly not be used but one would mention again that although it may occur soon after a traveller returns, on the other hand it may not occur until the traveller has left the tropics or subtropics for a long time.

Clinically diarrhoea with loose frothy pale fatty stools is the presenting feature and as such the patient goes to the doctor thinking he has an intestinal infection. Because of its fat and gaseous content the stool frequently floats similarly to a *Giardia lamblia* infection which it may well follow. The loose stools frequently occur in the morning, while abdominal distension and discomfort occur in the evening. In general there is no blood in the stools.

With the persistence of the diarrhoea and the failure to absorb fats and vitamins obvious signs of this malabsorption follow. Sore tongue; soreness at the angles of the mouth; weight loss; mild conjunctivitis and photophobia. The skin becomes dry. Dyspepsia and flatus becomes severe and lethargy increases.

Following on these symptoms a severe macrocytic anaemia ensues. Not unreasonably the patient becomes querulous, irritable and introspective. Diagnosis is dependent on the pathology. In tropical sprue the jejunal intestinal villi atrophy and this change of mucosal pattern shows up in a well conducted barium meal. Loops of small bowel also frequently become dilated showing pools of barium. If these findings are suggestive then a jejunal biopsy can be carried out by swallowing a Crosby capsule.

Further, the total fat excreted in the stools over a period of 72 hours will confirm whether or not there is malabsorption. The normal stool should not contain more than 5 g fat in 24 hours. In sprue it may well be 10-15 g. Also the ratio of split fats to unsplit fats is raised. Instead of 2:1 it may be up to 5:1. Similarly, absorption of sugars are of interest. In sprue glucose tolerance curves are usually flat, but fructose tolerance curves are normal.

With the xylose excretion and absorption test, the rate of xylose excreted in the urine is estimated. In the normal person 20-25 per cent is excreted in the first five hours. With malabsorption there is a low excretion in the first five hours.

Serum folic acid tends to be lowered as also serum calcium and serum vitamin B_{12}.

The blood picture is usually one of megaloblastic anaemia and if this anaemia is marked the marrow may be megaloblastic as well. Treatment is of a diet which is rich in protein and low in fat with the addition of folic acid and vitamin B_{12}. Broad spectrum antibiotics, usually tetracycline, have been found to bring about a rapid improvement which may well be associated with a bacterial cause.

We now pass to the metazoan infections and the first one, one must consider, is *schistosomiasis* or *bilharzia.* Called by either name but better by the former as the causative flukes are known as *Schistosoma haematobium, Schistosoma mansoni* and *Schistosoma japonicum.* All flukes need an intermediate host of a fresh water snail.

Infection occurs by paddling, bathing, or swimming in fresh water containing infected snails. It can also be spread by drinking or washing in infected water, as the cercaria penetrates undamaged skin or mucosa. Having penetrated either of these it graduates to the portal vein. Here the parasite matures for about six weeks—fertilisation by the male of the female occurs and the thinner females continue down into the small veins of the bladder or rectum where they lay their eggs. The ova then pass into the bladder or rectum. When passed into fresh water the embryo leaves the ovum and enters the snail. A parasite can remain active and produce viable eggs for up to 25 years. *S.haematobium* basically infects the urinary tract, while *S.mansoni* basically infects the intestinal tract. Although on occasions this may be reversed, *S.japonicum,* which only occurs in the Far East and is far less common, infects the spleen and liver as well as the intestinal tract.

Geographically, *S.haematobium* occurs in Africa, all along the Northern coast, down the Nile Valley, the entire East coast to Natal and the Cape, areas of the Congo and Niger rivers. It also occurs in the Sudan, Uganda, Rhodesia and Sierra Leone. It occurs in scattered areas in the Middle East, including parts of Saudi Arabia, the Yemen, Israel, Iran, Iraq, Northern Syria and Southern Turkey. In Europe it occurs in the southern part of Portugal and nearby Spain. There is a fairly high incidence in Madagascar, Réunion and Mauritius, especially the Black River area. It does not occur in the Americas. *S.mansoni* occurs all down the Nile Valley; right across Central Africa, from Sierra Leone to Zanzibar. It also occurs in Venezuela, North Eastern Brazil and in particular, in the island of St Lucia in the Caribbean which is fast becoming a very popular holiday resort.

S.japonicum occurs in the valley of the Yangtze River, some parts of Southern Japan, some of the Philippine Islands, also parts of Laos and Khmer Republic.

Clinically, there are the two different infections with different pictures but it is probable that in at least 15 per cent of cases a mixed infection occurs.

Initially, on invasion, when the cercariae penetrate the skin, there is localised irritation and small area of dermatitis. This may not be noticed at the time but if questioned later the patient may recall it.

Four to twelve weeks later there may be some constitutional symptoms which, basically, is a generalised allergic reaction. Such symptoms as irregular fever, generalised urticaria, cough, diarrhoea and vague muscular pains may occur. However, this generalised reaction may on the other hand be completely absent. If it occurs there is a leucocytosis with a high eosinophil count of 30-50 per cent. This stage lasts for two or three weeks.

The above initial phase occurs with both *S.haematobium* and *S.mansoni* infections, although it is more commonly apparent and severe with *S.mansoni.*

It is after this phase that the two infections go their own particular ways and as such they will now be described separately.

With *S.haematobium* infections ova usually appear in the urine round about the time of the generalised reaction, if this occurs. In other words, usually about four to seven weeks after invasion. At first their appearance does not cause symptoms. Symptoms rarely occur under three months and may not occur for up to two years. Initially symptoms are those of any irritating cystitis which of course is what is taking place. Thus dysuria, frequency and haematuria are classical. The blood is typically passed at the end of micturition. If any patient ever complains of this symptom a very careful long term geographical history must be obtained so that this progressively debilitating disease is not missed. There is also frequently pain in the perineum and penis after micturition. Haematuria is more frequent after violent exercise and although this point is not truly diagnostic it is a useful question to ask and the patient can be put to the test if young and otherwise fit. As the disease progresses and bladder inflammatory changes increase with the formation of papillomata and ulceration so the haematuria and frequency increase. Haematuria may become frank with clot formation but severe frank haematuria is more likely to be due to simple papillomata or carcinoma of the bladder. What is more frequent is that the bladder contracts down and the frequency becomes far more intense with inability to hold urine. Dribbling of urine and even incontinence occur. With the bladder changes increasing, further changes occur in the upper urinary tract with secondary infection almost always occurring and general ill health ensuing.

With *S.mansoni* infections, as mentioned earlier, the toxaemic state is more frequent and at this time eggs are passed in the stool with the onset of diarrhoeal symptoms. The timing of these symptoms is dependant on the severity of the infection. It may be after about two months but again it may not be for two years or so. However, symptoms do seem to start earlier with *S.mansoni* infections than with *S.haematobium.* The symptoms are suggestive of a chronic bacillary dysentery. There may be blood and mucus in the stools and abdominal colic occurs. Tenesmus is marked. Whether this is because the sharp lateral spined eggs are buried in the mucosa of the lower rectum is open to question. Bouts of this diarrhoea occur every few weeks with increasing severity and frequency.

With both infections, if the disease is not diagnosed and treated the ova can reach the liver and the lungs. Because of the intestinal infection more frequently being due to *S.mansoni* liver involvement is more common with this variety. Portal hypertension may follow due to fibrosis of the liver. Lung involvement is a definite late stage.

With the rare *S.japonicum* infection the initial allergic reaction is more marked. The second dysenteric stage is far more delayed and the third stage consists of hepatomegaly, splenomegaly, ascites and anaemia.

With the returning traveller from abroad it is obvious that the diagnosis of this slow but severely debilitating disease must be made early before any permanent damage has been done to the urinary or intestinal tracts.

Diagnosis of all types is of course automatic with the findings of the eggs: from the terminal urine in *S.haematobium,* from the blood in the stool for *S.mansoni* and *S.japonicum.* Other than the above, the most valuable diagnostic test in the searching for eggs is the rectal snip. Ova from *S.haematobium* are frequently found this way as well as with *S.mansoni* and *S.japonicum.* Eosinophilia is usually present but not necessarily so. Cystoscopy and I.V.P's should be carried out with *S.haematobium* and sigmoidoscopy with *S.mansoni* and *S.japonicum.*

Finally, the complement fixative test and the schistosomial skin test are of doubtful value.

The C.F.T. is usually only positive during the first three years of infection and not always even then. The skin test rather like the Casoni test can remain positive even after successful treatment. With schistosomiasis although the condition may be suspected, a conclusive diagnosis may not be made initially. If this is so, observation must be maintained. Treatment for all types of infection are basically the same.

In the past, various forms of antimony have been given with success.

Recently, Niridazole (Ambilhar) has been introduced. It is given orally and is very active against all forms of human schistosomes. It may cause psychoses, epileptiform attacks, E.C.G. changes and aspermogenesis so care has to be taken with its administration. Urine turns dark brown during the taking of Niridazole. In a survey of the various forms of treatment carried out by Professor Woodruff at the Hospital for Tropical Diseases in London, the following results were obtained:

1. Sodium Antimony Tartrate 25 mg per kg I.V. 77 cases—100 per cent cure.
2. Niridazole, 200 mg per kg. 32 cases—96.9 per cent cure.
3. Antimony Sodium Dimercapton Succinate (Astiban) 30 mg per kg. 47 cases—91.5 per cent cure.
4. Sodium Antimony Gluconate (Triostam) 24-37 mg per kg. 33 cases—79 per cent cure.

In highly endemic areas in developing countries where follow up is not possible, one injection of Hycanthone has been given with fairly high success with *S.haematobium* and some success with *S.mansoni.* It is not a treatment of choice when follow up is possible. It can be very hepatotoxic. In fact, follow up is one of the most important factors of satisfactory treatment. Tests of cure by looking for further viable eggs must be carried out after completion of treatment.

Other fluke infections are those of *Paragonimus westermanii, Fasciolopsis buski* and *Fasciola hepatica.*

Paragonimus westermanii is a further trematode or fluke infection. It affects the lungs and causes haemoptysis.

Geographically, it occurs in Japan, Korea, Taiwan, China, Manchuria and at the Philippine Islands. It also occurs in Thailand and India.

In its life cycle it has two intermediate hosts, a snail and crayfish or crabs. It is through the latter that man is normally infected by eating the uncooked meat. In man they enter the small intestine, bore through the jejunal wall, migrate through the diaphragm into the thoracic cavity where they end up in the lungs.

Symptomatology. It is usually two to three months before a cough develops which is usually associated with bloodstained sputum. There may be initial fever. Increasing dyspnoea occurs with general signs of bronchitis and subsequently bronchiectasis. As well as lung symptoms there may be liver involvement leading to hepatitis, and brain involvement leading to Jacksonian epilepsy.

Diagnosis is by finding the eggs in the sputum: sometimes they are found in the stools.

Treatment. The best is bithionol (Actamer, Bitin). The dose is 30 mg per kg daily in three doses for ten days or in one dose on alternate days for 20 days. Chloroquine and emetine hydrochloride have also been used.

Fasciolopsis buski is another fluke which is also known as the giant intestinal fluke. Again its intermediate host is a snail but it is spread by the cercariae attaching themselves to aquatic plants especially the lotus and water caltrop, where they develop into metacercariae. These plants are considered to be local delicacies. Geographically, it occurs in India, Thailand, China and Taiwan.

Symptomatology. Basically an intestinal infection, with severe diarrhoea developing about two months after infection leading to general wasting. If the infection is severe, anaemia, ascites and jaundice may ensue. With children there may be stunting of growth.

Diagnosis by demonstrating eggs in the stool.

Treatment is by tetrachlorethylene 2.0-4.0 ml in gelatine capsules. One dose repeated in two weeks.

Fasciola hepatica or the sheep liver fluke is another of the family that is rare in man but is spread by water cress. Adults attack the biliary and hepatic systems. Cirrhosis of the liver may occur at a later date.

Diagnosis by finding the eggs in the faeces.

Treatment is not very satisfactory, therefore several drugs have been tried. Bithional, tetrachlorethylene, emetine and chloroquine have all been used.

The eating of raw fish in Japan is considered a delicacy. With the development of Japan as one of the major economic countries in the world, more and more businessmen are visiting Japan and are being entertained with typical Japanese hospitality. Raw fish will frequently be put before them. Therefore its problems must be remembered, particularly the several infections that it can cause.

One of these is *Gnathostoma spingerum* which produces a single subcutaneous swelling practically anywhere in the body. It may vary in size and it may migrate. It is irritating, sometimes painless but sometimes painful.

There is a high eosinophilia. No chemotherapy has proven success but diethylcarbamazine may help. The swelling is due to the immature worm and as it is usually solitary removal of the worm cures.

Clonorchis sinensis is another Far Eastern raw fish infection, but it is an hepatic fluke. With a light infection, symptoms may be absent but with heavier infection there are varying degrees of cholangitis with hepatomegaly, jaundice and wasting.

Diagnosis is by finding the eggs in the stools.

Treatment is unsatisfactory. Chloroquine or intravenous sodium antimony tartrate are probably the most effective.

Opisthorciasis is a similar infection from raw fish in the East. Clinically the same as clonorchis but usually milder. Therapy is the same.

The next problems to pass on to are the cestodes or tapeworms.

These tapeworms should be divided into two groups. Firstly, those in which man is the definitive host, and as such the worm adult is in man. These are *Taenia saginata* or the beef tapeworm, *Taenia solium* the pork tapeworm, *Diphyllobothrium latum* (syn: *Dibothriocephalus latus*) the fish tapeworm and *Taenia nana* or *Hymenolepsis nana* the dwarf tapeworm whose intermediate hosts are rodents.

In the intermediate host group the one tapeworm that matters is *Taenia echinococcus* which causes hydatid cyst disease. The definitive host is the dog, jackal, wolf or cat, but it can also live in other intermediate hosts of which sheep and cattle are most important. It is where sheep and cattle are infected that hydatid disease is more common.

To consider *Taenia saginata* first. This is the usually found tapeworm in man. This infection occurs in the beef eating communities throughout the world but it is naturally more frequent where meat control is less satisfactory.

Geographically, therefore, there are no strict areas but the incidence is higher in the Middle East and the developing countries. This is sufficient reason to avoid underdone steaks and in particular steak tartare in these places.

Symptoms are vague and may be absent. Anorexia, loss of weight and vague diarrhoea may occur. The first the patient knows may be when he passes the proglottides. *Taenia saginata* rarely occurs in larval cysticercal form in man but when it does these cysticerci appear in muscles.

With *Taenia solium* the intermediate host is the pig but the very important larval cysticercal forms occur in man. (With *H.nana* and *D.latum,* it is more common to find eggs in the stool).

Geographically, Germany, India and parts of Africa. Rare in Britain and America. Symptoms of the adult worm are similar to *T.saginata* if they occur. However, in addition, the cysticerci in man not only lodge in connective tissue and muscles but in the central nervous system. Symptoms only occur after death of the larvae in three to five years. When they die in the muscles they calcify and can be seen radiologically.: when they die in the CNS they do not calcify. It is a very serious condition with multiple cysticerci in the brain. Jacksonian epilepsy and psychiatric disturbance occur.

Diphyllobothrium latum is the fish tapeworm particularly in pike. Also known as *Dibothriocephalus latus.*

Geographically, it occurs in Finland and Switzerland. Man only becomes infected by eating uncooked fish flesh. However, with a heavy infection there may be severe toxaemia, abdominal pain and diarrhoea. Convulsions may occur in children.

A true megalocytic anaemia can occur for which vitamin B_{12} and folic acid are needed in addition to the basic treatment for the worm.

Hymenolepis nana or Taenia nana, the dwarf tapeworm. Problems only occur if it is a very heavy infection.

Diagnosis of all tapeworm infections is finding the proglottides in the stools. Species identification of the worm before treatment is most important.

Surprisingly, eosinophilia only seems to appear with *Diphyllobothrium latum.*

Treatment is very successful and there are new remedies but certain limiting factors are necessary with the new remedies.

Treatment of choice for all tapeworms is Mepacrine by duodenal intubation. The patient is given a residue free diet for 48 hours. A duodenal tube is passed and one gramme of mepacrine dissolved in 100 ml of water is passed down it (adult dosage). 30 grams of magnesium sulphate are then given and the tube removed. Purgation occurs within two hours and the tapeworm is passed intact.

It is not essential to pass a duodenal tube but it is best. If this is not done then the mepacrine is taken by mouth over a period of half an hour.

The second form of treatment is the old established male fern. 15-30 grams of magnesium sulphate are given the day before male fern. The next day three doses or two millilitres of fresh extract male fern are given at 30 minute intervals, followed by a repeat dose as before, of magnesium sulphate. All stools for the next 24 hours are then searched for the head.

The other two forms of treatment cause disintegration of the tapeworm in the host and therefore spread of the eggs. As such they must *not* be used with *Taenia solium* else they may lead to the establishment of cysticercosis.

Niclosamide (Yomesan-FBA) is probably the most effective. Starvation overnight for 12 hours is followed by two 2.5 gram tablets which are repeated in one hour.

With Dichlorophen (Antiphen M & B) one dose of five grams is given in the morning without any preparation. There may be subsequent abdominal discomfort and diarrhoea. But remember neither of these two treatments with *Taenia solium*.

Taenia echinococcus infects man in the larval form, causing hydatid disease. The definitive host is the dog, wolf or jackal. However, the important factor in its spread is that there are other intermediate hosts in sheep and cattle. Dogs become infected by eating of egg infested viscera of these animals. Hence it is a disease where there is inadequate supervision of abattoirs.

Geographically, *T.echinococcus* occurs in Australia, parts of Central and South America, Argentina, Iceland, the northern coast of Africa, the Middle East and in particular Cyprus which is fact becoming one of the most popular holiday areas. In the U.K. it occurs in the Brecon Hills of Wales where sheep rearing is still popular.

Of 77 cases notified in England and Wales since 1966, 18 were thought to have been acquired in Wales. The origin of 23 was unknown and 25 came from the Middle East and Mediterranean area, of which the largest number were from Cyprus.

The human swallows the ova from soiled food and larvae migrate from the ova in the duodenum via the mesenteric glands mainly to the liver. The second most likely site is the lungs and after that the pleura, kidney and brain. However, rupture of the cyst may occur into the peritoneal cavity with involvement of the intestinal tract.

Symptoms are minimal, if any, when the cyst is small and when it gets large they are usually only those of pressure, such as abdominal pain, cough or enlarged abdomen due to hepatomegaly. After the death of the cyst, absorption of the fluid leads to allergic reactions such as asthma and urticaria. Rupture of the cyst into the lung can cause haemoptysis, suppuration and acute toxaemia leading to death. Rupture into the peritoneal cavity will cause peritonitis which can be fatal. Suppuration can also occur even without rupture. Rigors, sweats and pyrexia will follow.

Of the 77 cases previously mentioned, 48 patients had liver involvement only, while 17 had only lung involvement. The remaining 12 had multiple involvement.

Diagnosis is dependant usually on gross hepatomegaly. There is usually marked eosinophilia. Radiography is of value as also is a liver scan. The Casoni skin test in which antigens are used is specific. A positive reaction occurring within half and hour. There is also a complement fixation test.

Treatment is very difficult, especially of the liver. Aspiration with replacement by formal saline may be beneficial. Surgery of the lung is easier than with the liver. The problem with surgery is spread by damage to the cyst. Anthelmintics are valueless.

After the cestodes one must deal with the nematodes, some of which are worldwide in distribution but some are not. However, all of them which involve an intestinal infection are aggravated by bad food hygiene. The filarial infections are strictly nematode infections but as they are insect borne other than dracontiasis a guinea worm infection, they will be dealt with in Chapter 11.

The first to consider is *Ascaris lumbricoides* or the roundworm. One does not have to travel to find this infection. It is spread by uncooked food, soiled by ova. It also likes the humid tropics so East, Central and West Africa are high risk areas. To correlate all the symptoms one must, however, remember the life cycle of the ingested ova hatching in the small intestine and the larvae migrating through the veins to reach the liver, pass through the heart to the lungs into the bronchi, up the trachea, and down the oesophagus into the stomach and intestines to complete the circle and reach maturity after one to two months.

Symptoms are dependant on the heaviness of the infection and the stage of migration.

During migration there is frequently cough and urticaria. Diarrhoea and abdominal colic occur as well. Heavy infestations with adult worms in children have been known to cause intestinal obstruction.

More important though are the wandering habits of adult worms. The appearance of an adult worm in the bile ducts can be a cause of obstructive jaundice. The migration of one to the appendix can lead to an obstructive appendicitis. They have caused fatal pancreatitis by blocking the pancreatic duct.

Eosinophilia occurs in the invasive phase but dissappears later.

Diagnosis is by the passing in the stool the adult worm or more usually by finding the eggs in the stool.

Treatment is usually effective by the single dose methods with the piperazine salts.

In infections originating in the tropics a double infection along with hookworm is frequent. When this occurs Bephenium hydroxynaphthate (Alcopar) should be given as it is effective with both infections.

Infection with the *Enterobius (oxyuris) vermicularis* commonly known as the threadworm or pinworm, is again worldwide but once more far more frequent in dirty crowded areas in Asia and Africa.

Spread by infected water and uncooked foods. Ova can also be airborne. Main symptom is intense anal irritation.

Diagnosis by seeing the live worm. Eggs do not appear in the stool but sellotape put across the anus and then taken off will lift up eggs.

Treatment by piperazine salts for a week or by Viprynium (Vanquin) 50 mg per 10 kg body weight. This can be repeated in seven to ten days.

Probably one of the most important of the worm infestations commonly found in the tropics and subtropics is the *hookworm*. Of this worm there are two varieties *Ankylostoma duodenale* and *Necator americanus.*

This infestation is found in unsanitary conditions in temperate climates and in hot damp areas throughout the subtropics and tropics. *Ankylostoma duodenale* occurs in Southern Europe all around the Mediterranean, the Middle East, the coastal areas of India and throughout the Far East. It is also very prevalent throughout West, Central and East Africa as well as the Northern point of South Africa. It appears in the New World in South America. *A.brasiliense* may infect the subcutaneous tissues in man but not reach maturity. This is discussed under Larva migrans.

Necator americanus occurs in the Southern United States, throughout Cental America and the tropical areas of South America. In the old world it appears in the same areas of Africa as *Ankylostoma duodenade.*

Man is the natural host. It lives in the duodenum, and the eggs are passed in the faeces. The eggs hatch in about a couple of days and the free living larvae feed on the faeces in mud or sand. Subsequently the larva bores its way into the foot of man to find a new host. Within three days it reaches the lungs, up the bronchus and trachea and down into the oesophagus and through to the duodenum where it hooks itself on the wall. They mature in about four weeks.

The main pathological issue with hookworm infestation is that the worms absorb blood from the submucous tissues.

Diagnosis by finding eggs in the stool.

Clinically, mild or moderate infestation frequently cause no trouble as long as the patient's iron stores satisfactory. With heavy infestation or if already with a low iron store then a typical secondary microcytic anaemia ensues. However, initially there may be an erythematous rash turning to a small vesicular dermatitis at point of entry of the larva. If this occurs it is highly irritant and lasts for about two weeks. Popularly known as 'ground' itch it is more common with necator infections. It does not always occur. Sometimes there are signs of mild bronchitis while the larvae migrate through the lungs. However, the real symptoms occur when the worm has matured in the duodenum.

In Europeans symptoms occur with lesser infestations than with Africans: basically a secondary anaemia, which may be severe, with its concomitant symptoms. Epigastric discomfort, nausea and sometimes vomiting and diarrhoea, mental inertia and in children, poor development may be present with heavy infestation.

The haemoglobin can drop to five to six grams. Diagnosis by finding the ova in the stools. The blood picture as well as showing anaemia will usually show an eosinophilia of 15-20 per cent. Treatment is to treat the anaemia and eradicate the worm. Bephenium hydronaphthoate (Alcopar) is the drug of choice. A dose of five grams in adults, three grams in a child under 12, taken with water and followed by a saline purge in two hours. Repeat the dose in two hours.

Tetrachlorethylene is the second choice but it must not be used if there is an ascaris infection. For adults three ml in mucilage and flavouring agent on an empty stomach. Again followed by saline purge two to three hours later. Repeat in two to three days. Not to be used if there is gastroenteritis.

Trichuris trichiura or whipworm is a common nematode infection especially in the tropics. It is frequently one of a multiple infestation. It is faecal spread. In general it causes no symptoms. Only with very heavy infestations and with young children when it can cause a bloody diarrhoea with rectal prolapse. It is very difficult to eradicate and if symptom free it may well not be treated.

Diagnosis by finding eggs in the stools.

Thiabendazole 25 mg per kg body weight, twice daily for three days is one treatment and the other is Diathiazamine (Telmid) 200 mg t.d.s. for 14 days.

Trichiniasis or *Trichinelliasis* caused by the *Trichinella spiralis* is a nematode infection intitally causing gastritis but subsequently pain in the volountary muscles due to migration of the larvae. Spread by eating infected pork, the pig being the other host.

Geographically, North Germany and Kenya. It is spread by eating raw pig meat products. Symptoms are fever, oedema of the eyelids, muscle pains and eosinophilia.

Gastric irritation and possibly severe diarrhoea may occur within 24 hours of eating the pork, but it may be absent.

The muscle pains, fever and oedema of the eyelids, which is practically pathognomonic, occur after seven to 14 days. Leucocytosis of 20-30,000 with up to 50 per cent eosinophils.

Diagnosis by muscle biopsy, CFT, and skin test. It can be a very serious and even fatal disease. Treatment is non-specific. Purgation with calomel to discharge the worms: morphia may be necessary for the muscle pains.

Strongyloidiasis, an infection of man with *Strongyloides stercoralis* is one which gives a more complicated picture in view of the life cycle. It is also known as the dwarf threadworm.

Geographically, its distribution is basically the same as hookworm. Because of its free living stages in its need for further development an average temperature of a least 15°C (60°F) is necessary, so limiting its whereabouts.

The females live in the mucosa and submucosa of the small intestine and produce eggs parthenogenetically. Larvae emerge from the eggs, while still in the intestine. Some are passed in the stool where they can be easily identified as they are actively mobile. Outside the host they become the infective larvae which can penetrate intact skin. As well as by direct penetration and return to a host they can develop into the free living form in the soil and produce a further generation which can migrate back into the host. As well as this the larvae while still in the host's intestine, can develop into filaria and migrate to mesenteric lymph glands, the perianal skin and other internal tissues. With skin penetration the filariform larva proceeds up the venous system to the heart, through the lungs, up the bronchi and trachea to the epiglottis where it hitches onto food and is swallowed down to the stomach and intestines. Larvae migrating from the intestines may carry with them bowel micro-organisms.

Symptoms are frequently absent except with heavy infections. There may be abdominal colic, gastrointestinal irritation and, with severe infections, diarrhoea. Heavy infections in children may cause malabsorption. Invasion in the perianal skin will lead to irritable lesions like cutaneous larva migrans (see Chapter 10.)

Encysted worms in the lungs cause cough, sputum and pneumonitis.

Diagnosis by finding larvae in stools. There is usually a marked eosinophilia.

Treatment by dithiazine iodide (Telmid) 200 mg t.d.s. for 14 days.

Also thiabendazole 25 mg per kg body weight twice daily for three days.

Filariasis in all its forms is strictly a nematode infection but as it is not spread as an intestinal infection it is dealt with separately in Chapter 11.

10. Skin Problems, Bites, Stings and Venereal Diseases

Several of the fevers and other illnesses from the tropics and subtropics may manifest themselves first as a localised or generalised skin or subcutaneous problem. In the last chapter 'ground itch' as the first sign of a hookworm infection was mentioned. In this chapter it is intended to go through these various problems even although a fuller account of the infection or illness may be described elsewhere.

Fungal Infections

Fungal infections can be a very severe problem in the warm climates. Encouraged by the excess sweating the common ringworm infections which are normally seen in the temperate climates can appear in a far more severe form in someone who has recently returned from the tropics. One must look very seriously at anyone who has an active fungal skin infection as to whether they are a fit person to travel to hot and humid climates even on a short term basis.

Microsporon, tricphyton and epidermophyton are the groups that cause the fungal infections of the skin.

Epidermophytosis of the feet or tinea pedis is by far the commonest form as is well known in temperate areas. Greatly encouraged in the heat and an absolute contraindication to the wearing of nylon socks and even socks with a very small percentage of nylon in them. Thus encouraged by the heat, secondary infection may lead to pustules, lymphangitis, lymphadenitis and oedema of the feet. It also may spread to the hands.

Diagnosis by clinical appearance but positive proof by microscopy showing up the mycelia in skin scrapings.

Local treatment is the main line of attack. Lotions or paints are better than ointments. A paint such such as Monphytol containing salicylic acid, benzoic acid and undecylenic acid is most effective. Oral treatment is usually of little value. Many dermatologists consider griseofulvin does not reach a high enough blood content between the toes. Prophylaxis is of course by personal cleanliness, avoidance of nylon socks and the use of a dusting powder.

Fungal infections of the nails may spread from the hands or feet or be an original infection. Clinically the nails are pitted, scored, thickened and friable.

Treatment is usually best with oral griseofulvin in full dosage. If there is an improvement in one month then it should be given for a second month.

Tinea cruris or Dhobie's itch is another temperate climate fungal infection which is greatly encouraged in the hot and humid climates. Regular travellers to or long term residents in the tropics will say how it settles down and practically disappears on return to temperate climates but that it returns immediately with the heat.

An intensely itching and irritating red and scaly rash in the groin with an advancing serpiginous edge.

Treatment. Griseofulvin may be given orally. Whitfield's ointment, Castellani's paint or a paint such as Monphytol locally.

Tinea imbricata is a form of tinea corporis which occurs in the Far East, Ceylon, South Africa and South and Central America. It consists of slightly elevated concentric scaly rings with an ichthyotic appearance. These coalesce to form odd patterns.

Treatment is by griseofulvin and local antifungal paints or ointments.

In Africa where the patient may well not return for a second visit one dose treatment of 20 tablets of griseofulvin (10 g) has been given with fungal infections with success.

Tinea versicolor or pityriasis versicolor is a superficial fungal infection. The lesion is macular in type and originally is round or oval but with coalescence with other lesions the shape may change. In white skins the lesions are café-au-lait in colour while with the dark skinned the lesions are pale. The lesions are frequently scaly and are commonest on the neck and shoulders.

Diagnosis must be made from vitiligo. This can be done by finding the mycelia and spores in skin scrapings.

Treatment is by local applications of antifungal preparations or sodium thiosulphate 20 per cent in a 1 per cent solution of cetavlon daily for four weeks. Recently one application of selenium sulphide in the form of the shampoos for seborrhoea capitis has been found to be effective.

Fungal external otitis. This can be a very great problem in the tropics and subtropics if use has been made by the visitor of hotel, club and other swimming pools which have not been adequately cleansed. Anyone who develops an external otitis on return from overseas should have a swab taken to exclude fungal infection. Tinea infections and those of *Candida albicans* are frequent. Treatment by the necessary antifungicide including Nystatin.

Bacterial infections

Bacterial external otitis. The commonest varieties are *Staphylococcus aureus,* various streptococci, proteus and pyocyaneaus infections. With those who have been staying at tropical seaside resorts with swimming in the sea a coral external otitis occurs with ease when there is very severe irritation in the meatus which subsequently becomes secondarily infected.

Nematode infections

One of the results of holidaying on the beautiful Caribbean or East African beaches is that the holidaymaker may develop a larva migrans infection which is also known as creeping eruption or creeping itch. Just as with *Strongyloides stercoralis* the larva may migrate through the intestinal wall so also with *Toxocara canis* and *Toxocara catis* and cause a visceral larva migrans. Some larvae on penetrating the skin may migrate in the skin rather than make for its normal habitat. This may happen with *Strongyloides stercoralis, Ankylostoma duodenale* and *Necator americanus.* However it is more frequent with the larvae of nematodes who do not usually infect man. In particular *Ankylostoma brasiliensis,* the cat hookworm.

With the larva entering the skin a small papule may appear at the site. From this spot the larva wanders irregularly around actually in the layers of the skin. This wandering may go on for many weeks. The lesion is erythematous, raised, frequently scaly and finally vesicular. It is intensely irritating. With *A. brasiliensis* the larva tends to go round and about in a fairly circumscribed area but with Strongyloides it appears to run more in straight lines. As it progresses the lesion behind the larva tends to settle down and become dried and crusted, presumably due to the superficial layers of the skin being lifted. These tracks are always intensely irritating.

Diagnosis is the appearance of the tracks which are unmistakeable.

Treatment. The best treatment is Thiobendazole in a dose of 25 mg per kg body weight twice daily for two days. It is frequently necessary to repeat the dosage in 7-14 days.

Thiobendazole sometimes causes nausea which can be cleared with promazine.

Locally spraying the end of the run with ethylchloride or carbon dioxide snow frequently kills the larva but drug therapy is more certain.

As described in Chapter nine, ground itch, as the invasion by the *Ankylostoma duodenale* or the *Necator americanus* is called, is a very irritant erythema turning to a small vesicle. As the basic cause is the same as larva migrans it is not unreasonable that the initial skin changes are the same but with 'ground itch' the invading larva goes deeper on its appointed way.

Other infections which enter by the skin may show an initial localised lesion (pp. 130-131).

Filariasis

Filariasis in its three main forms has skin or subcutaneous manifestations early on.

With *Wucheria bancrofti* infection, a precursor of elephantiasis, the initial symptoms after an incubation period of anything from six months to two years is a typical lymphangitis. It usually is associated with fever and malaise. The lymphangitis may be retrograde in that it spreads distally. This is because of blockage of the lymphatic by a dead worm.

Loiasis usually shows itself first with the classical Calabar swellings. Sometimes prior to the swellings there are scattered erythematous areas all over the body. They may be followed by oedematous swellings or an allergic papular rash. Calabar swellings first appear from 3 to 24 months after infection and may continue to appear for many years although it is usual for there to be only one or two present at the same time. They appear principally around the medium size joints, in the face and in particular the orbit, also anywhere where there is repeated minor trauma. Before they occur there is usually irritation and a dull ache. They then swell, often being several inches across. The overlying skin is tense and reddened. They are uncomfortable and can well cause partial immobilisation of the nearby joint. They remain for three to four days and then gradually disappear. They may reappear in the same place or elsewhere. As well as these swellings adult worms may be seen moving around in subcutaneous tissues.

The third form of filariasis which has skin manifestations early is onchocerciasis. With this infection the earliest symptom is an irritant papular eruption. As is frequent the irritation is worse when warm in bed. There may be some thickening of the epithelium. Usually nodules appear later. These are actually in the subcutaneous tissues and contain a mass of worms surrounded by fibrous tissue. They classically appear over the iliac crest, the femoral greater trochanters and the lower ribs.

In addition to the three varieties of filaria mentioned there are two others which can be considered as only mildly pathogenic but with both there is skin involvement.

The first is *Dipętalonema perstans.* It can cause allergenic skin reactions similar to Calabar swellings. Geographically they occur in Central Africa and the northern part of South America.

The second is *Dipetalonema streptocercia.* This variety can cause generalised pruritus. Geographically it is found in Central Africa.

The main point to note with both these infections is to be sure that the other more important filarial infections are not present as well.

Dracontiasis or guinea worm disease, which is another filarial infection, starts with a generalised urticaria of allergic origin.

However all the filarial infections will be discussed in greater detail in the next chapter.

In schistosomiasis, initially, when the cercariae penetrates the skin there is a localised irritation and small area of dermatitis. This may not be noticed at the time but if questioned later the patient may recall it. Four to twelve weeks later there may be some constitutional symptoms including a generalised urticaria associated with a fever and possibly gastrointestinal symptoms. It is usually more severe with *S.mansoni* infections rather than *S.haematobium*. However it may not occur at all (pp. 116-118).

With trypanosomiasis the initial symptom is when a nodule appears with brown induration at the site of the bite. There may be a surrounding area looking like a bruise. This central area may ulcerate and become infected (pp. 99-100).

With tick typhus the black eschar usually on the lower limbs due to the low flying tick is a classical forerunner to the general symptoms of the disease. Later about the third to fifth day there is a generalised rash. Initially pink maculas but later petechial. Commencing at the wrists it spreads to the trunk but the face is usually clear (p. 104).

In typhoid one must remember the classical rose spots (pp. 110-113).

In toxoplasmosis there is a macula papular rash (pp. 100-101).

Dengue fever is characterised by the appearance of two rashes one after the other. The initial eruption is really a generalised erythema with suffusion of the face, congestion of the mucosae and conjunctivitis.

After five to seven days there may be the secondary eruption which again is a erythema but patchy in nature and classically starting on the palms and back of hands later spreading to the trunk, thighs and legs. The patches tend to coalesce. It is very irritating (pp. 102-103).

Jaundice occurs with infective hepatitis, serum hepatitis, leptospirosis and yellow fever.

Leprosy

Leprosy or Hansen's disease and its skin manifestations must be remembered but the chances of a short term traveller developing leprosy are very small. At a meeting of the Royal Society of Tropical Medicine and Hygiene held in January 1970 when there was a discussion on imported disease, Dr Stanley G. Browne, the leading leprologist, specifically answered the following question. 'What are the chances that a native of Britain spending a short time abroad may contact leprosy?' His answer was clear cut. 'The chances are remote, but not negligible. In general, the longer the sojourn abroad in a highly endemic area, the greater the chances of contracting leprosy. Other factors are naturally involved, such as the precautions taken against a recognised risk, the nature and duration of possible close contact, and genetic predisposition.'

'Notwithstanding the generally low risk, expatriates travelling abroad on holiday or on business should not forget the fact that a chance contact at a propitious time in auspicious circumstances may result in the transfer of *Mycobacterium leprae* to the skin of a susceptible subject and their subsequent percutaneous penetration to a nidus in the Schwann cells of the terminal nerve fibres in the dermis.'

Because of this one must briefly give the geography, the symptoms and the signs of leprosy.

Geographically it is commonest in India, Pakistan, Bangladesh, parts of South East Asia and Central and South America. Slightly less frequent in West, Central and East Africa: it also occurs in South Africa, the Middle East and North America.

There are two different types of leprosy with different skin manifestations. They are the lepromatous type and the tuberculoid type. Incubation period is probably from two to five years which makes the geographical aspect in the short term traveller very difficult.

However during this period there may be prodromal symptoms which occur both with the lepromatous and the tuberculoid types. These consist of general malaise, vague pains, attacks of fever with sweating and periodic short lasting macular lesions. Subsequently with the lepromatous type after an attack of fever lasting one to two weeks nodules and small masses appear scattered over the skin surface of the body. The face becomes leonine with coarseness and thickening of the skin. The hair falls out but the lepromatous changes do not affect the scalp. The most important point is there is always a nasal discharge usually with infiltration and ulceration of the tongue and pharynx.

In the early tuberculoid type the onset is very insidious as it usually occurs in someone with high resistance. Typically erythematous patches with very clear cut edges occur on the face, the buttocks and on the outer surfaces of the limbs. On quiescence the patches become either pigmented or depigmented *(lepra alba)*. Initially there is hyperaesthesia which subsequently becomes anaesthesia.

The ulnar and peroneal nerves become affected and thickened. The finding of a thickened ulnar nerve which can be 'rolled' with other symptoms and signs is practically pathognomonic.

There is also the dimorphus type which is basically a mixture of both types.

Diagnosis in the early lepromatous case is by finding the *Mycobacterium leprae* (Hansen's bacillus) in the nasal discharge or in excised pieces of skin. In the early tuberculoid type it is by the symptoms and signs described above. As well as a thickened ulnar nerve the presence of localised areas of anaesthesia is very typical of a leprous infection.

Once the possibility of leprosy has been queried it is essential that the patient is referred to a tropical diseases unit. This is not the place to go into the later problems of leprosy but briefly they include claw hand due to ulnar nerve involvement, perforating ulcers, loss of fingers and toes and rarely lesions of the fifth and seventh cranial nerves.

Treatment besides careful general treatment consists of the giving of diamino-diphenylsulphone (Dapsone). This is long term treatment with gradual increase to maximum dose and should take place only in a special centre.

Leishmaniasis

There are two forms of leishmaniasis which affect the skin:

Cutaneous leishmaniasis or dermal leishmaniasis

This is also known as tropical sore, oriental sore, Baghdad or Delhi sore or Aleppo boil. It is an infective granuloma of the skin and subcutaneous tissues caused by *Leishmania tropica*. Like kala-azar it is spread by the sandfly.

Geographically it occurs scattered around the entire Mediterranean littoral, the Middle East, the Southern Sahara, Southern Russia and North West India. It also occurs in Central and Southern America.

Incubation period is usually a few months but it may be weeks or years. It starts as an irritating papule, scabs over and then breaks down into an ulcer with raised, hard, clear cut edges. They are often multiple but near each other following several bites by one sandfly. Besides the ulcerated areas there may be warty granulomata which do not ulcerate. However it remains entirely localised and even the lymphatic glands are not involved unless there is secondary infection. Because the face and hands are exposed areas for the sandfly to bite these are the commonest sites. Diagnosis is confirmed by finding the Leishmania at the base of the ulcer.

Treatment is by giving antimony as with kala-azar (p. 98) and local dressings. However if untreated it usually heals spontaneously but with severe scarring.

Mucocutaneous leishmaniasis or espundia

This is another form caused by *Leishmania brasiliensis* and again spread by the sandfly.

Geographically it occurs only in South America. It is similar to the cutaneous variety but affects mucocutaneous junctions such as the nose and the mouth, leading to great destruction of tissue. Treatment is as for the other leishmanial infections. If untreated death will ensue.

Ulcers

One next should mention tropical ulcer. This is a different condition to tropical sore or dermal leishmaniasis which has just been discussed. Tropical ulcer is also known as tropical sloughing phagedena, Naga sore or Vincent's ulcer. There is reason in the last name because although many organisms may be present in the sore the commonest and most important in the *Trepanema vincentii* plus a fusiform bacillus. Very like Vincent's angina or 'trench mouth'.

It nearly always occurs in a previously untreated abrasion. Nutrition may be a factor but not necessarily so. It is a good reason to pay attention to all abrasions, however minor, which happen in the tropics. Hence the visitor may develop tropical ulcer because he may well pay no attention to an abrasion which would heal quite satisfactorily in a temperate climate without trouble. As well as an abrasion as the initial problem it can also be an insect bite. This irritates, the sufferer scratches it, and the skin surface is broken. The legs and ankles are the commonest areas for this type of trauma so they are the commonest areas for tropical ulcer. Usually starting with a painful blister which ruptures to form an ulcer with a sloughing base which produces a foul smelling discharge. Initially the edge spreads. It usually remains shallow but may become deep. Local lymphatic glands such as the inguinals become inflamed. With treatment the ulcer heals after a long time with extensive scarring and perhaps contracture depending on the position.

Treatment is by large doses of intramuscular penicillin. Tetracyclines are also usually effective. Local treatment rather depends on the views of the administrator. Some believe in active attack, others in rest and occlusion. Frequently skin grafting is needed at a later date.

Other ulcers occur with different causal organisms, such as *Corynebacterium diphtheriae, Mycobacterium tuberculosis* and *Mycobacterium ulcerans* being three in question. As well as these there are the pyogenic infections which may be primary or secondary.

Skin infections with *Corynebacterium diphtheria* causing diphtheritic ulcers are comparatively common in the dry areas of the Middle East, India and Africa. There is a particularly high incidence of diphtheria in one form or another in Nepal. These ulcers usually appear on the legs. They start as a vesicle, rapidly ulcerate but remain small. They are usually multiple. Frequently they become deep and the edges are usually undermined. The bottom of the ulcer is usually covered with a typical diphtheritic greyish slough which contains the organisms of diphtheria. There is usually secondary infection present.

Diagnosis by identification of *Corynebacterium diphtheriae.*

Treatment by one dose of 20,000 units of antitoxin.

A further type of ulceration occurring in the tropics but luckily in general occurring in small geographical areas and therefore less likely to be seen in the traveller, although recently cases have occurred on the campus of Ibadan University, is the ulceration due to *Mycobacterium ulcerans*. This type of ulcer is better known as the Buruli ulcer of Uganda.

It usually appears on the arms or legs. Diagnosis is by finding the organisms. Treatment by antituberculous drugs is ineffective but success has been obtained recently with new antibiotics. Plastic surgery is usually a subsequent necessity.

Coral Abrasions

When tropical ulcer was being discussed the question of untreated abrasions was mentioned. Abrasions are slow to heal in the tropics, especially with humidity when secondary infection is common, but one of the most important reasons for failure to heal is coral. So many of the wonderful holiday beaches of East Africa and the Caribbean are basically coral beaches. In the Caribbean the white sand is finely powdered coral while on the Kenya coast there is a coral reef just off shore where goggling is so popular. Abrasions caused by coral are very slow to heal and can be very troublesome.

Initially all pieces of coral must be cleaned away, if necessary washing out the wound with an antiseptic. Subsequently it may be necessary to give a parenteral antibiotic to prevent secondary infection (see also Chapter Six).

Bites

In the tropics and subtropics there are far more insects and animals which bite and cause local problems than there are in the temperate climates.

As well as the many fevers and other illnesses in these areas there are many localised bites and irritations which are caused by insects and animals.

The first of these to consider is the chigoe flea or jigger. *Tungu penetrans* is very like the common flea but is slightly smaller with a larger head. Both sexes bite warm blooded animals like any other flea but once the female becomes pregnant she buries herself in the skin of a human. Warmth there leads to development of the ova with the result that a highly irritant pea-like swelling appears in the skin nearly always of the foot and frequently in a toe or between the toes.

Geographically very common in South America and in East Africa. They live in the sand and dry dust, remaining near the ground surface.

Initially itching is the only symptom; this is followed by the presence of the pea-like swelling mentioned with subsequent ulceration which may become septic.

Treatment is by sterilising a needle and lifting the sac out without rupturing it. Once it ruptures sepsis is common.

This is a condition that the returning holidaymaker from the East African shores may well present to his practitioner at home.

Another egg laying fly which inhabits Africa is the tumbu fly or *Cordyloba anthropophaga.* Here again the visitor may be bitten while visiting Africa and the symptoms appear after return home.

Geographically this fly inhabits East, Central and West Africa south of the Sahara.

In its life cycle the fly lays her eggs on dry sand or soil which has been contaminated with the urine or excreta of animals, particularly rodents, or man. The larvae which hatch from the eggs can live for a week or two in the soil, until they become attached to a passing or resting host.

In Africa it is very common for the house boys or stewards to lay out the washing on dry soil to dry in the sun and fresh air. This is one of the commonest causes of spread of the larvae of the tumbu fly. The larvae climb on to the shirt, vest, pants or any other nether garment. When this garment is put on they burrow just under the skin leaving their posterior breathing openings on a level with the surface. The lesions resemble boils and they may be multiple. Each has a small hole in the centre. The larvae grow in their subdermal pockets for about 10-14 days and when mature wriggle out of the tissues and drop to the ground to form a puparium. Ten days later the adult fly, which is about the size of a blue bottle, but yellow, appears.

Clinically usually multiple boil-like lumps appear. They may become pustular. If undiagnosed the larvae later extrude themselves. There may be general malaise und slight pyrexia. Because the larvae have arrived on clothing they usually occur on the trunk or upper limbs unlike the jigger which is on the feet.

Once diagnosed the best treatment is to put liquid paraffin on the furuncles. The larvae move in an effort to bring their breathing apparatus to the air and paraffin enters the furuncle. After a few applications of liquid paraffin they can usually be extruded by pressure. Antibiotics may be necessary for secondary infection.

Fairly similar in his attack on the human as the tumbu fly is the warble fly *(Dermatobia hominis).* However he gets there differently. The larvae are deposited on the human skin by mosquitoes on which the warble fly has laid her eggs. The larvae penetrate the skin and produce boil-like lumps like the tumbu fly. The larvae take longer to emerge than with the tumbu as it takes about six weeks. Secondary infection is very frequent. Pain may be intense. They must be removed by stretching the opening with forceps when the larva will come out.

Venereal and Associated Diseases

Another group of diseases to be discussed in this chapter are the venereal diseases and in particular their associated diseases lymphogranuloma venereum (LGV), yaws (or frambaesia) and pinta, all of which are far commoner in the developing countries.

With regard to the more usual forms of venereal diseases there are regrettably many business travellers who once they are overseas 'on the loose' get ideas in their heads and seem to feel that because they are visiting developing countries they are arriving before venereal diseases have developed there. This, as we all know, is so wrong, and far worse than that there is a far higher percentage of antibiotic resistant strains because of far less control of the sale of antibiotics. Stories of medically inspected brothels is in general nonsense.

Lymphogranuloma venereum, also known as tropical bubo, climatic bubo, lymphopathia venereum, paradenitis nostras or Durand-Nicolas-Favre disease, is a venereal disease due to a virus characterised by inflammatory enlargement of the lymph glands draining the genitalia.

Geographically originally around the tropical coasts. Perhaps the ports encouraged this. However it is still commoner in the warmer climates and in the coloured races. But cases occur in temperate climates and have occurred in Britain.

Incubation period is a few days up to three weeks for primary lesion which is frequently unnoticed.

In males these are herpetiform vesicles turning to ulceration on the penis. In females they are rarely found because they are usually in the vagina. However in either sex they can be found anywhere around the genitalia or perineum. They are painless. Within about two weeks glandular enlargement occurs. In males it is the inguinal glands which are involved. In females the deeper pelvic glands and those around the rectum.

There may be a mild lymphangitis extending from the primary lesion to a first discretely enlarged gland but soon the glandular enlargement is multiple and coalescence takes place. Enlargement is insidious with periadenitis.

In the male this can be seen in the inguinal region and with fusion the glands become attached to the skin which becomes reddish blue in colour and subsequently ulceration takes place with the formation of multiple sinuses which excude a thick mucoid yellowish pus.

In females, as the deep lymphatics of the pelvis are involved this is even more serious especially as the condition may be even further advanced before advice is sought. Glands around the rectum can be involved leading to rectal stricture. Suppuration of the glands can lead to rectal and vaginal fistulae and involvement of all the pelvic glands.

While these local conditions are developing there are usually signs of generalised toxemia with low grade fever lassitude and general malaise. As well there may be tonsillar ulceration, scattered skin erythema and arthritis.

Diagnosis is naturally from other venereal diseases in particular.

Specifically there is the Frei intradermal test. Sterilised pus is injected intradermally. Positive reaction is a reddish papule with 48 hours. However it does not become positive until the adenitis has been present for one to three weeks. It further usually remains positive after treatment and may remain positive for life. LGV complement fixation test is carried out on the serum. However the availability of this test is rather limited.

Treatment is best by tetracyclines in the dosage of 500 mg six hourly for 10-14 days. Sulphonamides are also effective and may be given in conjunction with the tetracyclines.

Bed rest is essential to aid in healing.

A further venereal disease which must be mentioned which is rare in the developed countries is the *soft sore* or *chancroid*. Relatively common in the East particularly in the seaports it is only seen in the large seaports in Britain unless otherwise imported.

Causative organism is Ducrey's bacillus which is Gram-negative.

Clinically the incubation period is shorter than syphilis being only two days to two weeks. Initially small red papules appear on the genitalia or on the surrounding skin. Sometimes on both. After a few days they break down and an ulcer appears with undermined edges and surrounding erythema and oedema. There is no induration as with syphilis. Inguinal glands are usually enlarged and may even suppurate.

Treatment. A full course of sulphonamides is usually effective.

Yaws or frambaesia and pinta are not strictly venereal diseases as they are conveyed by direct contact rather than sexually but as they are both treponematous infections they must be distinguished from syphilis.

Yaws is a contagious disease caused by *Treponema pertenue.* Generally direct contact from person to person but flies may be involved.

It is never congenital and the lesions are extragenital.

Geographically Central America, the northern part of South America, the Caribbean area, North, West, Central and East Africa and scattered through the Far East.

It is relatively uncommon in towns and cities and is only likely to occur in the expatriate who has been living in primative up-country conditions such as engineers and surveyors.

Incubation period is about two to four weeks. Initially a papule occurs which increases in size, ulcerates and becomes a raspberry-like warty growth, hence frambaesia. There is usually mild toxemia.

The secondary stage may appear before the primary lesion has healed which is usually in about six weeks. In the secondary stage similar multiple lesions appear, usually in the sweat areas.

In the tertiary phase, which again may follow on directly, there may be gummata, irregular depigmentation, osteitis and hydrarthrosis.

Diagnosis. All serological tests for syphilis are positive in yaws.

Treatment is with massive doses of penicillin.

Pinta is an infection due to *Treponema carateum* causing round cell infiltration of the dermis leading to destruction of the melanophore cells.

Geographically in Mexico, Central America, Caribbean area and South America as far south as the Amazon.

Direct contact as with yaws is the cause but the sandfly (Phlebotomus) may be involved.

Clinically frequently not recognised until the tertiary stage but in the secondary stage pintids or maculopapules which are initially red and subsequently brown occur scattered over the exposed area. In the tertiary stage there are larger scattered areas of depigmentation frequently on hands, feet and genitalia.

Diagnosis. Serological tests for syphilis are positive.

Treatment. Penicillin, but no treatment will restore depigmentation.

Other Skin Problems

The commonest cause of depigmentation is *vitiligo.* It is one of the skin problems that can effect Caucasians visiting tropical climates. It causes psychological and social problems beyond its medical importance because of its cosmetic problem.

Clinically it may develop at any age but 50 per cent of cases occur in the second and third decades. Classically it consists of round or oval patches of skin, milk-white in colour. They vary in size and may coalesce thus forming irregularly shaped patches. Borders are always well defined and may be hyperpigmented. Naturally with darker skin people it is more noticeable. In fact it may be present in fair skinned people without being noticed and only when the sufferer moves into warm climates and the skin tans are the patches noticed. Hence the upset of the patient. It may be localised or with severity become generalised.

Aetiology is unknown but local trauma, contact dermatitis and alopecia areata are all possible factors. It may appear at the site of severe sunburn and be exacerbated in the summer.

Pathologically there is a localised absence of pigment. If vitiliguous skin has a high sun exposure a thickening of the skin occurs with erythema and scaling.

Treatment has been multiple in the past because of lack of success.

Over the last few years the giving of the psoralens by mouth along with controlled natural sunlight or ultraviolet light has been effective. Great care must be taken with the exposure to sunlight or UVL because there is a definite connection between vitiligo and excessive exposure.

8-methoxy psoralen (Meladine or Meloxine) is given in the form of three tablets per day increasing to five per day for approximately six weeks. With trimethylpsoralen (Trisoralen) the dosage is two to four tablets per day. A combination with topical psoralens gives a higher rate of repigmentation. Corticosteroids have also been used effectively with the psoralens but they are ineffective on their own.

Congenital leucoderma. This is purely mentioned so that it is not mistaken for vitiligo which could be considered to be acquired leucoderma. Albinism is the full example of congenital leucoderma with complete absence of pigment but albinism can be partial in distribution as well as in severity. As such larger patches of skin congenitally depigmented can occur.

Other skin conditions occur with excess exposure to the sun over long periods. In general premature ageing with wrinkles formation and a general leathery appearance occurs with many years of exposure.

These conditions however only occur in the long term resident of the tropics and subtropics: not in the short term visitor. In particular they occur with people such as farmers who are spending their life in the open.

Marshall (1972) from South Africa writes that 15 per cent of his new white patients are suffering from these problems.

Elastosis is the main change which occurs in the dermis due to excess solar radiation. With these changes the elasticity of the skin disappears and telangiectasia and erythema appear. The skin becomes yellow and thickened. It also becomes fragile and very minor trauma can be a problem. Spidery angiomas may appear also multiple small cysts and large comedos. In the epidermis atrophy occurs. Cell layers decrease in amount. The cells become disorderly in arrangement and inconstant in size, shape and staining properties.

Solar keratoses. Usually on the face or other exposed areas. May be single or multiple. Can start as telangiectasia or as brown pigmentation. Usually when on the face they are slightly raised pigmented areas with superficial scaling. When occurring elsewhere especially on the back of the hand they are thicker, more raised and with a harder adherent scale.

The main problem with keratoses are that a very definite percentage are precursors of either basal cell tumors or squamous cell carcinomata. Authorities vary on this but it is probably in the neighbourhood of 15-20 per cent.

Treatment. Because of malignant change solitary keratoses should be excised. If multiple this is difficult. Radiotherapy must not be employed. Cryotherapy, diathermy and cytotoxic drugs have all been used.

Solar cheilitis. This usually occurs in the lower lip rather than the upper. Scaling occurs in the lip but sometimes it is damp with oozing. The lip tends to become pale in colour and even turn yellow due to elastosis. Keratoses sometimes occur. Squamous cell carcinoma of the lip is a frequent result and radical treatment such as excision may well be indicated.

As already mentioned basal cell epithelioma and squamous cell carcinoma are frequent developments from solar keratoses and as such must be treated radically.

A *solitary keratoacanthoma* is usually caused by exposure to sunlight. They usually occur on the face but also on the arms and backs of the hands. They grow fairly rapidly over a few months and then regress leaving a scar. However because of their fairly rapid growth they are usually excised.

Chondrodermatitis nodularis helicis. This is a painful condition of the pinna due to exposure to the sun. Frequently associated with other solar dermatoses. It consists of a small hard yellowish nodule in the skin of the superior part of the pinna. It may become attached to the cartilage. It is not precancerous.

The writer recently had an overseas engineer who developed one such that he was unable to wear his noise protection ear muffs.

Treatment. The shaving off of the nodule. Bleeding is stopped by diathermy.

The above are conditions which only occur with prolonged exposure to the sun.

The conditions which occur after brief exposure to heat and sun such as sunburn, prickly heat and cheiropompholyx are described in Chapter Seven.

11. Other Infections, both Parasitic and Non-Parasitic

Probably the commonest and most important remaining infection is the group of diseases called filariasis. This group is an infection with a nematode.

There are four main varieties of this infection:

1. Bancroftian filariasis or the forerunner of elephantiasis due to an infection with *Wucheria bancrofti*.

2. Loiasis or loa-loa disease, caused by an infection with the loa-loa which, in its embryonic form, is the *microfilaria diurna*.

3. Onchocerciasis, also known as river blindness, caused by the *Oncocerca volvulus*.

4. This variety takes on a different form but is an infection with the guinea worm. It is called dracontiasis and is due to infection with the *Dracunculus medinensis*.

Bancroftian filariasis

This is an infection with a nematode, in which the adult worms infect the lymphatic system.

Geographically, it occurs along the North African Mediterranean littoral, throughout West, Central and East Africa, the Middle East, India, Burma, Malaysia, Thailand, Southern China, Japan, Indonesia, Samoa, Fiji, the Caribbean islands and the northern part of South America. A similar infection due to *Brugia malayi* occurs in Malaya and the surrounding countries.

Man is the definitive host and the mosquito is the intermediate host. In general the Culex species is the mosquito involved, in particular Culex pipiens fatigans (Culex quinquefasciatus), but some varieties of Anopheles and Aedes including Aedes aegypti are involved depending on the part of the world where the infection takes place.

On biting an infected human the mosquito takes in embryos which hatch in its stomach. The larvae are passed to a second man when the mosquito bites him. In fact they are left on the skin of the new host and penetrate the skin near, but not actually at, the site of the bite puncture. The cycle in the mosquito is about three weeks. On entering man these larvae reach lymphatics, mature and produce embryos which pass through lymphatics, entering the veins and peripheral circulation. It probably takes up to six months for the larval form to pass through the embryonic or microfilarial form to reach full maturity.

The typical, and most important point about the microfilariae, is their 'periodicity'. They are present in the blood only at night, in particular between 10 p.m. and 2 a.m. This has never been truly explained but it has been put forward that it is because they are spread by night biting mosquitoes. This is borne out by the fact that in Fiji there is no periodicity and they are spread there by an Aedes mosquito which, of course, bites by day.

In general, the symptoms are caused by the adult worms and the true rate of the circulating microfilariae is uncertain, although sensitivity reactions do take place. With the blockage by adult worms obliteration lymphangitis occurs.

It appears that repeated infection is usually necessary to develop any clinical picture and so it is uncommon in the brief visitor. It usually only occurs in an expatriate who has been resident in an endemic area for some time.

Incubation period is very variable but is probably six months to two years after the original mosquito borne infection when a lymphangitis is usually the first symptom. Typically and interestingly it is retrograde because it has been caused by a blockage due to a worm. In other words it runs distally whilst a lymphangitis, due to sepsis, usually runs proximally. There is associated pyrexia and malaise. There may be associated lymphadenitis and even abscess formation. These attacks tend to recur affecting the same lymphatics so progressing to a state of complete blockage. The femoral lymphatics are the commonest involved, but those of the spermatic cord and scrotum in man and the vulva in the woman are not infrequent. Both legs may be affected, but one usually more than the other. To a lesser extent it may affect the upper limbs or the trunk.

With involvement of the spermatic cord a painful orchitis may ensue, leading to an acute hydrocoele. As with the lymphangitis these symptoms settle down, but tend to recur. As time goes by the obstructive lymphangitis is present more and more of the time.

As well as the lymphatic varices occurring in the limbs and the scrotum they occur in the deep abdominal lymphatics leading to ascites and pleural effusion.

The most typical of these problems is the presence of chyluria. With this the lymphoid varix has ruptured into the urinary tract, usually the pelvis of the kidney, pouring chyle into the urine. This gives the pathognomonic sign of a milky urine. On standing, the urine separates into three layers. The bottom layer is a pink layer of erythrocytes and debris, the middle layer one of lymph and urine and the thin top layer consists of fat. Microfilariae are often found in chyluria.

This chyluria usually comes on suddenly. It may be preceded by loin pains and fever. It probably only last for a few days and then disappears only to return intermittently. As the condition progresses the skin of the limbs in which the lymphangitis has occurred becomes thickened and coarsened as also will the scrotum if this has been affected. This is a description of a *Wucheria bancrofti* type of a filarial infection. But what of elephantiasis?

In elephantiasis, microfilariae are not present in the blood; perhaps because the lymphatics are blocked.

Elephantiasis occurs when Wucherian infections are endemic. Both are lymphatic diseases with recurrent lymphangitis. The scrotum is particularly affected in both diseases. But *Wucheria bancrofti* or *Brugia malayi* are almost certainly not the only causes of elephantiasis.

Diagnosis is from the typical history described above. Confirmatory laboratory diagnosis is finding the microfilariae in the night blood.

Filarial complement fixation tests will give a positive reaction to present or past infections. There is nearly always an acute allergic response to the starting of treatment with diethylcarbamazine (Banocide) due to the sudden death of worms. Eosinophilia is usually present.

Treatment. Rest in bed is essential during the attacks of lymphangitis.

Specific treatment is diethylcarbamazine (Banocide, Meterazan). As described above an initial acute allergic reaction may occur with a fever for a few days. There may even be local reactions and flare up in the lymphatics, but treatment must be continued, giving antihistamines if necessary. Two mg per kg body weight, three times a day for 21 days is the usual course. But on the first day this dose is given only once and on the second day twice because of the early reactions.

Loiasis

Loiasis or filariform infection caused by loa-loa is the next to be considered. It is transmitted by various species of Chrysops flies. Also known as mangrove flies. Generally found in shady woodlands. Only the females bite man and then usually in the early morning and again in the late afternoon. Due to the type of terrain of the Chrysops fly, loa-loa infection, like onchocercal infections, are uncommon in the city workers and visitors but far commoner in the building engineer and surveyor and the worker in the agricultural projects such as student volunteers and peace corps workers.

Geographically, this infection is confined to tropical Africa between 10° North and 5° South, in particular around the shores of the Gulf of Guinea.

Adult worms wander in subcutaneous tissues and they may even be found by chance at surgical operations. The typical lesion in loiasis is the Calabar swelling which is a small mass of oedematous tissue below the skin, which may, or may not, contain an adult worm. It is thought to be an allergic response to the foreign protein of the worm. They last for two or three days then disappear, but other swellings may appear elsewhere. They are about three inches across and usually are near medium-sized joints or on the face, including the orbit. There is usually associated irritation or pain. Incubation period for these Calabar swellings is at least three months but may be up to two years. Sometimes before the appearance of these swellings there are scattered erythematous areas all over the body. They may be followed by oedematous swellings or an allergic papular rash. Adult worms may sometimes be seen migrating through subcutaneous loose tissue. Depending on sex they vary from 3 cm to 7 cm. Classically they can migrate across the conjuntivae. Usually with pain and oedema. It may cross the eye in a matter of seconds or it may take appreciably longer. However, it usually is a cause for the sufferer seeking medical assistance.

Diagnosis is by the typical Calabar swellings but confirmatory diagnosis should be by finding the microfilariae in the blood. The loa-loa microfilaria have a diurnal periodicity, fitting in with the diurnal biting habits of the Chrysops fly.

Eosinophilia is usually very high. Complement fixation test may be positive in light infections. Remember the infection only occurs in a comparative localised area.

Treatment is by diethylcarbamazine in exactly the same dosage as with *Wucheria bancrofti*. Once again, there may be fairly severe allergic reactions to the treatment and dosage may have to be cut temporarily. Antihistamines should be given to help with the allergic reactions during the first few days.

Onchocerciasis

This is the third filarial infection to be considered. Also known as river blindness, and caused by the filariae *Onchocerca volvulus*. This is spread by Simulium flies. Also known as buffalo and turkey gnats and black flies. They shun bright light and hence bite mainly in the early morning and towards evening, but in shady areas will attack any time of day. They are particularly vicious before or after storms or rain. They breed by preference in running water and shallow streams, even roadside ditches. Here again, the city or town worker or visitor is less likely to be affected than the roads surveyor or the hydroelectric engineer who are very likely to suffer.

Geographically, Africa is the main source of infection going right through from the west to the east in the tropical areas. As far north as Ethiopia and the Sudan, and as far south as Rhodesia and Malawi. It occurs in Tunisia as well. It is also present across the Red Sea in the Yemen. In the New World it occurs in Mexico, Guatemala and Venezuela.

Microfilariae are found in the skin, when dead. They produce small nodules which consist of inflammatory cells and eosinophils. Death in the eye causes keratitis, iritis and choroidoretinitis.

Symptoms may not occur for up to three or four years, but usually the first is an irritating papular eruption. As is frequent, the irritation is worse when warm, particularly in bed. At this time there may be some thickening of the epithelium. Usually subsequent to the above, but sometimes, previously, nodules appear. They are commonest over the iliac crest, femoral greater trochanters, lower ribs and in the scalp. The scalp is particularly affected with the New World infection.

With the eye manifestations, the earliest is a punctate keratitis. There is usually a conjunctivitis as well. This keratitis can be recognised by shining the light of the ophthalmoscope on to the eye with the use of a small magnifying lens, when small, milky areas will be noted. Subsequently an iritis occurs. In long standing cases the entire cornea may become opaque. Areas of choroidoretinitis also occur. They may be multiple and are usually fairly well demarcated. If untreated the prognosis of eye involvement is bad.

Diagnosis is by finding microfilariae in skin scrapings or adults in excised nodules.

Complement fixation test is of value in mild infections. Eosinophilia is usually marked.

Treatment. Diethylcarbamazine (Banocide) is effective as with other filarial infections. Again, allergic reactions may be violent and the dosage is small for the first few days, while at the same time, antihistamines are given. Dosage is the same as with the other infections but with even greater care, initially.

Diethylcarbamazine is mainly effective against Microfilariae. With anything other than a light infection several courses of treatment are necessary to kill adult worms.

Suramin or antrypol is effective against adult worms but acts only very slowly on the microfilariae.

Initially, 0.1 g IVI, followed weekly by 1.0 g IVI for six weeks. Again antihistamines should be exhibited. It is nephotoxic and the urine must be regularly tested for albumen, casts and blood.

Dracontiasis

The fourth filarial infection is dracontiasis or guinea worm disease, caused by an infection with *Dracunculus (Filaria) medinensis*.

Geographically, mainly in West Africa and Southern and Central India. It also occurs in the Middle East and northern part of South America.

Man is the definite host, while the Cyclops, which is a minute water crustacean, is the intermediate host.

The human becomes infected by swallowing infected Cyclops in water. The larvae are unaffected by gastric juices and migrate through the wall of the small intestine to subcutaneous tissue near the skin surface, where they develop over the course of approximately one year.

The leg is the most likely site for development. The developing worm secretes a toxin which penetrates the skin and produces a vesicle which ulcerates. Through this small ulcer the worm's head appears and the worm discharges hundreds of embryos when the erosion is covered with water. After all larvae have been ejected the worm can usually be removed. It frequently attains a length up to 80 cm and may calcify after it has extruded all its larvae.

Clinically, shortly before extrusion of the larvae, there is locally erythema, pain and tenderness. Sometimes there is general malaise and there may be generalised allergic reaction with pruritus and urticaria. There may even be vomiting, nausea and collapse. But all constitutional symptoms subside when the vesicle ruptures.

Eosinophilia is marked.

After rupture, secondary infection is common. The worm takes about three to six weeks to discharge all embryos. This is encouraged by regular douching of the area with water. Once all embryos have been discharged the ulcer usually heals.

The worm can sometimes be removed by rolling on a thin sterile stick. However, it must be kept moist with saline to prevent rupture. If it breaks, and then disappers into its track, secondary infection is almost inevitable.

Treatment. Niridazole (Ambilhar) is very effective, 25 mg per kg body weight daily for seven days. Alternative is Thiobendazole 50 mg per kg body weight daily for two days.

Tetracycline or other antibiotics should be given with secondary infection.

Toxocariasis

Toxocariasis is the human infection with the larvae of *Toxocara canis* and *Toxocara catis*. For some years the problem of visceral larva migrans due to the dog worm and cat worm, where the larvae migrate to the lungs and liver, has been accepted. One must remember that the toxocara is very like the *Ascaris lumbricoides* in which similar migration occurs. However, while one week after infection, the larva of the *A.lumbricoides* is 0.038 mm, at the same stage, that of the *T.canis* is 0.02 mm. Hence the *T.canis* can go on migrating into far smaller vessels.

It was in 1960 that Professor Ashton, at Moorfields, and Professor Woodruff, at the Hospital for Tropical Diseases, realised that *Toxocara canis* larvae could cause eye lesions. In a lot of ways these lesions are fairly similar to onchocerciasis but several cases have occurred in people, particularly children, who have never been out of Britain.

However, with the dog worm being far commoner in the tropics it is naturally a commoner occurrence in people returning from these parts than in full time inhabitants of the United Kingdom.

Between 1962 and 1969, 1107 stools of dogs from London and the Home counties showed ova of *T.canis* in 12.8 per cent, but the percentage was decreasing through the years. However, figures of 80 per cent in Calcutta, 93 per cent in Mexico in puppies, 37 per cent in Ibadan, Nigeria, and 28 per cent in Dar-es-Salaam show what a problem it can be.

Clinically, partial loss of vision due to choroidoretinitis usually near the macular region. This is caused by the embedding of a larva which has entered by the retinal artery. It is unilateral. It can also cause anterior uveitis. Strabismus due to macular involvement is often the presenting sign.

In addition to the eye, there may be liver and lung infection, the latter causing pneumonitis. It is also possibly a cause of some cases of epilepsy. Hepatomegaly may often occur. Eosinophilia is nearly always present.

Diagnosis is confirmed by a positive toxocaral skin test at dilution of 1/1000 and also by the toxocaral fluorescent antibody test.

Treatment is with a standard course of diethylcarbamazine, 3 mg per kg body weight, three times a day for three weeks.

Rabies

Rabies, also called hydrophobia, lyssa and la rage is a disease unknown nowadays in the United Kingdom, Scandinavia, the Iberian Peninsula and Australia. A virus infection affecting several warm blooded animals and birds. Traditionally occurring in the domestic dog, it also occurs in the fox, hyena, jackal, wolf, squirrel and vampire bat.

Geographically in Europe, it is fairly common in Russia and France, rare in Germany and absent in Spain and Portugal. Outside Europe it is present in many areas of Africa, Middle East, India, the Far East, Central and South America. It is not uncommon in North America where it can be spread by the squirrel. In Trinidad, it is spread by the vampire bat.

Pathologically caused by a neurotropic virus which affects the nervous system only. Virus travels slowly along the peripheral nerves from the site of infection. It is present in the saliva of the biting animal.

Incubation period depends on the site of the bite and the amount of infection. On the head or face, incubation is minimal: on the feet it is maximal. Usually about 35 to 50 days, but it has been as short as 12 days, and probably up to about six months. Much longer than this has not been proven. It is this long incubation period that must put the disease in the thoughts of the doctor who is attending someone who has returned from abroad. The severity of the wound and hence the absorption of toxin is a factor in the prognosis. Wolf bites have a higher incidence of subsequent infection than dog bites.

Due to the absolute quarantining of dogs from abroad, very little rabies has been seen in the United Kingdom in the last 50 years. In the period, 1946-69, there were eight fatal human cases: all brought in from abroad. Six had been infected by dogs, one by a wolf, and one by a cat. During the same period, in the United States, 240 cases had occurred. But, interestingly, 230 had occurred before 1963, when prophylactic vaccination of dogs in that country became established. Since 1963 only three of the indigenous cases were due to dogs.

Symptoms. Usually a premonitory phase, lasting one or two days, when the site of the bite usually becomes irritable. There is intense depression, irritability, intolerance of noise and a desire for solitude. The voice becomes husky and there may be difficulty in swallowing.

Rapidly, the fear and irritability increase, and muscular spasms ensue. Spasm of the larynx is marked and the fear of water starts.

Following the spasms, paralysis ensues. This is usually ascending in type, especially if the bite was at the extremities. Dementia, coma and death follow. The whole course of the illness is only four to five days. Until recently it was invariably fatal.

Prophylaxis after exposure. Due to the fact that once the illness is established there is little satisfactory treatment, and, also, there is usually a long incubation period, the benefits of the latter must be used to try and prevent the disease becoming established.

Locally, wounds must be thoroughly cleaned and irrigated with a detergent solution to remove all traces of saliva which contain the virus. They should not be sutured or cauterised. Antibiotics can be given to prevent secondary infection, although they will have no affect on the rabies virus. If the bite is severe, or if it is pretty certain the dog was rabid, then a single dose of antiserum is given, intramuscularly, as soon as possible. This is then followed by a course of the vaccine. This should not be started for 24 hours because the presence of passively circulating antibody from the serum may upset the effectiveness of the active immunisation, If the bite is small and it is only doubtful that the animal was rabid, then the vaccine is given alone, without the antiserum.

Antirabies serum (passive immunisation). Dosage is 40 iu per kg body weight. It is given intramuscularly and if given within 24 hours of the bite, part of it should be infiltrated into the area of the wound.

Serum sickness may follow within seven to ten days and should be treated by antihistamines from the date of injection.

If in an allergic person, then diluted serum must be given in graded injections, with the usual precautions.

Antirabies vaccine (active immunisation). Duck egg vaccine is the usual one used. Daily injections into the abdominal wall for 21 days. Two further doses should be given ten and 20 days after completion of the initial 21 day course.

Tetanus

Tetanus occurs in the United Kingdom, but it is commoner in continental Europe, and throughout Asia and Africa.

Described clearly by Hippocrates, the Greek word 'tetanos' means tension.

It is an infective disease caused by the toxins of *Clostridium tetani* and it is characterised by voluntary muscle spasm, usually in the jaw and neck, but they may occur in the rest of the body with progress of the disease.

The tetanus bacillus is a strict anaerobe and is only present at the site of inoculation or in the wound. Distal action is entirely due to the toxin.

The toxin is transferred by motor nerves to the spinal cord, up which it ascends. It is never transferred by sensory nerves.

Incubation period is variable but usually about seven to 12 days: very rare for it to be less than five days, but it can be a lot more than 12 days.

Premonitory symptoms of irritability, spasms, twitching and pain are unusual except when prophylactic serum has been given. Initial symptoms are usually a slight sore throat, but with difficulty in swallowing, far in excess of what should be expected for the severity of the sore throat. Pains and stiffness also occur in the back of the neck.

From these symptoms, definite spasm then occurs, primarily in the masseters and muscles of mastication, shortly spreading to the muscles of neck and the back of the neck. From there the spasm spreads in order to the abdominal recti, the back, and the legs. The important point is that there is *not* complete relaxation between spasms.

Along with these spasms there is excess sweating, pyrexia and abdominal rigidity. With advance of the condition, trismus and risus sardonicus ensue with inability to swallow. Rigidity of the abdomen, partial closing of the eyes, opisthotonos and extension of the legs all follow. Tachycardia ensues.

Without treating, vomiting and pneumonia occur.

Hippocrates considered major spasm meant death within four days. However, treatment has improved since then.

However, Cole very aptly suggested the period or rapidity of onset was most important. If the time between the first symptom and the first major spasm is less than 48 hours, then the prognosis is very bad. The old view that prognosis depended on length of incubation period is now not accepted.

Death occurs from exhaustion, cardiac failure, asphyxia or broncho-pneumonia.

Diagnosis in an established case should be obvious but tetany, hysteria and localised trismus must be considered.

As well as the above, there are types of poisoning. In the past, one would think of strychnine but now one must consider overdosage of or sensitivity to the phenothiazine group of drugs.

Treatment. There is no specific treatment of the established condition. The true treatment is prevention. Adequate immunisation throughout childhood and regular booster throughout life, at not more than five year intervals especially for overseas travellers.

Immediately after the wound occurs, further tetanus toxoid must be given, unless a booster dose has been given within the last six months.

The case must be treated at a special centre where respirators and high grade specialised nursing is available.

One final point which must be remembered, is that an attack of tetanus gives no immunity and active immunisation must be given to a patient who has recovered from an attack of tetanus.

12. Fitness to Travel by Air

Most cases of exotic disease encountered in this country arrive by air, and it seems appropriate, therefore, to include in this book a brief account of some of the medical aspects of air travel. In less than half a century aircraft have progressed from being a novelty to a widely accepted form of transport, and so readily is air travel accepted today that it is easy to forget that it requires man to venture into an alien and hostile environment. Fortunately the physiological problems caused by this have been largely overcome, and flying today presents no serious difficulties for most people, but when considering the unhealthy traveller it is necessary to examine more closely the aircraft cabin environment and its possible effects on these passengers. Before doing so, however, there are one or two points about an air journey which apply to all passengers and which should be considered when asked to advise on air travel.

The healthy traveller

An air journey, like any other, may be tiring, especially when several transit stops are involved, perhaps with a change of aircraft. The very speed of air travel brings with it the special problem of the rapid crossing of time zones and this may result in increased fatigue for the traveller who arrives at his destination at a local time quite out of phase with his own circadian rhythms. This is particularly important for businessmen and politicians travelling to meetings, and careful planning of journeys is needed to avoid arriving in a state where wrong decisions are likely due to fatigue. As a general guide it may be said that where a journey involves a time change of five hours (e.g. London to New York), at least 24 hours should elapse between arrival and commencing business. It should be noted that alcohol, especially if used as a hypnotic, tends to slow down a person's ability to adjust to a new time zone, and in general the elderly adjust less easily than the young.

Next, it is worth remembering that a long air journey involves prolonged sitting, with little opportunity to take even a minimum of exercise. The effects of the resulting venous statis in the legs can be relieved by advising travellers to get up for a short walk along the aisle every so often, and to avoid wearing constrictive shoes or boots for the flight. There is also a tendency amongst most passengers to eat and drink more than usual, if only to help time pass, and meals are often taken at physiologically unnatural times. The slight reduction in atmospheric pressure within the cabin of the aircraft leads to gaseous distension of the abdomen, and hence minor digestive upsets may result.

The slight reduction in cabin atmospheric pressure results also in a slight hypoxia, which will be referred to in greater detail later in the context of unhealthy passengers. With the healthy subject, if he is a smoker, this hypoxia will be exaggerated by the presence of carbon monoxide in his blood, and heavy smoking on a long flight should be discouraged.

To sum up, for the healthy passenger there is much to be said for moderation in smoking, eating and drinking (especially carbonated drinks), as well as careful planning of the timing of the journey. This subject was well covered in some detail by McGirr (1967), and in more general form for lay readers by Wright (1966) and Turner (1968, 1970).

The unhealthy traveller

General principles

When contemplating air travel for the unhealthy it is necessary to look more closely at the possible phsyiological stresses they may encounter. Cabin pressurisation overcomes most of the physiological problems encountered at high altitude, but it is not possible to produce a cabin atmosphere of sea level pressure without an enormous increase in aircraft weight. In practice, some reduction of cabin pressure is acceptable, and most modern airliners operate with a cabin pressure range equivalent to altitudes of 5,000 to 7,000 feet, with a ceiling of 8,000 feet.

At 6,000 feet the atmospheric pressure is just over 600 mmHg, and under this reduced pressure gas trapped in body cavities expands according to Boyle's law. Thus 100 ml of air trapped at sea level will occupy about 130 ml at 6,000 feet, and this may cause difficulties in the body. The commonest problems arise in the sinuses and the middle ear cavities where acute catarrhal conditions prevent free air flow and pressure equalisation. Pressure damage or barotrauma of these areas may be very painful, but serious damage is rare. Some of the other clinical implications of this decompression will be discussed later.

In passing, it may be of interest to mention that true subatmospheric sickness does not occur at altitudes below 17,000 feet and is extremely rare below 25,000 feet. However, it has been recorded on modern pressurised aircraft in persons undertaking an air journey immediately after scuba diving (Furry *et al.,* 1967), and travellers should be warned not to fly within 12 hours of any dive with an aqualung, and 24 hours should elapse before a flight when a deep dive (i.e. over 100 feet) has been made.

The second and much more important physiological consequence of reduced atmospheric pressure is hypoxia. At sea level the alveolar partial pressure of oxygen (pO_2 alv.) is 103 mmHg, whereas at 6,000 feet it is about 75 mmHg. Since the amount of oxygen taken up by the haemoglobin is related to the pO_2 alv., this fall might be disastrous were it not for the sigmoid shape of the oxygen dissociation curve. Reference to this will show that in fact the fall of over 25 per cent on the pO_2 alv. leads to a reduction in carried oxygen of only about 3 per cent. Unless the pO_2 alv. begins to fall below 60 mmHg there is relatively little effect on the oxygen saturation of the blood, but below this partial pressure hypoxia becomes severe. The fall in pO_2 alv. experienced in a modern airliner cabin, with the 3 per cent desaturation of arterial blood, is not noticed by the healthy passenger at rest, although the effects on night vision and on the learning of new tasks have been reported in experimental subjects. (Goldie, 1942; Dennison *et al.*, 1966).

For certain groups of unhealthy passengers, however, the sudden exposure to such an atmosphere may prove to be the final step over the threshold into significant tissue hypoxia. Conditions such as cardiac failure, myocardial ischaemia, severe anaemia, severe respiratory disease, and cerebral arterial insufficiency are among those which may react badly to such hypoxia, and these will be discussed later. The problems of this hypoxia may be largely overcome by the use of supplementary oxygen in flight, and a portable oxygen set or the aircraft's main supply can be used to increase the pO_2 alv. in such cases. It must be remembered, however, that continuous oxygen for a 10 hour journey, even at a low flow rate, may not be practical; it requires a lot of equipment which is both heavy and bulky in a situation where weight and space are expensive commodities.

Besides the peculiar physiological problems of air travel, some mention must be made of the physical difficulties that may be encountered for the disabled or handicapped traveller.

The ergonomic problems of fitting the passenger into the space available cause most trouble. Passengers with long leg plasters, ankylosed knees or hips, and similar disabilities may simply not fit in. Even if they can be accommodated with some effort, they may then have to maintain an uncomfortable position for many hours. It is true that there are seats in the aircraft with a little more leg room than normal, at the front of the economy class cabin and in the so-called 'emergency exit' row. Most airliners, however, reserve the forward seats for mothers with infants in cots, and safety regulations preclude the allocation of emergency row seats to handicapped passengers.

To sum up, space is severely limited and passengers unable to occupy a normal economy class seat may be restricted in some way. Sometimes the only solution is for the passenger to travel first class, or on a stretcher.

Fatigue in travelling has already been mentioned, but for the air traveller this may be compounded by problems at the airports where he may have a long and slightly anxious wait in queues at Customs and Immigration desks, while at the same time feeling slightly apprehensive about the flight itself. Added to all this are the distances that may have to be walked within the airport buildings. The International Air Transport Association recommend a maximum walking distance of 1230 feet from aircraft to kerbside, and similarly the United States Federal Aviation Administration recommend maximum gradients for ramps in airports of 1 in 12. Many airports exceed these suggested maxima, and this adds to the fatigue of the air traveller. An airliner's medical department working with its passenger services section can do much to relieve the elderly or invalid passenger of the physical and mental stresses that may occur. Baggage, ticket and passport formalities can be undertaken by the passenger services staff, and a wheelchair provided, or just a friendly arm to lean on, making the whole process much less tiring. For those who may find the aircraft steps difficult, special lifting arrangements can be made and, of course, all of these facilities can be more readily available if the airline has some prior notification.

Aesthetic considerations are of great importance to an airline carrying invalid passengers alongside normal passengers on scheduled services. In this respect particularly an airline differs from a military flight, a point not always recognised by doctors with service experience who are accustomed to the flying ambulance of the Royal Air Force Aeromedical Evacuation Service. However, in many major commercial airlines seriously ill patients, and those who physically cannot occupy a normal seat, can be carried on a stretcher. In these cases the area is curtained off and as many as nine seats may be occupied by the specially designed aircraft stretcher, and the space available around the stretcher permits the basic nursing functions. The patient must be escorted by a trained person who can undertake any necessary nursing care and treatment in flight. In this context it must be remembered that airline stewardesses are not trained nurses, and can only be expected to offer first aid to passengers. They cannot be required to undertake nursing duties, administer injections or supervise treatment without seriously restricting their service to other passengers. Furthermore, as food handlers, it is not appropriate for them to be handling bedpans or urinals in flight.

Finally, when requests are made to the airline for the carriage of critically ill patients humanitarian considerations must be made. An air journey may be the only link between the patient and life saving treatment, and such cases are always carried, albeit sometimes with very elaborate precautions. Similarly, some patients with a terminal illness may wish to travel home to die, and this is a right that no one wishes to deny them. Only if it seems likely that death will occur during the journey are such cases refused. This is because the administrative and practical problems which surround an in-flight death may be distressing and inconvenient to other passengers, and very costly to the airline.

Clinical considerations

So far the general principles of fitness to fly have been discussed, and the application of these to some clinical conditions can now be examined. The following notes are of necessity only a brief guide, but most major airlines have a department where specialist advice can be obtained on individual cases.

Contraindications to air travel. It may be useful to start by disposing of the conditions which are usually regarded as absolute contraindication to flying on scheduled airline services. Infectious disease during the infectious phase is an obvious one, and in the case of chickenpox it is desirable that all the facial lesions have cleared lest the passenger should be quarantined as a smallpox suspect. Moribund passengers are not acceptable because of the difficulties created by death in flight. Expectant mothers near to term are not acceptable because of the risk of the patient going into labour in flight, and because premature labour does seem to be sometimes induced by an air journey. In practice most airlines are agreed that such passengers are not acceptable after the end of the 35th week of pregnancy, although for short domestic journeys this is extended to the end of the 36th week.

Cardiovascular disease. The effects of slight hypoxia on air travellers with impaired cardiovascular systems is now well recognised and documented (Richards, 1973; Beighton and Richards, 1968). Conditions likely to give trouble are congestive heart failure, myocardial ischaemia (especially with evidence of infarction in recent weeks). pulmonary hypertension, and severe systemic hypertension with complications. Supplementary oxygen may overcome some of the difficulties, but such cases need careful assessment before allowed to fly. Uncontrolled cardiac failure and recent myocardial infarction (i.e. within four weeks) are usually regarded as contraindicative to air travel.

Respiratory disease. Chronic bronchitis, emphysema, bronchiectasis and cor pulmonale are similarly at risk to the effects of hypoxia and supplementary oxygen may be necessary for such passengers. If a pneumothorax is present the problem of gaseous expansion arises, and ideally such cases should not fly until all the air has been reabsorbed.

Blood disorders. Severely anaemic patients may not tolerate the slight hypoxia, and generally a haemoglobin level of 50 per cent is regarded as the lowest acceptable. Much depends, however, on the cause of the anaemia, the chronicity of the condition, and the length of flight. The sickle cell diseases require special consideration as the more severe forms may be affected by the slight hypoxia and a sickling crisis provoked (Green *et al.*, 1971) and such cases should be discussed with the airline's medical department before travel.

Gastrointestinal disease. Recent gastrointestinal surgery may be affected by the expansion of gas in the gut, and similarly abdominal wounds may be subject to stress. Such cases should generally not fly until at least ten days after the operation, and if recovery has been complicated by paralytic ileus this period may need to be extended. Recent gastric or duodenal haemorrhage may be reawakened by gut distension, and in such cases three weeks should elapse after a major haemorrhage before major air travel is considered. Gas expansion may also cause difficulties in controlling colostomies or ileostomies, and such patients should be aware of this and take a good supply of bags and dressings in their hand luggage.

Neurological disease. The neurological disorders which require special attention are those in which cerebral hypoxia is a feature. Thus any cerebral infarction, whether from thrombosis or haemorrhage, should be regarded cautiously until the acute stage is past. In this context should be mentioned the elderly person whose cerebral oxygenation is adequately maintained at sea level, despite arteriosclerosis. It is a common experience in airlines that such passengers become confused after some time at altitude, and this must be remembered when such a person wishes to make a long journey alone. Epileptics may be slightly more liable to attacks during air travel. One possible factor which lowers their convulsion threshold is hypoxia, but probably much more important are fatigue, excitement, and the disturbance of routine which leads to irregular medication. The usual advice to such passengers is that they should take extra anticonvulsant medication on the day of travel. Recent air encephalography is a contraindication to flying as the expanding air would be dangerous. Patients with severe head injuries, and with cerebral tumours, appear to tolerate air travel very well, although, of course, they need special attention en route.

Diabetes mellitus. Diabetic patients often seek advice before travel. Airlines can usually make a suitable diet available but the main problem is one of time zone changes, with the risk of mistiming insulin injections. Where large time changes are involved, it is better for the passenger to remain on his own local time throughout the journey, and only attempt readjustment when at his destination. Some very severe diabetics may even need to change to a twice daily dose of soluble insulin for the journey. A problem, rare nowadays, is that of airsickness adding to the diabetics' problems, and should this occur it is clearly better to omit the insulin for the journey, and restabilise the condition on arrival.

Ears and sinuses. Apart from the acute catarrhal conditions which may prevent equalisation of pressure in the ears and sinuses, the most serious problem is for patients after recent middle ear surgery. Until the middle ear cavity is dry and normally aerated it is not desirable for these patients to fly, and especial care is necessary after stapedectomy.

Some disasters have occurred when the prosthesis has been driven into the labyrinth by barotrauma, with severe vertigo. Recent faciomaxillary surgery with fixed wiring of the jaws is a contraindication to air travel because of the risk of vomiting.

Psychiatric disorders. As passengers, the mentally ill may have trouble for two reasons. The obvious one is usually foreseen and relatively easily avoided, that is the dangerous psychotic who may be a risk to himself or others in the close confines of an aircraft cabin. Providing such a patient is well sedated and adequately escorted for the journey there is no contraindication to travel. The second group, less easily detected, are those psychotics and psychoneurotics for whom air travel may be very stressful and who may become bewildered or lost during their journey. Psychiatric patients who are well controlled in the sheltered environment of hospital or home, with a regular routine of meals, rest and medication, are ill-equipped to deal with the mental stresses of airline travel. A long intercontinental flight may involve several transit stops, perhaps a change of aircraft, considerable fatigue, and some natural anxiety about personal safety. Unexpected delays due to technical troubles and adverse weather add further to the stress. These factors, added to the hustle and bustle of a busy airport, are enough to disturb even the most placid person at times, and this is often overlooked by the doctor who has assessed the patient in the calm of hospital or consulting rooms.

A useful guide to suitability for air travel when assessing these patients is whether the doctor feels he would be happy to have them make a long rail journey, involving changes of trains at mainline stations, entirely alone. If this sort of stress would be considered unacceptable then an air journey may be unwise unless the patient is accompanied by a very sensible companion.

Summary

Fitness to travel by air is often taken for granted by both patient and physician, and this is justifiable for the vast majority of travellers. However, even for them, the journey can be made more comfortable by simple advice. In the very few unhealthy travellers some special care may be needed. Most major airlines have specialist advice available and welcome enquiries from doctors or prospective passengers, since their experience is that with advance planning there are very few patients who cannot travel safely by air.

13. Medical Assessment for Living in Warm Climates

'We must export to live.' These words or words very like them have been said by successive Prime Ministers and their fellows in the successive Governments of Great Britain since the end of World War Two.

Since then also the majority of our colonies and dependencies that once made up the British Empire have become independent states within or without the Commonwealth. This has not only affected the British Empire. Independence has come to the former colonies of France, Belgium, Italy, Holland and the United States.

With these countries gaining their independence and developing into progressive modern states they have needed help and assistance in the form of trained professional people.

And so with the businessmen selling their wares to the developing countries and the professional men offering their knowledge to create new situations or train local people to takeover, the need for expatriates in the developing countries has increased rather than decreased.

As well as these there are the student and graduate voluntary organisations who send people overseas for one or two years to teach and help in the developing countries in various ways. In Britain we have Voluntary Service Overseas (V.S.O.). In the United States there is the Peace Corps. France, Germany, Denmark and many other countries have similar organisations. Besides the above, with more countries independent, the Diplomatic Corps must send more representatives to many countries.

The majority of the developing countries to which these various people are sent, either for short visits or for longer residence, are in the subtropics and tropics.

Up to now we have been considering the short term visitor, if anything, more than the long term resident. In this chapter it is the long term resident who is the major object of our interest, although certain conditions mentioned should be very seriously considered also in the case of assessing a person's suitability for a short visit to the tropics.

Besides the major medical point of whether someone's health is going to be affected adversely by living in a tropical climate and environment, there are other subsidiary factors which must be considered.

A good employer covers the employee for medical expenses when he sends him overseas. An even better employer covers the cost of sickness in a man's wife and family as well.

As such any condition present at the time that a man goes abroad which may produce a cost factor has to be considered.

Large organisations like the oil companies have their own fully equipped hospitals on certain stations but in general local facilities have to be used. Therefore any surgical conditions, although not urgent at the time, should be put right before the employee goes abroad. Treatment will probably be costly overseas and may not even be satisfactory.

Besides the employee it is equally, if not more, important for the man's wife and any children to be assessed as fully fit to go abroad before the man is offered the appointment.

If either his wife or any of his children are judged as unfit to go abroad then the company should on no account offer the man the appointment. It is absolutely wrong for a company to put itself in the position of dividing a family, even if temporarily, after initially offering to send all the family overseas. This may be the start of a marriage break-up in which the company is by no means innocent.

Certain appointments, normally due to the actual job, are unaccompanied. However, as long as they are advertised as unaccompanied this is entirely different in that the man and his wife have been put fully in the picture from the start.

Many companies send the man overseas on his own for an initial period of three to six months to see that he is suitable and fits in to the job and environment satisfactorily. This is quite understandable. The cost of repatriating the man by air from half way round the world is bad enough but to repatriate the whole family could be very expensive. However, the writer considers that three months is the maximum that a company should expect for this separation.

Psychiatric Disease

Psychiatric problems are far the major reasons for costly repatriation of employees and families from subtropical and tropical areas. Napier Malcolm, in a survey of patients repatriated through the Queen Elizabeth Hospital in Aden, found the following figures: 11 per cent of all admissions to the hospital in expatriate staff were psychiatric cases; 13 per cent of admissions of over 21 days were psychiatric; approximately 30 per cent of cases repatriated were psychiatric.

Naturally any overt psychiatric disease would obviously be an absolute bar to acceptance. However it is the lesser forms of psychiatric problems which cause so many of the troubles.

Symptoms or signs of any psychoneurotic disease, especially if there is a history of inpatient, or even outpatient, treatment under the care of a psychiatrist must be very seriously considered.

Regrettably, if the patient tells the psychiatrist that they are considering going abroad the latter's response, if he has no experience of life overseas, tends to be that a change of environment will do the patient good. However in practice usually nothing is farther from the truth and subsequent breakdown is very frequent.

This is because many few factors enter into the patient's life and a high percentage of these factors may be difficult. To look at them reasonably one may think that they are all very unimportant but one must remember that the psychiatric patient does not consider them reasonably and multiple factors in the psychiatric patient seem to 'add up' by geometric progression rather than by arithmetical progression.

The following are some of the factors which count.

1. The sudden separation from Mum and Dad. If there has been a close-knit relationship, particularly between the wife and her parents, a sudden and primary break in this relationship due to going abroad may precipitate a relapse. One has known of the employee's wife who has worried because they would not have the return air fare if her elderly mother or father were to be taken ill suddenly.

2. Good public transport is something which the residents of the cities of the developed countries accept without thought. In the developing countries it is, in general, very inadequate. Let us be fair; in some of the developing countries the expatriate's wife is not very welcome on some of the public transport and may well get an unpleasant 'buffeting'. This means that if the man needs his car for his work and has it away all day then his wife is tied down to the house and cannot get out. The writer has known of a wife who had a further breakdown and had to be repatriated because she did not hold a driving licence and public transport was impossible. Solitude like this can be impossible.

3. Within the developing countries today there are politicians who are highly critical of the western world and the developed countries such that expatriates from the western world, and their families, are not popular. They may be literally and metaphorically 'jostled' when they go out and this can cause anxiety.

4. One of the benefits in the past in living in the developing countries has been the availability of domestic staff in the home. However these staff can be a problem in themselves. Their attitude to their employers has changed with the years and they may well come in the category just described above such that they may 'jostle'. Further many wives who are new overseas have never had the experience of either employing domestic staff or of having come from a house where domestic staff were employed when they were young. As such they may well go about it in the wrong way such that more anxiety is caused by employing staff than would be caused by doing the work themselves. At least if they did the work they would be mentally and physically occupied. Lack of being mentally occupied in itself can be a factor.

5. Another most important point which may cause anxiety in the matter is the problem of the children's health. Besides all the added problems which occur in the tropics and subtropics which we have just

been discussing, there is the problem of medical attention. Not all employers cover the families of their expatriates against medical costs and hence the high charges for medical attention which prevail in many places can in itself be a cause for worry. It is when this happens that mothers realise what a wonderful institution the much maligned National Health Service really is. As well as this the actual medical facilities in themselves may not be of a particularly high standard. There may also be a language problem between the patients and the doctor. In some developing countries where there are governmental financial problems there may be limitation of import licences such that baby foods and drugs can be in short supply. All these points can cause anxiety to a mother who, if there is an underlying instability, can break down.

6. The housewife who has been brought up entirely in an enclosed terrain such as suburbia and who has not been 'out and about' frequently does badly, especially if she has revelled in suburbia. Naturally the one who has been brought up this way but has always wanted to 'break out' does very well when she does 'break out', and this is information that the selecting medical practitioner must try and evaluate. Beware of the young woman who lives for the telly and the supermarket and over the fence chit chat.

7. In general people who go abroad to the tropics to live for the first time when they are over forty frequently find the changes and new stresses too much for them and they are unable to adjust to the new ways of life.

If people are going to break down they generally break down on their first tour which can be very expensive for the employer. Return air tickets for the entire family can easily reach four figures in pounds. If on top of this the man was given a course of training before he went abroad one can understand the annoyance of the employers if they had slipped through a medical net.

One rider I would add to the above. If a wife has not enjoyed her first tour but at the time is quite psychiatrically stable and is obviously fit to return overseas, then I would recommend her not to persuade her husband to chuck it in. When practising in the tropics the writer frequently found that although the woman might not enjoy their first tour when they got back home for their first leave they longed to get back overseas again so much that they greatly enjoyed the second and subsequent tours.

The final difficulty with psychiatric problems is that in many of the developing countries the psychiatric services can be a serious problem. In many places they are geared entirely to looking after the nationals of the country whether it be in Africa or the Arab States of the Middle East. As such the arrangements may be entirely unsuitable for dealing with a psychosis in an expatriate. The psychiatric 'nurses' may well be quite unable to speak the language of the expatriate patient.

Where the psychiatric facilities are suitable, as in the New World, they are normally very expensive and they may be necessary on a fairly long term so putting the employer or the unfortunate patient, if he is self-employed, to great expense.

The final point with regard to psychiatric problems is that there can be great difficulties in transporting the patient by air. Naturally if suicidal or maniacal no airline will carry them. Even if they are accepted for carriage it is very usual for the patient or his family to provide an attendant which means an extra air fare. Sometimes in fact the attendant may have to be qualified — either a nurse or a doctor — which puts the cost up even more.

Malignant Disease

The main problem here is the need for frequent checks on people who have been diagnosed and treated for malignant disease. Obviously it is best for these regular checks to be done by the physicians or surgeons who originally treated the patient. When initially the checks are at three or six month intervals it is quite uneconomic for a company to fly one of their staff back and forth from, say, the Middle East at the shortest at this sort of frequency. It is only of value if the patient is a very senior man overseas whom they know is very difficult to replace. The airlines are luckier in this respect with their own employees because, provided there is a seat unoccupied, then it costs them nothing to fly someone home.

It depends entirely on the type of organisation whether they can find a job for an employee back in their home country for perhaps a year after treatment when the checks are more frequent. Then after that time when the checks may be annually they can send them overseas again. The other point of great importance here is whether the patient is told that he is suffering from malignant disease. As we all know, there are still two very different schools of thought although perhaps the 'don't tell' school is losing the day and beginning to dwindle. In the case of the 'don't tell' it is very difficult to tell a patient he is unfit to go abroad but at the same time he is told there is nothing serious to worry about. The writer considers that everything should be done to let the patient go back overseas. It helps his morale and one must remember that on the whole he earns far more money abroad. As such if he does know he has had a malignancy then he is in a better position to save more money for his family.

Alimentary System

In the upper alimentary tract active peptic ulceration must debar someone from taking up employment overseas. This, however, need only be a temporary setback. Any history of serious indigestion must be very fully investigated. If a gastric or duodenal ulcer is found on a barium meal then after medical treatment it is essential to see that it is healed on a second barium meal.

There are many places where expatriates are living where the medical facilities are such that a haemorrhage or a perforation could not be adequately treated.

Similarly for the businessman going on visits overseas a sudden admission to hospital for a gastric haemorrhage or a duodenal perforation could cause a lot of worry and expense to his employer and family at home.

In the past it was considered that once someone had suffered from tropical sprue or the malabsorption syndrome of the tropics it was an absolute ban to their going to the tropics again. Now, however, with more being known about its origin and causes, treatment is far more satisfactory. Hence once fat absorption is completely back to normal their return can be considered.

However a persisting steatorrhoea whatever the aetiology should bar the sufferer from tropical residence. This, of course, includes coeliac disease and idiopathic steatorrhoea.

Probably one of the most serious contraindications to residence in the tropics, on even brief visits, is a confirmed ulcerative colitis. Even a history of previous attacks should prevent someone living there long term. A minor bacillary dysentery infection or something less severe than that such as an episode of traveller's diarrhoea can set off a recurrence of ulcerative colitis which could be very serious indeed to the patient. Along with this, anyone with an active Crohn's disease should not be allowed to live in the tropics.

Cardiovascular System

The untreated hypertensive is a poor risk in tropical climates. He is also a poor risk living at altitude so this excludes tropical areas where the climate is better because of the altitude. Such places are Nairobi, Johannesburg and Bogota. Another point one must remember with the hypertensive is the fact that he usually is instructed to cut down his salt intake. This is something that the resident in the tropics must increase rather than decrease because of the increased sweating and so it is a contraindication to him living there. It is naturally difficult and invidious to lay down hard rules but once the diastole is maintained at over 100, doubts must be roused as to suitability. Malcolm referred to this very point with atheromatous changes in his survey of people repatriated from Aden. The patient who has had a previous coronary thrombosis is also a problem. In the past many cardiologists have gone on the principle that someone who had a myocardial infarction should remain in his temperate home environment for at least one year afterwards for complete stabilisation.

Recently with the success of the coronary rehabilitation scheme as practised by the RAF Rehabilitation Unit at Hedley Court and by

Nixon of the Charing Cross and Fulham Hospitals it has been found that stabilisation has come far quicker and in fact within about four months the patient is far fitter than he has been for probably the last two years.

Rheumatic heart disease is far less common than it used to be a generation or two ago but established mitral disease and in particular double valvular disease are contraindications, especially as fluid balance problems are involved.

Children with congenital heart disease must be very carefully assessed by a paediatrician who is interested in the whole problem. Naturally if surgery is considered it must be carried out before the child goes overseas.

One must remember that until acclimatisation has taken place satisfactorily there is an added burden thrown on the cardiovascular system. Hence any doubt in the system's efficiency to cope with the added strain must be very carefully considered.

Respiratory System

Pulmonary tuberculosis is a great problem and before chemotherapy was available was, of course, an absolute ban to further overseas service. With the advent of chemotherapy and its remarkable cure rate the whole picture has changed but authoritative sources do say that if there is a recurrence of the disease then there is a very great likelihood that the patient may have developed a resistance to the specific chemotherapy which was so successful before. The result is that the recurrence is far harder to treat. Therefore everything must be done to prevent such a recurrence.

The policy then must be long term. There is the initial full two years of chemotherapy. This must be followed by at least two and preferably three years in temperate climates depending on the extent of the initial infection and its rapidity to respond to treatment. With this regime it is four to five years before the patient can be considered to return to the subtropics and tropics. Even then the really humid areas such as the West and East African coastal areas, Colombo and Singapore are problematical. Obviously the chest X-ray findings are most important and before someone goes back to the tropics the film must show either absolute clearance or calcification, no doubtful shadows.

Asthma is a very difficult problem to assess. This problem comes up far more frequently with the children but it can also be a problem with the employee or his wife although in his long experience the writer has only infrequently seen it in the employee. With the children the anxious mother, worried about her husband going abroad and the effect on the child, will frequently consult her general practitioner. He, knowing what problems the child has in the cold winters, will in all honesty assure her that the warm weather will help him. This is not always so and because the mother has been reassured it makes the problem far harder for the assessing doctor.

Some asthmatics are better in a dry heat while they are worse if it is humid. Others react the opposite way in that they are better with humidity and worse in the sandy type of area.

Hence you will get the child or adult who is fine if stationed along the North African coast and along the Arabian Gulf, or even in up-country Kenya, being far worse if moved to West Africa, Ceylon coastal areas or Singapore. Similarly the opposite can happen just as easily.

Hence an asthmatic, or parent of an asthmatic, should be warned in advance that it is quite impossible to say whether the patient will be better or worse. It is only right to put this fairly and squarely to the family because if the applicant has given up a good job at home to go overseas to what he thinks is a better job, and then within a year he has to return home having lost his first job and perhaps sold his house, he will wish he had never gone abroad.

The possibility of this problem arising must be made clear in advance of him giving notice so he can decide to take or not to take the risk.

Nervous System

Epilepsy is a condition which must be seriously considered before acceptance for overseas service.

No epileptic should be considered as suitable to work on isolated projects away from good pharmaceutical supplies in case they run out of their anticonvulsants and new supplies can not be obtained.

This includes 'up-country' engineering projects and isolated work by organisations such as Voluntary Service Overseas and the American Peace Corps.

It is not fair either on the patient or on the people with whom he is living or working if his supply of essential drugs suddenly dries up. As well as this there is the problem that a percentage of epileptics are emotionally unstable.

Migraine sufferers come in the same category even if to a lesser extent. There can well be the need of essential medicaments and also the possible emotional instability. Myasthenia gravis is again an essential drug problem.

If any of these people are confined to city areas these problems do not arise unless there is a severe drugs import restriction.

The demyelinating diseases are another neurological problem. Authorities will assure one that disseminated sclerosis is rare in the tropics. This is so but it is because it is rare in the native races. These figures do not relate to expatriates. What is important is that relapses occur in disseminated sclerosis associated with intercurrent infections.

Intercurrent infections are commoner in the tropics than in temperate climates and so the acceptance of a patient suffering from disseminated sclerosis for living in the tropics must be very seriously considered and preferably they should not be accepted.

Collagen and Rheumatic Diseases

Patients with systemic lupus erythematosus are reported as doing badly in the tropics. Rheumatoid arthritis is another problem. Obviously the amount of disability and the activity, or not, are most important. The problem will come far more with the employee's wife than the employee. If severely incapacitated then she is not suitable for regular air travel to distant places.

Similarly if on long term corticosteroid treatment they must be very seriously considered not only because of the provision of drugs problem but also of the added complications of steroids if surgery were to become necessary for anything.

Gout is a further problem in the group. Raised serum uric acid levels are fairly common in people who have lived in the tropics for some time. This may be due to increased alcohol intake while there. It is a very different thing to accept someone to go to the tropics for the first time with a raised serum uric acid. It may be because his alcohol intake is already too high.

Frequently this type of person is obese as well which is a bad point.

A further point with gout is that there is a known association between raised serum uric acid and an increased incidence of renal calculi. As these occur more frequently in hot climates anyway due to dehydration from increased sweating the last thing one wants is to possibly increase the chances even more.

Diseases of the Urinary Tract

These are extremely important in the assessment of fitness to reside in warm climates. Obviously anyone suffering from a condition in which fluid balance is a problem is unfit for the tropics. The adequate maintenance of fluids and salt is the basic necessity for acclimatisation and subsquent living in the tropics.

Hence any degree of chronic nephritis rules out someone as a possibility. Similarly a history of severe recurring pyelonephritis is a contraindication.

Recurring renal calculi is an absolute contraindication because of the far higher incidence of this trouble in the tropics due to failure to maintain fluid intake. Anyone who has manufactured a renal calculus in the tropics needs to be fully investigated to make sure he has no abnormal calcium metabolism or any other problem likely to encourage stone formation.

Because of the higher incidence of stone formation, nephrectomy for any condition at all, including trauma, must preclude service in hot climates. One ureteric calculus could be fatal, especially if medical facilities were indifferent. Similarly any congenital renal abnormalities which lead to urinary statis and hence to calculi should also be excluded.

Diseases of Metabolism and the Endocrine System

Diabetes mellitus is another of the conditions in which permanent essential drug supply in the form of insulin is a factor. Here again once more there is the point that a diabetic must remain close to very adequate medical facilities where they can deal with hypoglycaemia or hyperglycaemia. Also the problem of any need for surgical interference. As such they must not be considered for any projects remote from good facilities and adequate insulin supply. Thyrotoxicosis is always made worse in a tropical environment. The opposite, the myxoedematous, can not cope either with the excess heat.

Excessive obesity renders anyone quite unsuitable for residence in tropical climates.

Diseases of the Haematopoietic System

Haemophilia is normally an absolute bar unless the person is going to live entirely where there are very good medical facilities which can deal with him adequately in his emergencies. Even so it may be in a place where such treatment could be costly, especially if recurrent.

Anaemia must be seriously considered. Obviously having found the applicant to be anaemic then the next thing is to find out why. If it is a secondary iron deficiency microcytic anaemia due to bleeding from a chronic peptic ulcer, haemorrhoids or menorrhagia the primary condition must be treated satisfactorily before the patient is allowed to go abroad. If it is of a primary macrocytic type then the necessary treatment such as vitamin B_{12} should be instituted and the blood picture be satisfactory again before travel.

Leukaemia and Hodgkin's disease are again problems like malignant disease in that they require frequent and regular follow up preferably at the centre in the patient's home country where they were first treated. As well as this there is the very definite problem of probable reduced immunity.

Tropical Diseases

In World War Two in the services it was said that there were only three guaranteed 'Blighty' illnesses for servicemen serving overseas. They were psychosis, tuberculosis and blackwater fever. The first two have been discussed. A psychotic should not go back overseas. A patient cured of tuberculosis can now go back after a comparatively long interval. Someone who has suffered from blackwater fever must never go back to a malarious area. This is quite final.

Skin Conditions

Infected psoriasis does very badly in the tropics while psoriasis itself does very well. As such any infected condition must be cleared up prior to going overseas.

Any skin condition which interferes with the ability to sweat freely is a natural bar to residence in the tropics. Acne vulgaris with extensive scarring as a residuum, so upsetting natural sweating, can cause a problem. Besides the problem of scarring it has been put forward as a theory that with acne there is an imbalance in the androgen/oestrogen ratio which might aid keratinisation of the ducts and pores of some sweat glands with the result that occlusion occurs when waterlogged during profuse sweating.

Severe seborrhoeic dermatitis is another bar to the tropics as it always does badly there and here again the sweating mechanism can be upset. Congenital ectodermal dysplasia is a rare condition but it is an absolute bar to residence in warm climates because in this condition the sweat glands are defective if not completely absent depending on the severity of the condition. On the other hand excess sweating, although excellent in preventing heat disorders, may well make life intolerable for others. The true sufferer from hyperidrosis can be a social problem in the tropics. Similarly his skin can become so continuously sodden that maceration will occur. Along with this condition, if there is any evidence of an epidermophytosis infection then the whole situation becomes most unpleasant with a foul smell. As such any condition like this is an excluder from tropical climates. Cheiropompholyx, if severe, can be a necessary bar.

Surgical Conditions

This section mainly recapitulates items that have occurred in other sections but one puts together conditions which should be treated surgically before the patient goes abroad.

Renal calculi are one of the first one must consider. If there is any possibility of renal calculi becoming ureteric calculi they must be removed surgically first. As well as this, as stated previously, anyone suffering from this condition must be fully investigated before going abroad to make sure they are not likely to continue to make stones in the heat. Prostatic enlargement must be treated as well as urine stasis is bad.

Any simple herniation of the peritoneal cavity such as inguinal and femoral herniae must be treated surgically before going abroad. Chronic suppurative otitis media is a condition which must be very seriously considered as a bar to the tropics in that it frequently deteriorates in this type of climate, especially if it is humid.

Strictly anyone with a perforated drum and a discharge should not be allowed to go to the tropics until the infection has been cleared up and preferably the perforation healed. In view of the severity of some tropical external otitis with its ability to perforate a drum, anyone who is completely deaf in one ear can be considered as a dubious problem. A further ear condition which can cause a problem in the tropics if severe is Menière's disease due to the essential need in this condition to maintain a satisfactory salt balance. Splenectomised patients have a decreased resistance to malaria and so their acceptance in highly endemic areas must be open to doubt. The amputee is another serious problem with the difficulties of excess sweating and skin maceration in the shell of the prosthesis.

Educational Problems in Handicapped Children

Under the welfare state in the United Kingdom free or subsidised special education is probably better than in any other country in the world. Other developed countries have excellent facilities but in general they are expensive. As such every effort should be made to persuade parents of these children to remain in the U.K. for the special education of their children. Such conditions include all forms of mental deficiency, educationally subnormal children, dyslexia, spastic disease, partial and complete blindness, partial and complete deafness, mutism and all other severe physical disabilities including phocomelia.

By careful selection one should avoid costly repatriation. In Malcolm's article to which reference has already been made it is interesting that he stresses that psychiatric problems are so often the cause of repatriation. He puts the question 'Will his psyche and his circulation stand the strain?' This is very true and apt.

Some of the diseases one has mentioned are absolute bars to residence in warm climates but others are only in a matter of degree but all of them have to be considered very seriously.

A. Vaccination Requirements for, and Climate of Various Countries

After the name of each country, paragraph A states the vaccination requirements on January 1st, 1975, and paragraph B briefly states the usual climate. Asterisk, thus*, signifies that transiting, without leaving the airport, exempts one from the regulation.

As of January 1st, 1975, the following countries have been declared to be infected areas:

Cholera

Africa

Angola, Cameroon, Chad, Dahomey, Ghana, Liberia, Malawi, Mali, Mozambique, Niger, Nigeria, Rhodesia, Upper Volta.

Asia

Bangladesh, Burma, India, Indonesia, Khmer Republic, Malaysia, Nepal, Philippines, Sri Lanka, Thailand.

Smallpox

Africa

Ethiopia

Asia

Bangladesh, India, Nepal, Pakistan.

Yellow Fever

Africa

Angola, Ghana, Nigeria, Sierra Leone, Sudan, Zaire.

South America

Bolivia, Brazil, Colombia.

However, vaccination requirements for various countries are liable to change at short notice, and the following information is a guide only for travellers. As such, the author and publishers can not accept responsibility for errors or omissions or their consequences. Final confirmation can be obtained by contacting the respective Embassies or High Commissions. Vaccinations are required for infants if no minimum age limit is stated.

Afars and Issas (formerly French Somaliland)

A. *Smallpox*. Exempt are children under three months. Otherwise, everyone.

B. Hot and dry.

Afghanistan

A. **Smallpox.*
Cholera. If arriving within five days from or departing to India or Pakistan.
B. Hot in the summer (July-August). Cold in the winter. Rainy season, March and April.

Albania

A. **Smallpox.* If arriving within 14 days after leaving or transiting all countries, excluding Europe, Oceania, Canada, China, North Korea, Morocco, Turkey, U.S.A. and North Vietnam.
Yellow Fever. If arriving within six days after leaving or transiting infected areas.
B. Mediterranean type. Fairly dry on coast, but cooler and wetter inland.

Algeria

A. **Smallpox.* If arriving within 14 days after leaving or transiting all countries, excluding those in Europe, Canada, Morocco, Tunisia and U.S.A.
**Cholera.* Recommended.
**Yellow Fever.* If arriving within six days after leaving or transiting infected areas. Children under one year exempt.
B. Mediterranean on coast, with hot summers and mild winters. Hot and dry inland.

Angola

A. *Smallpox.* Everyone except children under three months.
Yellow Fever. If arriving within six days after leaving or transiting infected areas. Recommended for all other passengers. Children under one year exempt.
B. Tropical; hot and humid.

Argentina

A. *Smallpox.*
B. Subtropical in North. Subantarctic in South. All variations in between. Buenos Aires can be very hot and humid between December and March.

Australia

A. *Quarantine.* Passengers without valid cholera, smallpox or yellow fever certificates, or proof of no active pulmonary tuberculosis (required on immigration) are subject to quarantine.
Doctors' certificates stating that vaccination would be injurious to health does not necessarily absolve passengers from quarantine (e.g. smallpox, see below). Examples of such cases which are still liable to quarantine if arriving from a proclaimed infected area are those with conditions which contra indicate smallpox vaccination, pregnant women, and those holding certificate of exemption from smallpox vaccination for travel by sea. This does not authorise entry into Australia by air.

Smallpox. Exemptions are:

1. Those who spent the last 14 days before arrival in Australia in American Samoa, Antarctic Territories, Australia, Canada, Christmas (Indian Ocean) and Cocos (Keeling) Islands, Cook Islands, Fiji, French Polynesia, Gilbert and Ellice Islands Colony (including Ocean and Fanning Islands), Hawaii, Lord Howe Island, Nauru, New Caledonia, New Hebrides, New Zealand, Niue, Norfolk Island, Papua and New Guinea, Society Archipelago, Solomon Islands, Tokelau Islands, Tonga, U.S.A., Western Samoa. However, vaccination required for all infected areas. Full quarantine requirements are strictly enforced for passengers originating in the U.S.A. or Canada who travel to Australia other than by the direct Trans Pacific route.

2. Children under one year.

3. Travellers who cannot be vaccinated because of a medical condition may be exempt under the following conditions:

a. Must have a medical certificate issued within the 12 months before embarkation and signed by a registered medical practitioner stating that vaccination against smallpox was unadvisable due to a medical condition. The condition must be specified and only the following are recognised by the Australian Health Authorities. These conditions are pregnancy, eczema or other skin condition considered by the traveller's doctor as a contra indication, states of immunological deficiency which are either subsequent to treatment depressing immunity such as deep x-ray therapy, corticosteroids, alkylating or cytotoxic drugs or due to hypogammaglobulinaemic conditions such as nephrosis, organ transplants and general malignant disease. In addition, travellers accompanied by a doctor or nurse for whom hospital care is likely for 14 or more days after arrival would be exempted.

b. The passenger has not come from a country where smallpox was endemic, or where the disease has not been recorded in the previous 12 months, except in direct transit.

Cholera. If arriving within six days after departure from countries any part of which is infected. Exempt are children under 12 months.

Yellow Fever. Everyone regardless of age coming from a proclaimed yellow fever infected area or endemic zone. Violators will be isolated for up to six days.

Austria

A. **Smallpox.* If arriving within 14 days after leaving or transiting infected areas and countries in Africa (except Algeria, Egypt, Libyan Arab Republic, Morocco, Tunisia), in America (except Canada, U.S.A.) and Asia (except Israel, Jordan, Lebanon, Syria, Turkey and U.S.S.R.). Exempt are children under one year.

B. Temperate. Cold at altitude in the winter.

Bahamas

A. **Smallpox.* Unless the 14 days prior to arrival have been spent in countries outside infected areas.

**Yellow Fever.* If arriving within six days of leaving or transiting infected areas.

B. Subtropical. Fairly high humidity.

Bahrain

A. **Smallpox.*

**Yellow Fever.* If arriving within six days after leaving or transiting infected areas. Children under one year are exempt.

B. July-October. Very hot and humid. Rest of the year, mild to warm, but may be cold in January and February.

Bangladesh

A. **Smallpox.* Also required for those leaving Bangladesh.

**Cholera.* Recommended for all passengers.

**Yellow Fever.* If arriving within nine days after leaving or transiting infected areas.

B. Hot and humid. Very hot and very humid immediately prior to monsoon, which is generally July-September.

Barbados

A. **Smallpox.* Required except if last 14 days prior to arrival were spent in Antigua, Bahamas, Bermuda, British Virgin Islands, Canada, Dominica, Grenada, Montserrat, St Kitts-Nevis-Anguilla, St Lucia, St Vincent, Trinidad and Tobago, U.S.A. Children under one year exempt.

**Yellow Fever.* If arriving within six days after leaving or transiting infected areas. Children under one year exempt.

B. Semi-tropical. Maximum temperature varies very little, usually being in the eighties Fahrenheit. Rain, June-November (heaviest, August-November). Fairly humid.

Belgium

A. **Smallpox.* Required if arriving within 14 days after leaving or transiting all countries outside Europe *except* Algeria, Azores, Bermuda, Canada, Canary Islands, Caribbean Islands, Egypt, French Guiana, Greenland, Guadeloupe, Guyana, Israel, Libyan Arab Republic, Maderia, Martinique, Mexico, Morocco, Netherlands Antilles, Réunion, St Pierre and Miquelon, Surinam, Tunisia, Turkey, U.S.A., U.S.S.R. Australia, Japan and New Zealand are also excluded if travelling via transpolar, transpacific or transsiberian routes.

B. Temperate.

Belize

A. **Smallpox.*

**Yellow Fever.* If arriving within six days after leaving or transiting infected areas.

B. Tropical, hot and humid.

Bermuda

A. **Smallpox.* Required except for those who have spent the 14 days prior to arrival in Aruba, Bahamas, Barbados, Bonaire, British Virgin Islands, Canada, Cayman Islands, Curacao, Dominica, Dominican Republic, Greenland, Grenada, Haiti, Iceland, Jamaica, Mexico, Montserrat, Panama

Canal Zone, Puerto Rico, St Kitts, St Lucia, St Pierre and Miquelon, St Vincent, Trinidad and Tobago, U.S.A.

B. Semi-tropical but cold winds prevail, especially in September.

Bhutan

A. *Smallpox.*

Cholera. If arriving within five days after leaving or transiting an infected area. Recommended for all.

Yellow Fever. If arriving within six days after leaving or transiting an infected area.

B. Varies according to altitude. In the South, hot and humid in summer. In the North, in the mountains, cold in the winter.

Bolivia

A. *Smallpox.*

N.B. The above requirements are necessary for all passengers who are only transiting Bolivia.

B. Entirely dependent on altitude. Can be tropical, temperate or cold.

Botswana

A. *Smallpox.*

Yellow Fever. If arriving after leaving or transiting infected areas. Children under one year exempt provided they have a medical certificate of contraindication.

B. Sub-tropical. Low humidity.

Brazil

A. **Smallpox.* Children under three months are exempt.

**Yellow Fever.* If arriving in Belem area only within six days of leaving or transiting infected areas.

N.B. Also required, *poliomyelitis*—all children from three months to six years inclusive who are returning to live in Brazil. X-ray of chest for all temporary visitors other than tourists.

B. All variations, from tropical in the North to cool in the South. Rain throughout the year.

British Honduras—see Belize.

British Solomon Islands Protectorate

A. *Smallpox.* If arriving within 14 days after leaving or transiting countries outside Australia, Cook Islands, Fiji, French Polynesia, Gilbert and Ellice Islands, Nauru, New Caledonia, New Hebrides, New Zealand, Niue, Norfolk and Tokelau Islands, Samoa (American and Western) and Tonga. If travel from Australia is via Papua-New Guinea, with or without stopover, vaccination is required.

**Cholera.* If arriving within five days after leaving or transiting infected areas. Exempt are children under six months.

**Yellow Fever.* If arriving within six days after leaving or transiting infected areas.

B. Tropical. hot and humid. Wettest, December-March.

Brunei

A. *Smallpox.*

**Cholera.* If arriving within five days after leaving or transiting infected areas. Persons without a cholera certificate, when required, are liable to quarantine.

**Yellow Fever.* If arriving within six days after leaving or transiting infected areas. Children under one year are exempt.

Bulgaria

A. *Smallpox.* Required except if immediate 14 days prior to arrival have been spent in Europe, Canada or U.S.A. Children under six months exempt.

B. Hot and dry in summer. Cold in winter.

Burma

A. *Smallpox.* (Also for everyone leaving Burma.)

Cholera. Only if leaving Burma for a country requiring a certificate.

Yellow Fever. If arriving within nine days after leaving or transiting infected and endemic areas.

B. Tropical. Hot, February-May. Monsoon, May-October. Warm, November-January. Rainfall may be over 20 inches per month in June, July and August. Humidity is always high.

Burundi

A. **Smallpox.* Children under three months exempt.

**Cholera.* If arriving within five days after leaving or transiting infected areas. Children under six months exempt.

**Yellow Fever.* If arriving within six days after leaving or transiting infected areas. Children under one year are exempt.

N.B. Local authorities recommend vaccination against typhoid, paratyphoid and typhus.

B. Tropical. Hot and humid.

Cameroon

A. **Smallpox.* If arriving within five days after leaving or transiting countries, any parts of which are infected areas.

Cholera. If arriving within five days after leaving or transiting infected areas. Also if leaving for an infected area.

Yellow Fever. Children under one year and visitors staying less than 15 days are exempt.

B. Tropical. Hot. Very humid in the South; less so on the plateau.

Canada

A. **Smallpox.* If arriving within 14 days after leaving or transiting infected areas or any country habitually infected.

B. Complete variation according to time of year and position. From very hot to very cold.

Canary Islands

A. **Smallpox*. Required, unless 14 days immediately prior to arrival were spent in Europe, Morocco, U.S.A. or U.S.S.R. Children under six months are exempt.

**Yellow Fever*. If arriving within six days after leaving or transiting infected areas.

B. Generally warm and dry.

Cape Verde Islands

A. **Smallpox*. Children under three months exempt.

**Cholera*. Children under three months are exempt.

**Yellow Fever*. If arriving within six days after leaving or transiting infected areas. Not required for entering Sao Vicente, Sal, Maio, Boa Vista and Santiago. Children under one year are exempt.

B. Generally moderately warm and dry.

Cayman Islands

A. **Smallpox*. If arriving within 14 days after leaving or transiting all countries other than Canada, the U.S.A. and the continent of Europe.

B. Subtropical to tropical. Torrential showers. Humidity fairly high.

Central African Republic

A. *Smallpox*.

Cholera. If arriving within five days after leaving or transiting infected areas.

Yellow Fever. Children under one year are exempt.

N.B. The above requirements are necessary for all passengers who are only transiting the Central African Republic.

B. Hot and humid.

Chad

A. *Smallpox*. Children under one year exempt.

**Cholera*. If arriving within five days after leaving or transiting infected areas.

Yellow Fever. For those arriving within six days after leaving or transiting infected areas, including airport transit. However, it is recommended for all passengers. Children under one year are exempt.

B. Tropical. Very hot in northern desert.

Chile

A. **Smallpox*. Required for everyone, including airport transit passengers.

N.B. A general certificate of health may be required, even for a transit visa.

B. Tropical in the North. Very cold in the South. Rainy season, May-August.

Chinese People's Republic

A. *Smallpox*.

Cholera. If arriving within five days after leaving or transiting infected areas, plus Burma, India, Indonesia, Malaysia, Pakistan, Philippines, Singapore, Thailand. Required for passengers in transit.

Yellow Fever. If arriving within six days after leaving or transiting infected areas, plus all countries in Africa, Central and South America.

B. Climate can vary from one extreme to the other.

Colombia

A. **Smallpox*. Children under three months are exempt.

B. Tropical, but temperature varies according to altitude; but little variation throughout the year.

Comores Islands

A. **Smallpox*.

B. Tropical. April-October, warm and fairly dry. November-March, very hot; humid; rain.

Congo (Brazzaville)

A. **Smallpox*. Children under six months are exempt.

Yellow Fever. If arriving within six days after leaving or transiting infected areas, plus Central African Republic, Chad or Gabon. Also all passengers staying in Congo (Brazzaville) longer than two weeks. Children under one year are exempt.

B. Tropical. Hot and humid.

Cook Islands

A. *Smallpox*. Required if arriving by aircraft or ship from countries in South America and Asia, and by aircraft only from all other countries.

B. Tropical. Wet, December-March. Dry, April-November.

Costa Rica

A. *Smallpox*. Including transit passengers.

B. Subtropical. Little variation throughout the year.

Cuba

A. **Smallpox*.

**Yellow Fever*. If arriving within six days after leaving or transiting infected areas plus the following countries: In Africa: Angola, Burundi, Cameroon, Central African Republic, Chad, Congo (Brazzaville), Dahomey, Ethiopia, Gabon, Gambia, Ghana, Guinea, Kenya, Liberia, Mali, Mauritania, Niger, Nigeria, Portuguese Guinea, Rwanda, Sao Tóme and Principe, Senegal, Sierra Leone, Somalia, Tanzania Togo, Uganda, Upper Volta, Zaire, Zambia. In America: Bolivia, Brazil, Colombia, Ecuador, French Guiana, Guyana, Panama, Peru, Surinam, Venezuela.

B. Subtropical. Rainy season May-October.

Cyprus

A. **Smallpox.* Required except if immediate last 14 days before arrival have been spent in Europe or North America. Children under one year are exempt.

**Yellow Fever.* If arriving within six days after leaving or transiting infected areas.

B. Mediterranean. Summers hot and dry but increased humidity at coast.

Czechoslovakia

A. **Smallpox.* Required except if last 14 days have been spent in Canada, Cuba, European countries, U.S.A., Turkey, Mongolian People's Republic or the U.S.S.R.

B. Warm summers; cold winters.

Dahomey

A. **Smallpox.* Required for those arriving within 14 days after leaving or transiting infected areas, and also travellers staying in Dahomey more than two weeks. Children under one year are exempt.

Yellow Fever. Required for those arriving within six days after leaving or transiting infected areas plus all travellers staying in Dahomey more than two weeks.

B. Tropical. Hot and humid. Cooler in North.

Denmark

A. **Smallpox.* Required if arriving within 14 days of leaving or transiting any country other than Azores, Canada, Canary Islands, Madeira, Morocco, U.S.A. or U.S.S.R. and European countries.

B. Temperate.

Dominican Republic

A. **Smallpox.* Required unless last 14 days have been spent in the U.S.A.

B. Tropical. Little variation in year.

Ecuador

A. **Smallpox.*

**Yellow Fever.* If arriving within six days after leaving or transiting infected areas.

B. Subtropical on coast. Tropical inland. Temperate in mountains.

Egypt

A. **Smallpox.* If arriving within 14 days after leaving or transiting infected areas *and* if leaving Egypt. Children under three months are exempt.

**Cholera.* If arriving within five days after leaving or transiting infected areas. Children under one year exempt.

**Yellow Fever.* If arriving within six days after leaving or transiting infected areas plus the following countries:

In Africa: Angola, Botswana, Burundi, Cameroon, Central African Republic, Chad, Congo (Brazzaville), Dahomey, Equatorial Guinea, Ethiopia,

Gabon, Gambia, Ghana, Guinea, Ivory Coast, Kenya, Liberia, Malawi, Mali, Mauritania, Niger, Nigeria, Portuguese Guinea, Rwanda, Sao Tóme and Principe, Senegal, Sierra Leone, Somalia, Súdan (South of 15°N), Tanzania, Togo, Uganda, Upper Volta, Zaire, Zambia.

In America: Bolivia, Brazil, British Honduras, Colombia, Costa Rica, Ecuador, French Guiana, Guatemala, Guyana, Honduras (Republic), Nicaragua, Panama, Panama Canal Zone, Peru, Surinam, Trinidad, Venezuela.

Passengers coming from Khartoum (not in the Yellow Fever Zone) must hold a certificate from the Sudan Medical Authorities dated the day before or day of departure certifying that the traveller has not been south of 15°N within six days of embarkation.

N.B. Lack of valid certificates render travellers to quarantine.

B. Cool and dry winters; hot and fairly dry summers.

Equatorial Guinea

A. **Smallpox*.

**Yellow Fever*. If arriving within six days after leaving or transiting infected areas.

B. Tropical. Hot and humid. Drier in North.

Ethiopia

A. **Smallpox*. Also when leaving Ethiopia.

Yellow Fever. Also when leaving Ethiopia.

N.B. Invalid certificates may cause quarantine or deportation.

B. Lowlands hot and humid. Hill country warm and pleasant. Central uplands cool.

Fiji

A. **Smallpox*. Required if arriving by air unless last 14 days spent in Australia, British Solomon Islands, Cook Islands, French Polynesia, Gilbert and Ellice Islands, Nauru, New Caledonia. New Hebrides, New Zealand, Niue, Norfolk and Tokelau Islands, Samoa (American and Western), or Tonga. Required by passengers arriving from India by sea or air.

Cholera. If arriving within five days after leaving or transiting infected areas. Children under one year exempt.

Yellow Fever. If arriving by air within six days after leaving or transiting infected areas. Children under one year exempt.

B. Tropical. Very humid in Suva. Drier on Nandi coast. Monsoon November-May.

Finland

A. **Smallpox*. Required if arriving within 14 days after leaving or transiting all countries excluding Europe, Azores, Canada, Canary Islands, Madeira, Morocco, U.S.A. and U.S.S.R.

B. Summer mild. Winter very cold.

France

A. **Smallpox*. Required if arriving after leaving or transiting all infected areas plus countries outside Europe except Algeria, Azores, Bermuda,

Canada, Canary Islands, Caribbean Islands, French Guiana, Greenland, Guadeloupe, Guyana, Israel, Libyan Arab Republic, Madeira, Martinique, Mexico, Morocco, Netherlands Antilles, Réunion. St Pierre and Miquelon, Surinam. Tunisia, U.S.A. and U.S.S.R.

Australia, Japan and New Zealand also excluded if arriving by transpolar, transpacific or transsiberia routes.

B. Temperate in the North to Mediterranean in the South.

French Guiana

A. **Smallpox*. Regulations as for France.

**Yellow Fever*. If arriving after leaving or transiting infected areas and for all arrivals staying in French Guiana for more than two weeks. Children under one year exempt.

B. Tropical. Hot and humid.

French Polynesia

A. **Smallpox*. Required unless last 14 days prior to arrival were spent in Australia, British Solomon Islands, Cook Islands, Fiji, Gilbert and Ellice Islands, Nauru, New Caledonia, New Hebrides, New Zealand, Samoa (American and Western) and Tonga.

**Yellow Fever*. If arriving within 14 days after leaving or transiting infected areas. Children under one year exempt.

B. Subtropical. Little variation. Occasional storms.

French West Indies

A. **Smallpox*. As for France.

B. Subtropical. Sunny but some wind. Rain August-November.

Gabon

A. **Smallpox*. Required for everyone except children under one year.

**Yellow Fever*. If arriving within six days after leaving or transiting infected areas or if staying in Gabon for longer than two weeks. Children under six months exempt.

B. Tropical. Hot and humid.

Gambia

A. **Smallpox*. Also if leaving Gambia. Exempt are children under one year.

Cholera. If arriving within five days after leaving or transiting infected areas.

**Yellow Fever*. If arriving within six days after leaving or transiting infected areas. Children under one year are exempt.

B. Tropical. In general, hot and humid.

Germany—Berlin (East)

See German Democratic Republic (East).

Germany—Berlin (West)

See German Federal Republic (West).

German Democratic Republic (East)

A. **Smallpox*. If arriving within five days from or via infected areas and countries in Africa, America (except Canada and U.S.A.) and Asia (except Asiatic part of U.S.S.R.).

B. Temperate. Warm summers. Fairly cold winters.

German Federal Republic (West)

A. **Smallpox*. If arriving by air within 14 days after leaving or transiting infected areas and countries in Asia (except U.S.S.R.), Africa (except Azores, Canary Islands, Madeira) and America (except U.S.A. and Canada).

B. Temperate. Warm summers. Fairly cold winters.

Ghana

A. **Smallpox*. Children under one year exempt.

**Yellow Fever*. If arriving after leaving or transiting infected areas but recommended for all passengers. May be required on leaving Ghana. Children under one year exempt.

B. Tropical. Hot and humid, except in the North where it is dry.

Gibraltar

A. **Smallpox*. If arriving within 14 days after leaving or transiting an infected area.

B. Temperate. Warm summers. Cool winters.

Gilbert and Ellice Islands

A. **Smallpox*. If arriving within 14 days after leaving or transiting any country other than Australia, British Solomon Islands, Cook Islands, Fiji, French Polynesia, Nauru, New Caledonia, New Hebrides, New Zealand, Niue, Norfolk and Tokelau Islands, Samoa (American and Western) and Tonga.

**Cholera*. If arriving within five days after leaving or transiting infected areas. Children under six months are exempt.

**Yellow Fever*. If arriving within six days after leaving or transiting infected areas. Children under one year are exempt.

B. Hot. Humid December-March.

Greece

A. **Smallpox*. If arriving within 14 days after leaving or transiting infected areas, also countries outside Europe except Algeria, Australia (if via transpolar, transpacific or transsiberian flights), Azores, Bermuda, Canada, Canary Islands, Carribean Islands, French Guiana, Greenland, Guadeloupe, Guyana, Japan (if via transpolar, transpacific or transsiberian flights), Libyan Arab Republic, Madeira, Martinique, Mexico, Morocco, Netherlands Antilles, New Zealand (if via transpolar, transpacific or transsiberian flights), Réunion, St Pierre and Miquelon, Surinam, Tunisia, U.S.A. and U.S.S.R.

**Yellow Fever*. If arriving within six days after leaving or transiting infected areas. Children under six months are exempt.

B. Mediterranean, but cold in winter in North. In South in summer the temperature may rise to 110°F. Rain November-March.

Guam

A. For requirements see U.S.A.
B. Tropical. Hot and humid.

Guatemala

A. **Smallpox.*
B. Coastal, hot and humid. Mountains, cool and dry.

Guinea (Republic of)

A. **Smallpox.*
Cholera.
**Yellow Fever.* If arriving within six days after leaving or transiting infected areas, also for anyone staying in Guinea for longer than two weeks.
B. Tropical. Hot and humid. Drier in North.

Guyana

A. **Smallpox.* Children under three months are exempt.
Yellow Fever. If arriving within six days after leaving or transiting infected areas plus:
In Africa: Angola, Burundi, Cameroon, Central African Republic, Chad, Congo (Brazzaville), Dahomey, Ethiopia, Gabon, Gambia, Ghana, Guinea, Kenya, Liberia, Mali, Niger, Nigeria, Portuguese Guinea, Rwanda, Sao Tóme and Principe, Senegal, Sierra Leone, Somalia, Togo, Uganda, United Republic of Tanzania, Upper Volta and Zaire.
In America: Bolivia, Brazil, British Honduras, Colombia, Costa Rica, Ecuador, French Guiana, Guatemala, Honduras, Nicaragua, Panama, Peru, Surinam, Venezuela.
N.B. Passengers without valid certificate will not be allowed to disembark.
B. Tropical. Hot and humid.

Haiti

A. **Smallpox.* Required for everyone except if last 14 days prior to departure for Haiti were spent in the U.S.A.
**Cholera.* If arriving within five days after leaving or transiting infected areas.
**Yellow Fever.* If arriving within six days after leaving or transiting infected areas.
B. Subtropical. Cooler in mountains.

Honduras (Republic of)

A. **Smallpox.* Everyone except children under six months.
**Yellow Fever.* If arriving within six days after leaving or transiting infected areas.
B. Tropical. Hot and humid on coast. Cooler in mountains.

Hong Kong

A. **Smallpox.*

N.B. Refusal to be vaccinated or inoculated on arriving if required will lead to quarantine, or refusal to land.

B. Subtropical. Summer hot and humid. Winter sunny and dry.

Hungary

A. **Smallpox.* If arriving within 14 days after leaving or transiting any infected area plus all countries except those in Europe plus Canada, Mongolia, U.S.A. and U.S.S.R.

**Cholera.* If arriving within five days after leaving or transiting countries in which any part is an infected area. Children under six months are exempt.

B. Summer very warm. Winter very cold.

Iceland

A. **Smallpox.* If arriving within 14 days after leaving or transiting any infected area plus all countries excluding Europe, the Azores, Canada, Canary Islands, Madeira, Morocco, U.S.A. and U.S.S.R.

B. Temperate with cool summers. Strong winds and gales in the winter.

India

A. *Smallpox.* Recommended for everyone.

Cholera. Recommended for everyone.

Yellow Fever. If arriving within six days after leaving or transiting infected areas or any one of the following countries—including not leaving the airport.

Africa: Angola, Botswana, Burundi, Cameroon, Central African Republic, Chad, Congo (Brazzaville), Dahomey, Equatorial Guinea, Ethiopia, Gabon, Gambia, Ghana, Guinea, Ivory Coast, Kenya, Liberia, Malawi, Mali, Mauritania, Niger, Nigeria, Portuguese Guinea, Rwanda, Sao Tóme and Principe, Senegal, Sierra Leone, Somalia, Sudan (South of 15°N), Tanzania, Togo, Uganda, Upper Volta, Zaire, Zambia.

America: Bolivia, Brazil, British Honduras, Colombia, Costa Rica, Ecuador, French Guiana, Guatemala, Guyana, Honduras (Republic), Nicaragua, Panama, Panama Canal Zone, Peru, Surinam, Trinidad and Tobago, Venezuela.

B. Considerable variation. Very hot immediately prior to monsoon. Monsoon in Delhi, Bombay and Calcutta June-September. Madras heaviest October-November.

Indonesia

A. **Smallpox.* Everyone except children under one year.

Yellow Fever. If arriving within six days after leaving or transiting infected areas.

B. Tropical. Dry May-September. Wet October-April.

Iran

A. **Smallpox.*

Cholera. (1) If arriving within five days after leaving or transiting an infected area or from Afghanistan, Burma, India, Italy, Malawi, Malaysia, Pakistan,

Philippines, Singapore, Thailand, Tunisia, Vietnam (South). (2) Also if the aircraft has transited an infected area. Children under six months are exempt.

**Yellow Fever.* If arriving within six days after leaving or transiting infected areas. Children under one year are exempt.

N.B. Authorities are very strict on regulations. Passengers without valid certificates are subject to quarantine.

B. High plateau. Warm spring; hot summer; cold winter. Coast areas hot and humid.

Iraq

A. **Smallpox.* If arriving within 14 days after leaving or transiting infected areas. Children under one year are exempt.

**Yellow Fever.* If arriving within six days after leaving or transiting infected areas.

B. Summers extremely hot and dry except coast (Basra) which is humid. Winters cool to cold.

Ireland (Republic of)

A. **Smallpox.* If arriving within 14 days after leaving or transiting infected areas plus countries in Africa (except Algeria, Azores, Canary Islands, Libyan Arab Republic, Madeira, Morocco, Réunion, Tunisia) and in America (except Bermuda, Canada, French Guiana, Greenland, Guadeloupe, Martinique, Netherlands Antilles, St Pierre and Miquelon, Surinam and U.S.A.).

B. As in U.K. but slightly milder.

Israel

A. **Smallpox.* If arriving within 14 days after leaving or transiting countries, any part of which are infected areas.

B. Mediterranean. Humidity fairly high in summer.

Italy

A. **Smallpox.* If arriving within 14 days after leaving or transiting infected areas plus countries outside Europe except Algeria, Australia, Azores, Bermuda, Canada, Canary Islands, Caribbean Islands, French Guiana, Greenland, Guadeloupe, Guyana, Israel, Japan, Libyan Arab Republic, Madeira, Martinique, Mexico, Morocco, Netherlands Antilles, New Zealand, Réunion, St Pierre and Miquelon, Surinam, Tunisia, U.S.A. and U.S.S.R.

**Cholera.* If arriving within five days after leaving or transiting countries, any part of which is an infected area. Children under one year are exempt.

B. Mediterranean. Winters can be cold in the North.

Ivory Coast

A. **Smallpox.* Also when leaving Ivory Coast.

Yellow Fever. Children under one year are exempt.

B. Hot and very humid at coast. Drier in North.

Jamaica

A. **Smallpox.* If arriving from any country other than Aruba, Bahamas, Bermuda, British Virgin Islands, Canada, Cuba, Curacao and the U.S.A.

*Cholera. If arriving within five days after leaving or transiting infected areas. Children under one year are exempt.

**Yellow Fever.* If arriving within six days after leaving or transiting infected areas. Children under one year are exempt.

B. Tropical and humid at coast. Subtropical and humid inland.

Japan

A. **Smallpox.* Children under one year are exempt.

B. Very cold in the North in winter: subtropical in the South in summer. Hot and humid July and August.

Jordan

A. **Smallpox.* If arriving within 14 days after leaving or transiting infected areas.

**Cholera.* If arriving within five days after leaving or transiting infected areas or the Gulf Area.

B. Extremely hot in the valley of River Jordan. Cooler in the hills; arid.

Kenya

A. **Smallpox.*

**Cholera.* If arriving within five days after leaving or transiting infected areas. Required if not leaving airports in infected areas. Children under one year exempt.

**Yellow Fever.* If arriving within six days after leaving or transiting infected areas. Children under one year are exempt.

In addition, if leaving Kenya and arriving within six days in Australia, Burma, Central African Republic, Cuba, Egypt, Greece, Guyana, India, Indonesia, Iran, Iraq, Ivory Coast, Lebanon, Libyan Arab Republic, Madeira and Azores, Malaysia, Malta, Mauritius, Oman, Nigeria, Pakistan, Papua and New Guinea, Portuguese Guinea, Saudi Arabia, Singapore, South African Republic, South West Africa, Sri Lanka, St Lucia, Sudan. However, it is recommended for all arriving and departing passengers.

N.B. Persons without valid certificates are liable to quarantine.

Authorities also recommend vaccination against typhoid and paratyphoid fevers.

B. Hot and humid at the coast. Hot and dry in the Northern territories. Pleasantly warm in the highlands.

Khmer Republic (formerly Cambodia)

A. **Smallpox.*

**Cholera.* Persons without valid certificates are subject to quarantine.

B. Tropical. Hot and dry November-May. Hot and humid June to October.

Korea (Democratic People's Republic) North

A. *Smallpox.*

Cholera. If arriving within five days after leaving or transiting infected areas.

B. Winters dry and cold. Summers hot. July and August humid.

Korea (Republic) South

A. **Smallpox*. Children under one year are exempt.
B. Winters dry and cold. Summers hot. July and August humid.

Kuwait

A. **Smallpox*. Children under three months are exempt.
**Yellow Fever*. If arriving within six days after leaving or transiting countries, any part of which is infected. Children under one year are exempt.
N.B. Persons without valid certificates are subject to quarantine.
B. Tropical. Extremely hot in summer: humid in August. Winters comparatively cool.

Laos

A. **Smallpox*. Also required for passengers leaving Laos.
**Cholera*. Also required for passengers leaving Laos.
B. Subtropical with great variations. Rainy season August-January.

Lebanon

A. **Smallpox*.
**Yellow Fever*. If arriving within six days after leaving or transiting endemic areas.
B. Mediterranean. Warm winters. Hot summers. Humid at coast. Snow in the mountains.

Leeward Islands

(Anguilla, Antigua, Monserrat, Nevis, St Kitts, and the British Virgin Islands).
A. **Smallpox*. Unless coming directly from stay of at least 14 days in the U.S.A. without leaving airports *en route* in other countries.
**Cholera*. If arriving within five days after leaving or transiting infected areas. Children under one year exempt.
**Yellow Fever*. If arriving within six days after leaving or transiting infected areas. Children under one year exempt.
B. Subtropical. Sunny but some wind. Rain August-November.

Lesotho

A. *Smallpox*. Children under one year are exempt.
Cholera. If arriving within five days after leaving or transiting infected areas.
Yellow Fever. If arriving within 14 days after leaving or transiting infected areas.
B. Subtropical. Rather dry.

Liberia

A. **Smallpox*. Also if leaving Liberia.
**Yellow Fever*.
B. Tropical. Hot and humid.

Libyan Arab Republic

A. **Smallpox.* Children under one year are exempt if coming from a smallpox-free country.

**Yellow Fever.* If arriving within six days after leaving or transiting endemic areas.

B. Mediterranean on the coast. Hot, dry and arid inland.

Luxembourg

A. **Smallpox.* If arriving within 14 days after leaving or transiting infected areas plus countries outside Europe except Algeria, Australia (if via transpolar, transpacific or transsiberian flights), Azores, Bermuda, Canada, Canary Islands, Caribbean Islands, French Guiana, Greenland, Guadeloupe, Guyana, Israel, Japan (if via transpolar, transpacific or transsiberian flights), Libyan Arab Republic, Réunion, St Pierre and Miquelon, Surinam, Tunisia, U.S.A. and U.S.S.R.

B. Temperate. Cool summers and mild winters.

Macao

A. **Smallpox.* Children under three months are exempt.

**Yellow Fever.* If arriving within six days after leaving or transiting infected areas. Children under one year are exempt.

B. Subtropical. Summer hot and humid. Winter sunny and dry.

Malagasy Republic

A. **Smallpox.* Children under three months are exempt.

**Cholera.* If arriving within six days after leaving or transiting infected areas, and sanitary surveillance for the five days following departure from infected areas. Children under six months are exempt.

**Yellow Fever.* If arriving within six days after leaving or transiting infected areas. Children under one year are exempt.

B. Tropical. April-October dry and warm at coast. Cold in the highlands. November-March very hot on the coast: hot inland.

Malawi

A. **Smallpox.* If staying in Malawi for more than one month: but recommended for all.

**Yellow Fever.* If arriving by air after leaving or transiting infected areas.

B. Tropical, but wide variation according to altitude.

Malaysia

A. **Smallpox.* Children under six months are exempt.

**Yellow Fever.* If arriving within six days after leaving or transiting infected areas.

B. Tropical. Hot and humid; little variation in the year.

Mali

A. **Smallpox.*

**Cholera.*

**Yellow Fever.*

B. Tropical. Hot and humid in South. Hot and dry in North.

Malta

A. **Smallpox.* If arriving within 14 days after leaving or transiting infected areas plus all countries in Africa, Asia, and America except U.S.A. and Canada.

**Cholera.* If arriving within five days after leaving or transiting infected areas. Children under six months are exempt.

Yellow Fever. If arriving within six days after leaving or transiting infected areas. Children under six months are exempt.

B. Mediterranean. Hot in summer, cool in winter.

Mauritania

A. **Smallpox.*

**Yellow Fever.* If arriving within six days after leaving or transiting infected areas plus all other passengers staying in Mauritania for longer than two weeks. Children under one year are exempt.

B. Tropical. Hot and humid at the coast. Warm and dry in the north.

Mauritius

A. **Smallpox.* Except if coming from Réunion.

**Cholera.* If arriving within five days after leaving or transiting countries any part of which are infected areas.

**Yellow Fever.* If arriving within six days after leaving or transiting endemic areas. Children under one year are exempt.

B. Tropical maritime, but no extremes. Humid at coast.

Mexico

A. *Smallpox.* Everyone unless last 14 days have been spent in U.S.A. and/or Canada.

B. Varies to extremes with altitude.

Morocco including Tangier

A. **Smallpox.* If arriving within 14 days after leaving or transiting infected areas plus all countries in Africa and Asia.

B. Mediterranean in coastal areas. Hot and arid inland.

Mozambique

A. **Smallpox.* Children under three months are exempt.

**Yellow Fever.* If arriving within six days after leaving or transiting infected areas, plus all passengers staying in Mozambique for more than two weeks. Children under one year are exempt.

B. Tropical. April-September warm and dry. October-March hot, wet and very humid.

Nauru

A. *Smallpox.* If arriving within 14 days after leaving or transiting any country outside Australia, British Solomon Islands, Cook Islands, Fiji, French Polynesia, Gilbert and Ellice Islands, New Caledonia, New Hebrides, New

Zealand, Niue, Norfolk Island, Papua and New Guinea, Samoa (American and Western), Tokelau Islands and Tonga. Children under six months are exempt.

Cholera. If arriving within five days after leaving or transiting infected areas. Children under one year are exempt.

Yellow Fever. If arriving within six days after leaving or transiting infected areas. Children under one year are exempt.

B. Hot and humid. Wettest December-March.

Nepal

A. *Smallpox.*

**Cholera.* If arriving within five days after leaving or transiting infected areas.

**Yellow Fever.* If arriving within six days after leaving or transiting infected areas.

B. Varies greatly—altitude and monsoon.

Netherlands

A. **Smallpox.* If arriving within 14 days after leaving or transiting infected areas, plus all countries outside Europe except Algeria, Australia†, Azores, Bermuda, Canada, Canary Islands, Caribbean Islands, French Guiana, Greenland, Guadeloupe, Guyana, Israel, Japan†, Libyan Arab Republic, Madeira, Martinique, Mexico, Morocco, Netherlands Antilles, New Zealand†, Réunion, St Pierre and Miquelon, Surinam, Tunisia, U.S.A. and U.S.S.R.

B. Cool summers and moderate winters.

Netherlands Antilles

(Aruba, Bonaire, Curacao, Saba, St Eustatius, St Maarten).

A. **Smallpox.* If arriving within 14 days after leaving or transiting infected areas, plus all countries in Africa, America and Asia except Azores, Bahamas, Bermuda, British Virgin Islands, Canada, Canal Zone, Canary Islands, French Guiana, Greenland, Guadeloupe, Jamaica, Madeira, Martinique, Mexico, Puerto Rico, Réunion, St Croix, St John, St Pierre and Miquelon, St Thomas, Surinam, U.S.A. Children under three months are exempt.

**Yellow Fever.* If arriving within six days after leaving or transiting infected areas. Children under six months are exempt.

B. Sunny and pleasant all the year with low humidity.

New Caledonia

A. **Smallpox.* Except for those who have spent the last 14 days before departure to New Caledonia in Australia, British Solomon Islands, Cook Islands, Fiji, French Polynesia, Gilbert and Ellice Islands, Nauru, New Hebrides, New Zealand, Samoa (American and Western), Tonga, provided that there are no infected areas in these countries.

**Yellow Fever.* If arriving within six days after leaving or transiting infected areas.

Recommended: Vaccinations against typhoid and paratyphoid fevers.

B. Tropical. Hot and humid. Cyclones.

†Only if journey has been transpolar, transpacific or transsiberian flight.

New Hebrides

A. **Smallpox*. Except for those who, prior to departure for the New Hebrides, spent the last 14 days in Australia, British Solomon Islands, Cook Islands, Fiji, French Polynesia, Gilbert and Ellice Islands, Hawaiian Islands, Lord Howe Island, Nauru, New Caledonia, New Zealand, Niue, Norfolk Island, Tonga, Samoa (American and Western), provided these areas are free from smallpox. Children under one year are exempt.

**Yellow Fever*. If arriving within six days after leaving or transiting infected areas. Children under one year are exempt.

B. Tropical, hot and humid.

New Zealand

A. *Smallpox*. Except for those who, prior to arrival, have spent the last 14 days in Australia, British Solomon Islands, Canada, Cook Islands, Fiji. French Polynesia, Gilbert and Ellice Islands, Hawaii, Nauru, New Caledonia, New Hebrides, Niue, Norfolk Island, Samoa (American and Western), Tokelau Islands, Tonga and U.S.A., provided there are no infected areas in these countries. Children under three months and those holding medical certificates of contraindication may be accepted. However, they and any without valid certificates may be subject to surveillance or quarantine.

B. Great variation between North and South. Summers generally dry. Snow in winter in South.

Nicaragua

A. **Smallpox*.

B. Tropical. Hot throughout the year. Dry November-May. Wet and humid May-November.

Niger

A. **Smallpox*. Also recommended for those leaving Niger. Children under six months are exempt.

**Yellow Fever*. Children under one year are exempt.

B. Tropical. Hot.

Nigeria

A. **Smallpox*. Also required for persons leaving Nigeria. Children under three months are exempt.

**Cholera*. Also required for persons leaving Nigeria. Children under three months are exempt.

**Yellow Fever*. Also required for persons leaving Nigeria.

B. Hot. Humid in the South: dry in the North.

Niue

A. **Smallpox*. If arriving within 14 days after leaving or transiting any country other than Australia, British Solomon Islands, Fiji, French Polynesia, Gilbert and Ellice Islands, Nauru, New Caledonia, New Hebrides, New Zealand, Norfolk Island, Samoa (American and Western), Tokelau Islands and Tonga.

**Cholera*. If arriving within five days after leaving or transiting infected areas. Children under one year are exempt.

**Yellow Fever*. If arriving within six days after leaving or transiting infected areas. Children under one year are exempt.

B. Tropical. Wet December - March. Dry April - November.

Norfolk Island

A. No health regulations.

B. Tropical. Hot and humid.

Norway

A. **Smallpox*. If arriving within 14 days after leaving or transiting all countries except those in Europe, the Azores, Canada, Canary Islands, Madeira, Morocco, U.S.A. and U.S.S.R. Children under one year are exempt.

B. Summers cool, winters cold.

Oman

A. **Smallpox*.

**Cholera*. If arriving within five days after leaving or transiting infected areas.

**Yellow Fever*. If arriving within six days after leaving or transiting infected areas.

B. Very hot and humid in summer. Mild in winter.

Pakistan

A. **Smallpox*. If arriving within 14 days after leaving or transiting infected areas, but recommended for all passengers.

Cholera. If arriving within 14 days after leaving or transiting infected areas.

With both of the above, passengers leaving Pakistan or changing aircraft must be vaccinated.

Yellow Fever. If arriving within nine days after leaving or transiting endemic or infected areas or one of the non-endemic towns or a country considered as infected by the Government of Pakistan, viz:

In Africa: Angola, Botswana, Burundi, Cameroon, Central African Republic, Chad, Congo (Brazzaville), Dahomey, Equatorial Guinea. Ethiopia, Gabon, Gambia, Ghana, Guinea, Ivory Coast, Kenya, Liberia, Malawi, Mali, Mauritania, Niger, Nigeria, Portuguese Guinea, Rwanda, Sao Tóme and Principe, Senegal, Sierra Leone, Somalia, Sudan (south of 15°N), Tanzania, Togo, Uganda, Upper Volta, Zaire, Zambia.

In America: Bolivia, Brazil, Colombia, Costa Rica, Ecuador, French Guiana, Gautemala, Guyana, Honduras (Republic), Nicaragua, Panama. Panama Canal Zone, Peru, Surinam, Trinidad and Tobago, Venezuela.

Certificates must be in English, stating origin and batch number of vaccine. They must be stamped officially at least ten days prior to arrival in Pakistan.

N.B. Transit in international airports in endemic areas considered exempt by W.H.O. are not so accepted by Pakistan.

Persons without valid yellow fever certificates, when required, are subject to quarantine.

B. Very hot and dry except July - September, when it is humid.

Panama

A. **Smallpox.*
B. Tropical. Hot all the year. Heavy rain October and November.

Papua and New Guinea

A. **Smallpox.* Everyone except those who, for the last 14 days prior to arrival, have been in Antarctic Regions, Australia, Christmas Islands, Cook Islands, Fiji, Gilbert and Ellice Islands, Lord Howe Island, Nauru, New Caledonia, New Hebrides, New Zealand, Niue, Norfolk Island, Society Archipeligo, Samoa (American and Western), Tonga. Children under six months are exempt.

**Cholera.* Everyone except those who, for the last seven days, have been in the following countries, and if these countries are free of cholera: Australia, Australian Antarctic Territories, Cook Islands, Fiji, Gilbert and Ellice Islands, Lord Howe Island, Nauru, New Zealand, Norfolk Island, Samoa (American and Western), Society Archipelago and Tonga. Children under six months are exempt.

**Yellow Fever.* If arriving within six days after leaving or transiting infected and endemic areas.

B. Hot. Humid December-March.

Paraguay

A. **Smallpox.* Children under six months are exempt.

**Yellow Fever.* If arriving within six days after leaving or transiting infected areas.

B. Subtropical. Sunny and warm.

Peru

A. **Smallpox.* Everyone. Children under six months are exempt.

**Yellow Fever.* If arriving within six months after leaving or transiting infected areas. Children under six months are exempt.

A general health certificate is not required for entry, but may be required by the consulate from passengers applying for a visa.

B. Varies from temperate to tropical according to region, but generally humid or wet.

Phillipines

A. **Smallpox.*

**Yellow Fever.* If arriving within six days after leaving or transiting infected areas. Children under one year are exempt.

B. Tropical. Hot, and always humid.

Poland

A. **Smallpox.* Exemptions: (1) children under ten months who have not been in an infected area during the preceding 14 days; (2) those who have spent the preceding 14 days in Canada, Morocco, U.S.A., U.S.S.R. and/or European countries, provided there are no infected areas in these countries.

B. Temperate, but summers very warm and winters cold.

Portugal

A. **Smallpox*. If arriving within 14 days after leaving or transiting infected areas. Children under six months are exempt.

**Yellow Fever*. Only if arriving in the Azores or Madeira (excluding the airports) within six days after leaving or transiting infected areas. Children under one year are exempt.

B. Varies from north to south. In general hot summers, mild to cold winters.

Portuguese Guinea

A. **Smallpox*. Children under three months are exempt.

**Yellow Fever*. If arriving within six days after leaving or transiting infected areas, also all passengers staying in Portuguese Guinea more than two weeks. Children under one year are exempt.

B. Tropical. Wet mid-May to mid-November. Dry mid-November to mid-May.

Portuguese Timor

A. **Smallpox*. Children under three months are exempt.

**Yellow Fever*. If arriving within six days after leaving or transiting infected areas, also all passengers staying in Portuguese Timor longer than two weeks. Children under one year are exempt.

B. Tropical. Always hot and humid.

Puerto Rico

A. For requirements see U.S.A.

B. Subtropical. Little annual variation.

Qatar

A. **Smallpox*.

**Cholera*. if arriving within five days after leaving or transiting infected areas. Children under one year are exempt.

**Yellow Fever*. If arriving within six days after leaving or transiting infected areas. Children under one year are exempt.

B. Very hot and humid in summer. Mild in winter.

Réunion

A. **Smallpox*. If arriving aftr leaving or transiting infected areas, plus countries outside Europe except Algeria, Australia†, Azores, Bermuda, Canada, Canary Islands, Caribbean Islands, French Guiana, Greenland, Guadeloupe, Guyana, Israel, Japan†, Libyan Arab Republic, Madeira, Martinique, Mexico, Morocco, Netherlands Antilles, New Zealand†, St Pierre and Miquelon, Surinam, Tunisia, U.S.A. and U.S.S.R.

**Yellow Fever*. If arriving after leaving or transiting infected areas. Children under one year are exempt.

B. Tropical. Hot and humid. Cooler in the hills.

†If coming from Australia, Japan or New Zealand, provided travelling on transpolar, transpacific or transsiberian flights.

Rhodesia

A. **Smallpox.*

**Yellow Fever.* If arriving within six days after leaving or transiting infected areas. Children under one year are exempt.

B. Subtropical in plains. Temperate on the plateaux.

Romania

A. *Smallpox.* Except for those who have spent the immediate past 14 days in Australia, Canada, China (People's Republic), European countries, North Korea, Mongolian People's Republic, Turkey, U.S.A. and U.S.S.R. Required if leaving Romania for infected areas.

Yellow Fever. If arriving within 14 days after leaving or transiting Mauritania, Mozambique, Paraguay, Timor or countries any part of which are endemic areas: also required for passengers leaving Romania for infected areas.

B. Hot summers and long cold winters.

Rwanda

A. **Smallpox.* Required for all arriving and departing passengers. Children under three months are exempt.

Yellow Fever. If arriving within six days after leaving or transiting infected areas, and also if leaving the country and intending to arrive within six days in a fever receptive area. It is also recommended in all other cases. Children under one year are exempt.

N.B. Vaccination against typhoid and paratyphoid is recommended by the authorities.

B. Tropical. Hot and humid.

El Salvador

A. **Smallpox.* Children under one year are exempt.

**Yellow Fever.* If arriving within six days after leaving or transiting infected areas. Children under six months are exempt.

B. Tropical, humid. Temperate in mountains.

Samoa (American)

A. *Smallpox.* If arriving within 14 days after leaving or transiting countries outside Australia, British Solomon Islands, Cook Islands, Fiji, French Polynesia, Gilbert and Ellice Islands, Nauru, New Caledonia, New Hebrides, New Zealand, Niue and Tokelau Islands, Trust Territory of the Pacific Islands, U.S.A. and Western Samoa.

Yellow Fever. If arriving within six days after leaving or transiting infected areas. Children under six months are exempt.

Additional requirements

Passengers who are not American Samoan or Nationals of the U.S.A. and who are arriving from and have resided in, for more than 12 months, Fiji,

Tokelau, Tonga or Western Samoa, must provide proof of treatment for filariasis or acceptance to undergo treatment on arrival in the country.

However the following are exempt:

(1) Remaining for less than 72 hours and hold confirmed onward reservations.

(2) Have completed a full course of treatment for filariasis within one year of their arrival and hold a Public Health Authority certificate of the country in question.

(3) Proof of residence for less than 12 months in Fiji, Tokelau, Tonga or Western Samoa.

(4) If European residence in Fiji, Tokelau, Tonga or Western Samoa has been less than two years.

B. Tropical. Wet December-March. Dry April-November.

Samoa (Western)

A. *Smallpox.* Except those who have spent last 14 days before departure in Australia, Cook Islands, Fiji, French Polynesia, Gilbert and Ellice Islands, Nauru, New Caledonia, New Hebrides, New Zealand, Niue, Norfolk Island, Samoa (American), Solomon Islands, Tokelau Islands, Tonga, provided there are no infected areas in the above named places and they have not left the airports *en route.*

**Yellow Fever.* If arriving within six days after leaving or transiting infected areas.

B. Tropical. Wet December-March. Dry April-November.

Sao Tome and Principe

A. **Smallpox.* Children under three months are exempt.

**Yellow Fever.* If arriving within six days after leaving or transiting infected areas plus all other passengers who are staying in Sao Tome and Principe for more than two weeks. Children under one year are exempt.

B. Tropical. Hot and humid.

Saudi Arabia

A. **Smallpox.*

Cholera. Requirements are dependent on whether it is the Haj pilgrimage season or not. Non-pilgrimage — normally February-October approximately. *If arriving within five days after leaving or transiting countries, any parts of which are infected areas. Pilgrimage — normally late October to early February. Cholera vaccination certificate showing a single dose was administered not less than one week and not more than three months prior to arrival in Saudi Arabia. *In addition those arriving within five days after leaving or transiting a country, any part of which is an infected area, require:

(1) 'Five-day certificate' showing that prior to arrival they have spent five days in an area free of cholera designated by the health authority and notified in advance to Saudi Arabia as a cholera-free area.

(2) Certificate from the health authority that they have taken adequate dosage of tetracycline for four consecutive days prior to departure.

**Yellow Fever.* If arriving within six days after leaving or transiting countries, any parts of which are infected areas.

N.B. *Quarantine.* Persons without valid smallpox, cholera or yellow fever certificates when required will be vaccinated on arrival. Further, if coming from an infected area they will be quarantined. Further if they do not hold the necessary five-day certificate they will be quarantined. These regulations are applied rigidly.

B. Tropical. Coastal areas hot and humid. Inland hot and dry in summer: cool in winter.

Senegal

A. **Smallpox.* Only exemptions are children under six months and passengers transiting Senegal without leaving the airport.

**Yellow Fever.* If arriving within six days after leaving or transiting infected areas plus all passengers staying in Senegal for more than two weeks. Children under one year are exempt.

B. Tropical. Coastal hot and humid: inland hot and dry.

Seychelles

A. **Smallpox.*

**Cholera.* Children under one year are exempt.

**Yellow Fever.* If arriving within six days after leaving or transiting infected areas. Children under one year are exempt.

N.B. Subject to quarantine for those without valid certificates.

B. Tropical. Hot and humid.

Sierra Leone

A. **Smallpox.* Also recommended for those leaving Sierra Leone.

Yellow Fever. May be required for those leaving Sierra Leone. Children under one year are exempt.

B. Tropical. Hot and humid.

Singapore

A. **Smallpox.* Children under one year are exempt.

**Yellow Fever.* If arriving within nine days after leaving or transiting countries, any part of which are endemic or infected areas.

N.B. Persons without valid smallpox certificates when required will be inoculated on arrival and put under observation: without a valid yellow fever certificate when required will be quarantined.

B. Tropical. Hot and humid. Probably the most monotonous climate in the world.

Solomon Islands

N.B. Kieta, Bougainville which is geographically located in the Solomon Islands is administered by Australia and documentation is as for Papua and New Guinea.

A. **Smallpox.* If arriving within 14 days after leaving or transiting countries outside Australia, Cook Islands, Fiji, French Polynesia, Gilbert and Ellice Islands, Nauru, New Caledonia, New Hebrides, New Zealand, Niue, Norfolk and Tokelau Islands, Samoa (American and Western), Tonga.

N.B. If travel from Australia is *via* Papua-New Guinea vaccination certificates are required.

**Yellow Fever.* If arriving within six days after leaving or transiting infected areas.

B. Tropical. Hot and humid. Wettest December-March.

Somalia

A. **Smallpox.*

**Cholera.* If arriving within five days after leaving or transiting countries, any parts of which are infected areas plus Egypt, Guinea, Iraq, Korea (North), Qatar, Thailand, Vietnam (North), Yemen.

**Yellow Fever.* If arriving within six days after leaving or transiting infected areas. However not required for those arriving in and remaining in Berbera or Hargeisa.

N.B. Persons without valid cholera and yellow fever certificates when required are subject to quarantine.

B. Hot and dry in the North: more humid in South.

South Africa (Republic of)

A. *Smallpox.* Everyone unless holding duly authorised medical certificate of contraindication or objections on religious grounds. However either of the above may be placed under surveillance if coming from non-infected areas or isolated if coming from infected areas. Also required for residents of South Africa when leaving South Africa.

**Yellow Fever.* If arriving after leaving or transiting infected areas or African countries in the endemic area. Children under one year are exempt *provided* a medical certificate is submitted saying it is undesirable to inoculate the baby. Persons arriving in Johannesburg *en route* for Natal or the Transvaal Lowveld without a valid certificate, when required, will be subject to six days surveillance in Johannesburg.

B. Temperate to subtropical. The veld hot and dry. Natal coast hot and humid. Cape Province Mediterranean but can be cold in winter.

Spain

A. *Smallpox.* Required except for those who immediately prior to arrival have spent the last 14 days in a European country, Canada, Morocco, Puerto Rico, U.S.A. or U.S.S.R., provided there are no infected areas in the above countries. Children under six months are exempt.

B. Temperate in North. Hot and dry in South.

Sri Lanka (Republic of). Previously Ceylon

A. **Smallpox.*

**Cholera.* If arriving within five days after leaving or transiting infected areas. Children under six months are exempt.

**Yellow Fever.* If arriving within nine days after leaving or transiting infected areas. Children under one year are exempt.

N.B. Persons without valid smallpox or yellow fever certificates, when required, are subject to quarantine.

B. Tropical, and fairly high humidity in coastal areas. Cooler in hills. South-west area monsoon December-February.

Sudan

A. **Smallpox.*
Yellow Fever. If arriving within six days after leaving or transiting infected areas. Children under one year are exempt. Also necessary for those leaving Sudan for Middle East countries and Greece.
N.B. Passengers travelling to Egypt from Khartoum must have a location certificate issued on the day of or the day before departure by the Sudan Medical Authorities in Khartoum attesting that they have not been south of latitude 15°N within six days of embarkation.
B. Tropical. Very hot in summer; moderate in winter.

Surinam

A. **Smallpox.*
**Cholera.* If arriving within five days after leaving or transiting infected areas.
**Yellow Fever.* If arriving within six days after leaving or transiting infected areas.
B. Tropical. Hot.

Swaziland

A. *Smallpox.*
Cholera. If arriving within five days after leaving or transiting infected areas.
Yellow Fever. If arriving within 14 days and after leaving or transiting infected areas.
B. Subtropical. Drier in high land, more humid in the eastern half.

Sweden

A. **Smallpox.* If arriving within 14 days after leaving or transiting all countries except those in Europe, the Azores, Canada, Canary Islands, Madeira, Morocco, U.S.A. and U.S.S.R., provided there are no infected areas in the above countries.
**Cholera.* If arriving within five days after leaving or transiting infected areas. Children under one year are exempt.
B. Very cold in North. Summer in central districts may be rather warm. Winter cold throughout.

Switzerland (and Lichtenstein)

A. *Smallpox.* If arriving within 14 days after leaving or transiting an infected area or a country in Africa (excluding Algeria, Egypt, Libyan Arab Republic, Morocco, Tunisia), in the Americas (excluding Canada and U.S.A.) or Asia except Israel, Jordan, Lebanon, Syria, Turkey and the U.S.S.R.). Children under six months are exempt.
B. Generally warm summers. Cold winters.

Syria

A. **Smallpox*. Exempt are children under six months.

**Yellow Fever*. If arriving within six days after leaving or transiting infected areas.

B. Mediterranean basically. Damascus hot in summer, cold in winter.

Taiwan (Formosa)

A. **Smallpox*.

**Cholera*. If arriving within five days after leaving or transiting infected areas. Children under one year are exempt.

B. Subtropical. Humidity high.

Tanzania (United Republic of) Mainland and Zanzibar

A. **Smallpox*.

**Cholera*. If arriving within five days after leaving or transiting infected areas. Children under one year are exempt.

**Yellow Fever*. If arriving within six days after leaving or transiting infected areas. Children under one year are exempt.

N.B. Recommended are vaccinations against typhoid and paratyphoid fever.

B. Tropical. Hot and humid. Cooler with altitude.

Thailand

A. *Smallpox*. Passengers transiting Thailand are exempt even if they make a night stop provided they continue their journey by the same aircraft.

Yellow Fever. If arriving within six days after leaving or transiting infected areas. Exemptions are as for smallpox also children under one year.

B. Tropical. Warm in northern mountains. Hot and humid in South.

Togo

A. **Smallpox*. Children under one year are exempt. Also required when leaving Togo.

**Cholera*. If arriving within five days after leaving or transiting infected areas. Children under one year are exempt.

Yellow Fever. If arriving within six days after leaving or transiting infected areas: also all passengers staying in Togo longer than two weeks. Children under one year are exempt.

B. Tropical. Hot and humid especially at coast.

Tonga

A. *Smallpox*. If arriving within 14 days after leaving or transiting countries outside Australia, British Solomon Islands, Cook Islands, Fiji, French Polynesia, Gilbert and Ellice Islands, Nauru, New Caledonia, New Hebrides, New Zealand, Niue, Norfolk and Tokelau Islands, Samoa (American and Western).

**Cholera*. If arriving within five days after leaving or transiting infected areas. Children under six months are exempt.

**Yellow Fever*. If arriving within six days after leaving or transiting infected areas. Children under one year are exempt.

B. Tropical. Hot and humid.

Trinidad and Tobago

A. **Smallpox* required except if last 14 days before departure were spent in Bahamas, Barbados, British Virgin Islands, Canada, Dominica, Great Britain and Northern Ireland, Grenada, St Kitts-Nevis-Anguilla, St Lucia, St Vincent, U.S.A. and territories under its administration.

**Yellow Fever*. If arriving within six days after leaving or transiting infected areas. Children under one year are exempt.

B. Hot and humid.

Trucial States — see United Arab Emirates

Tunisia

A. **Smallpox*. If arriving within 14 days after leaving or transiting infected areas. Children under one year are exempt.

**Yellow Fever*. If arriving within 14 days after leaving or transiting infected areas. Children under one year are exempt.

B. Mediterranean.

Turkey

A. **Smallpox*. If arriving within 14 days after leaving or transiting infected areas and countries in Africa (excluding Morocco) and Asia.

N.B. Persons without valid smallpox or cholera certificates when required will be subject to quarantine.

B. Very cold to subtropical.

Uganda

A. **Smallpox*.

**Cholera*. Recommended.

**Yellow Fever*. If arriving within six days after leaving or transiting infected areas.

B. Tropical. Hot and humid.

United Arab Emirates (Formerly Trucial States)

Following Sheikdoms Abu Dhabi, Ajman, Dubai, Fujairah, Ras al Khaimah, Sharjah and Umm al Qawain.

A. *Smallpox*.

Cholera.

Yellow Fever. If arriving within six days after leaving or transiting infected areas.

B. Hot and humid in summer; warm spring and autumn; cool in winter.

United Kingdom (Great Britain)

A. **Smallpox*. If arriving within 14 days after leaving or transiting infected areas and all countries outside Europe except Algeria, Australia†, Azores, Bermuda, Canary Islands, Caribbean Islands, French Guiana, Greenland, Guadeloupe, Guyana, Israel, Japan†, Libyan Arab Republic, Madeira, Martinique, Mexico, Morocco, Netherlands Antilles, New Zealand†, Réunion, St Pierre and Miquelon, Surinam, Tunisia, U.S.A. and U.S.S.R.

B. Temperate.

†Provided air travel is by transpolar, transpacific and transsiberian flights.

Upper Volta

A. **Smallpox.*
**Cholera.*
**Yellow Fever.*
B. Tropical. Hot. Dry in North. Very high humidity in South.

Uruguay

A. **Smallpox.* Also required if leaving Uruguay.
B. Mediterranean type climate. Extremes rare.

U.S.A.

A. **Smallpox.* If arriving within 14 days after leaving or transiting countries, any parts of which are infected areas.
Yellow Fever. Vaccination recommended for passengers travelling to infected areas.
N.B. (1) Those entering on a K-1 or K-2 Visa (fiancée or child of a fiancée of a national of the U.S.A.) must hold a medical form FS398 and X-ray plates of chest (full size or MMR).
(2) Persons having conscientious objections to vaccination (eg Christian Scientists) are allowed to travel to the U.S.A. without vaccination, but if from an infected area they may be quarantined on arrival.
B. Through all ranges.

U.S.S.R.

A. **Smallpox.* Exempt if previous 14 days have been spent in Canada, Mainland China, Mongolia, Turkey, U.S.A. or European countries provided there are no infected areas in the countries concerned.
B. Subarctic to subtropical.

Venezuela

A. **Smallpox.* Children under six months are exempt.
B. Tropical. Varies with altitude but not with season. Carcacas mild and pleasant. Maracaibo hot and humid.

Vietnam (North) (Democratic Republic)

A. *Smallpox.*
Cholera.
N.B. Also required for transit passengers not leaving the airport.
B. Tropical. Hot and humid.

Vietnam (South)

A. **Smallpox.*
**Cholera.* If arriving within five days after leaving or transiting infected areas. Children under one year are exempt.
**Yellow Fever.* If arriving within six days after leaving or transiting infected areas. Children under one year are exempt.
B. Tropical. Hot and humid.

Virgin Islands (U.S.A.)

A. Requirements as for U.S.A.
B. Subtropical. Sunny but some wind. Rain August-November.

Windward Islands (Dominica, Grenada, St Lucia and St Vincent)

A. *Smallpox.* If arriving within 14 days after leaving or transiting infected areas plus all countries other than Antigua, Barbados, British Virgin Islands, Canada, Dominica, Grenada, Guyana, Jamaica, Montserrat, St Kitts, St Vincent, Trinidad and Tobago and U.S.A. Children under three months are exempt if arriving in St Vincent.
Yellow Fever. If arriving within six days after leaving or transiting infected areas. Children under one year are exempt.
B. Subtropical to tropical with high humidity.

Yemen Arab Republic

A. *Smallpox.*
Cholera.
Yellow Fever. If arriving within six days after leaving or transiting infected areas. Children under one year are exempt.
B. Tropical. Coastal hot and humid. Inland hot and dry in summer; cooler in winter.

Yemen (People's Democratic Republic)

A. **Smallpox.*
**Cholera.*
**Yellow Fever.* If arriving within six days after leaving or transiting infected areas.
B. Tropical. Coastal hot and humid. Inland hot and dry in summer; cooler in winter.

Yugoslavia

A. **Smallpox.* If arriving within 14 days after leaving or transiting infected areas and countries in Africa (except North Africa) and South America. Children under one year are exempt.
B. Coastal: mild winters and hot summers. Mountains and North: cold winters, warm summers.

Zaire (Republic of)

Formerly called Congo (Kinshasa)

A. *Smallpox.* Children under three months are exempt.
**Yellow Fever.* If arriving within six days after leaving or transiting infected areas and arriving in or being destined for that part of the country south of 10°S. Children under one year are exempt.
N.B. However yellow fever vaccination certificate is recommended for all passengers. Also recommended vaccination against typhoid and paratyphoid fevers.
B. Tropical. Hot and humid.

Zambia

A. **Smallpox.*

**Cholera.* If arriving within five days after leaving or transiting infected areas.

**Yellow Fever.* If arriving within six days after leaving or transiting infected areas. Passengers holding medical certificates contraindicating vaccination on health grounds are exempt.

N.B. Satisfactory chest X-ray certificate is compulsory for all new residents entering Zambia for the first time. Not required for tourists, transit passengers and returning residents.

B. Subtropical in plains. Temperate on the plateaux.

Transit Passengers

In certain cases the authorities may even require transit passengers proceeding by the same flight and not leaving the airport to hold valid vaccination certificates. The following table shows the countries in question and their possible requirements.

Name of Country	Smallpox	Cholera	Yellow Fever
Australia	*	*	*
Bolivia	*	*	
Botswana	*	*	
Canada	*		
Cayman Islands	*		
Central African Republic	*	*	*
Chad	*	*	*
China (People's Republic)	*	*	*
Cook Islands	*		
Costa Rica	*		
Gilbert and Ellice Islands	*	*	*
Guam	*		
Korea (Democratic People's Republic)	*	*	
Lesotho	*		*
Mexico	*		
Nauru	*	*	*
New Zealand	*		
Nicaragua	*		
Niue	*	*	*
Puerto Rico	*		
Romania	*		*
Samoa (American)	*		*
Samoa (Western)	*		*
South Africa	*	*	*
Swaziland	*	*	*
Tonga	*	*	*
U.S.A.	*		
Vietnam Democratic Republic	*	*	
Virgin Islands	*		

B. Yellow Fever Vaccination Centres*

United Kingdom

N.B. It is best to telephone the appropriate centre prior to attending.

London

British Airways Medical Service, Immunisation Centre, Victoria Air Terminal, Buckingham Palace Road, London, SW1. 01-834 2232.
British Broadcasting Corporation, Yellow Fever Vaccination Centre, Broadcasting House, London, W1A 4WW. 01-580 4468.
British Caledonian Airways Medical Department. 01-283 8755.
British Petroleum Co. Ltd., Yellow Fever Vaccination Centre, Britannic House, Moor Lane, London, EC2. 01-920 7198.
Cable & Wireless Yellow Fever Vaccination Centre.
Commonwealth Development Corporation, Medical Centre, 33 Hill Street, London, W1. 01-629 8424.
Corporation of London Yellow Fever Vaccination Service, Unilever House, Blackfriars, London, EC4. 01-353 7474.
Costains Industrial Health Services, Yellow Fever Vaccination Centre, 111 Westminster Bridge Road, London, SE1. 01-928 4977.
C.P. Ships, Yellow Fever Vaccination Centre, Medical Department, 62-65 Trafalgar Square, London, WC2. 01-930 5100.
De La Rue Company Ltd., Medical Service, London, Yellow Fever Vaccination Centre, 84 Regent Street, London, W1. 01-734 8020.
Dolphin Square Vaccination Centre, Dolphin Square, Grosvenor Road, London, SW1. 01-834 3800.
Financial Times Yellow Fever Vaccination Centre, Bracken House, Cannon Street, London, EC4. 01-248 8000.
Health Services of Norway, 41 Lancaster Gate, London, W2. 01-262 3385.
London Borough of Camden, Yellow Fever Vaccination Service, Hospital for Tropical Diseases, 4 St Pancras Way, London, N1. 01-387 4411.
London (Heathrow) Airport, Health Control Unit, Yellow Fever Vaccination Centre, London (Heathrow) Airport. 01-387 4411.
Marble Arch Yellow Fever Vaccination Centre, 53 Great Cumberland Place, London, W1. 01-723 6482 and 01-262 6456.
Mobil Oil Co., Medical Department, Yellow Fever Vaccination Centre, 54 Victoria Street, London, SW1. 01-828 9777.
N.A.A.F.I. Yellow Fever Vaccination Centre, Headquarters, Imperial Court, Kennington Lane, London, SE11. 01-735 1200.
Norfolk Place Yellow Fever Vaccination Centre.
Rank Organisation Ltd., Medical Service, London, Yellow Fever Vaccination Centre, 7 Guildhouse Street, London, SW1. 01-828 3327.
Shell International Petroleum Co. Ltd., London Medical Division, Vaccination Centre, Shell Centre, London, SE1. 01-934 1234.

*As of January 1st 1975

Shipping Federation and London Port Health Authority Vaccination Centre, 20 Prescott Street, London, E1. 01-480 5021.

St George's Hospital Medical School, Yellow Fever Vaccination Centre, Hyde Park Corner, London, SW1. 01-235 1716.

Westminster City Council Yellow Fever Vaccination Service, City Hall, Victoria Street, London, SW1. 01-828 8070.

Provinces

Aberdeen: City Hospital, Yellow Fever Immunisation Service.

Ballymena: Divisional Healh Office, Yellow Fever Vaccination Centre.

Barnsley: County Borough Council Yellow Fever Vaccination Centre.

Barrow-in-Furness: Vickers Armstrong (Engineers) Ltd., Medical Department.

Belfast: Belfast Corporation Yellow Fever Vaccination Centre.

Birmingham: Public Health Department Yellow Fever Vaccination Centre.

Blackburn: County Borough Yellow Fever Vaccination Centre.

Bournemouth: County Borough Yellow Fever Vaccination Centre.

Bradford: Yellow Fever Vaccination Centre.

Brighton: Yellow Fever Vaccination Centre, County Borough Health Dept.

Bristol: Yellow Fever Vaccination Centre.

Cambridge: Clinic 2, Addenbrookes Hospital.

Cardiff: Yellow Fever Vaccination Centre.

Carlisle: County Borough Yellow Fever Vaccination Centre.

Chemsford: County Council Yellow Fever Vaccination Centre.

Coventry: Health Department Yellow Fever Vaccination Centre.

Croydon: Geophysical Service International Ltd., Yellow Fever Vaccination Centre.

Derby: Area Health Authority Yellow Fever Vaccination Centre.

Doncaster: County Borough Yellow Fever Vaccination Centre.

Dundee: King's Cross Hospital, Yellow Fever Vaccination Centre.

Edinburgh: Public Health Department.

Exeter: Health Care District Vaccination Centre.

Gatwick Airport: British Caledonian Airways Medical Department. 01-283 8755, or Crawley 27890.

Glasgow: Glasgow Corporation Immunisation Centre.

Gloucester: Royal Hospital Yellow Fever Vaccination Centre.

Grimsby: Yellow Fever Vaccination Centre, Queen Street.

Guernsey: Health Department, Lukis House.

Gwent: Area Health Authority, South Gwent Health District.

Harlow: Industrial Health Service Yellow Fever Vaccination Centre.

Haverfordwest: Pembrokeshire County Council Health Department.

Isle of Man: Clegg Pathological Laboratory, Noble's Hospital, Douglas.

Jersey: Medical Officer of Health, Public Health Committee Laboratory.

Kingston-upon-Hull: City and County Yellow Fever Vaccination Centre.

Kingston-upon-Thames: Yellow Fever Vaccination Centre, Royal Borough of Kingston-upon-Thames.

Lancaster: County Council Vaccination Centre, Ashton Road Clinic.

Leeds: City Council Immunisation Centre.

Leicester: County Borough Yellow Fever Vaccination Centre, City Health Department.

Leyland: Motor Corporation Yellow Fever Vaccination Service.
Lincoln: Area Health Authority Vaccination Centre.
Liverpool: Area Health Authority (Teaching) Vaccination Centre, School of Tropical Medicine, Pembroke Place, Liverpool, 3. 051-709 7611.
Maidstone: Kent Area Health Authority Yellow Fever Vaccination Centre.
Manchester: Yellow Fever Vaccination Centre, Town Hall.
Newcastle-upon-Tyne: Yellow Fever Vaccination Centre.
Northampton: Area Health Authority Yellow Fever Vaccination Centre.
Norwich: Health Department Yellow Fever Vaccination Centre.
Nottingham: Medical Officer of Health, Yellow Fever Vaccination Centre.
Omagh: The Clinic, Yellow Fever Vaccination Centre.
Oxford: County Borough Yellow Fever Vaccination Centre.
Penzance: County Council Yellow Fever Vaccination Centre.
Plymouth: Yellow Fever Vaccination Centre, Local Health Authority.
Sheffield: Metropolitan District Yellow Fever Vaccination Centre.
Shrewsbury: Salop County Council, Yellow Fever Vaccination Centre, County Health Department.
Southampton: Cunard Steamship Co. Medical Department, Southwestern House, Canute Road, Southampton. 0703 29933.
Swansea: City of Swansea Yellow Fever Vaccination Centre.
Taunton: County Council Yellow Fever Vaccination Centre.
Tilbury: Shipping Federation and London Port Health Authority Vaccination Centre, Tilbury Dock.
Truro: County Council Yellow Fever Vaccination Centre.
York: Health Services Centre (Vaccination and Immunisation).
All United Kingdom Government Vaccination Centres.

Australia

The Commonwealth Health Department through its Divisional Offices in each State.

Canada

Astra, Ontario: Canadian Forces Base, Trenton.
Calgary, Alberta: Department of Veterans Affairs.
Cornwallis, Nova Scotia: Canadian Forces Base.
Edmonton, Alberta: Regional Director, Alberta Regional Medical Services, Department of National Health and Welfare.
Halifax, Nova Scotia: Halifax Clinic, Department of National Health and Welfare.
Kingston, Ontario: Canadian Forces Hospital.
Lazo, British Columbia: Canadian Forces Base, Comox.
Malton, Ontario: Department of National Health and Welfare, Canadian National Railway Medical Clinic.
Montreal, Province of Quebec: Medical Officer in Charge, Port of Montreal Building.
Ottawa, Ontario: National Capital Zone, Department of National Health and Welfare.
Quebec, Province of Quebec: Quebec Clinic, Medical Services, Department of National Health and Welfare.

Regina, Saskatchewan: City Health Department.
Richelieu, Province of Quebec: Canadian Forces Base, St Jean.
Saint John, New Brunswick: Saint John Clinic, Medical Services, Department of National Health and Welfare.
St John's, Newfoundland: St John's Clinic, Medical Services, Department of National Health and Welfare.
Saskatoon, Saskatchewan: Veterans Home, Department of Veterans Affairs.
Thunder Bay, Ontario: Lake Superior Centre, Medical Services, Department of National Health and Welfare.
Toronto, Ontario: 1. Canadian National Railways, Medical Clinic;
2. Southern Ontario Zone, Medical Services, Department of National Health and Welfare.
Vancouver, British Colombia: Vancouver Clinic, Medical Services, Department of National Health and Welfare.
Vedder Crossing, British Colombia: Canadian Forces Base, Chilliwak.
Victoria, British Colombia: Victoria Clinic, Medical Services, Department of National Health and Welfare.
Victoria, British Colombia: Canadian Forces Base, Esquimalt.
Winnipeg, Manitoba: Manitoba Region, Medical Services, Department of National Health and Welfare.

Eire

Athlone: Military Hospital, Custume Barracks.
Blackrock (Co. Dublin): Dr John Fleetwood, 'Glenvera', Proby Square.
Cork: Chief Medical Officer, Health Authority, City Hall, Military Hospital, Collins Barracks.
Curragh: General Military Hospital, Curragh Training Camp.
Drogheda: Our Lady of Lourdes International Missionary Training Hospital.
Dublin: Arthur Guinness Ltd., Medical Department.
Irish Shipowners Association.
St Bricin's Hospital.
Trinity College, Department of Bacteriology, School of Pathology.
Dr Joseph Bernes, 47 Fitzwilliam Square.
Dr Ivor Hooper, 2 Mount Harold Terrace, Leinster Road.
Dublin Airport: Irish International Airlines Medical Centre.
Ennis: County Medical Officer.
Limerick: City Medical Officer.
Shannon: Airport Medical Officer.

New Zealand

Government Centres

(a) Medical Officers of Health of the Health Department at:

Auckland	Invercargill	South Auckland
Christchurch	Napier	Takapuna
Dunedin	Nelson	Timaru
Gisborne	New Plymouth	Wanganui
Hamilton	Palmerston North	Wellington
Hutt	Rotorua	Whangarei

(b) Ministry of Defence: All Commissioned Medical Officers of the Royal New Zealand Navy, Army and Air Force.

Private Vaccination Centres

Auckland: Public Hospital, Director of Laboratory Services.
Laboratory Diagnostic Service, 43 Symonds Street.
Port Health Officer.
Christchurch: Public Hospital, Clinical Pathologist.
Christchurch Airport, Port Health Officer.
Lyttelton Port Health Officer.
Dunedin: Medical School, Professór of Preventive and Social Medicine.
Gisborne: Public Hospital, Clinical Pathologist.
Greymouth: Public Hospital, Medical Superintendent.
Hamilton: Public Hospital, Clinical Pathologist.
Invercargill: Dr N. G. Prentice, 119 Don Street.
Lower Hutt: Valley Diagnostic Laboratory, 24 Kings Crescent.
Napier: Public Hospital, Clinical Pathologist.
Public Hospital, Medical Superintendent.
Public Hospital, Hastings, Medical Superintendent.
Nelson: Dr B. A. Kaye, 284 Hardy Street.
Public Hosptial, Blenheim, Medical Superintendent.
New Plymouth: Public Hospital, Clinical Pathologist.
Palmerston North: Public Hospital, Clinical Pathologist.
Ohakea Airport, Port Health Officer.
Rotorua: Public Hospital, Medical Superintendent.
Public Hospital, Tauranga, Medical Superintendent.
South Auckland: Middlemore Hospital, Otahuhu, Clinical Pathologist.
Takapuna: North Shore Hospital, Medical Superintendent.
Whenuapai Airport, Port Health Officer.
Timaru: Public Hospital, Clinical Pathologist.
Wanganui: Public Hospital, Clinical Pathologist.
Wellington: Public Hospital, Clinical Pathologist.
Port Health Officer.
Dr M. Kronfeld, Mayfair Chambers, 48 The Terrace.
Medical Laboratory, Kelvin Chambers, The Terrace.
Whangarei: Public Hospital, Medical Superintendent.
Port Health Officer.

Republic of South Africa (R.S.A.)

Any of the following Medical Officers of the Department of Health stationed at the centres listed below:
District Surgeons; Government Pathologists; Medical Inspectors; Medical Officers of Health; Port Health Officers.
Regional Director and Assistant Regional Director, State Health Services.

Belleville	Germiston	Louis Trichardt
Benoni	Grahamstown	Mossel Bay
Bethlehem	Johannesburg	Nelspruit
Bloemfontein	Katima Mulilo	Nylstroom
Bronkhorstspruit	Kimberley	Paarl
Cape Town	Klerksdorp	Pietermaritzburg
Durban	Knysma	Pietersburg
East London	Kroonstad	Piet Relief
Port Elizabeth	Rustenburg	Upington

Potgeitersrust	Tzaneen	Vereeniging
Pretoria	Umtata	Welkom
Queenstown		

Johannesburg: South African Railway Sick Fund, Headquarters.
Director of Health Services, South African Railways, Health and Industrial Welfare Section.
Umtata: Tembuland Hospital, Medical Superintendent.

Military Establishments

C.O. No. 1. South African Military Hospital, Voortrekkermoogte, Pretoria.
C.O. No. 2. South African Military Hospital, Wynberg, Cape.
Deputy Assistant Surgeon General, Natal Command, Durban.

United States of America

Alabama

Birmingham: Jefferson County Department of Health.
Mobile: Alcoa Steamship Co. Inc.
National Bulk Carriers.
U.S. Public Health Service Outpatient Clinic.
Montgomery: State Department of Health.

Alaska

Anchorage: Greater Anchorage Area Borough.

Arizona

Flagstaff: Coconino County Health Department.
Phoenix: Maricopa County Health Department.
Tucson: Pima County Health Department.

Arkansas

Little Rock: State Health Department.

California

Alameda: U.S. Coastguard Training and Supply Centre, Government Island.
Bakersfield: Kern County Health Department.
Burbank: Lockheed Aircraft Corporation, Medical Department.
Davis: Cowell Student Health Centre, University of California.
El Centro: Imperial County Health Centre.
El Segundo: Sepulveda Medical Group.
Fresno: County Department of Public Health.
Hollywood: Medical Clinic for Immunization.
Loma Linda: School of Health, University Department of Preventive Medicine.
Los Angeles: American Airlines, Medical Department.
Overseas Medical Centtre.
UCLA Student Health Services, Centre for Health Sciences.
White Memorial Hospital.
Napa: County Health Department.
Oakland: Dr Thomas Reich, 411, 30th Street, 94609.
Palo Alto: Medical Clinic.
Redding: Shasta County Health Deent.
Sacramento: County Health Department.
San Bernardino: County Health Department.

San Diego: Public Health Service Outpatient Clinic, Central Medical Group.
San Francisco: International Medical Centre.
Financial District Medical Centre.
Overseas Medical Centre.
Pan American World Airways, Medical Department, International Airport.
Seafarers Medical Centre.
U.S. Public Health Service Hospital.
San José: Santa Clara County Health Department.
San Luis Obispo: County Health Department.
San Pedro: Seafarers Medical Centre.
U.S. Public Health Service Outpatient Clinic.
Santa Ana: Orange County Health Department.
Ventura: James M. Hunter, M.D., 1590 East Main Street. 93003.

Colorado
Colorado Springs: City-County Health Department.
Denver: Department of Health and Hospitals, Disease Control Service.
Stapleton International Airport Clinic.
Fort Collins: Vector Borne Diseases Branch, Centre for Disease Control.
Grand Junction: Mesa County Department of Public Health.

Connecticut
Hartford: State Department of Health, Health Services for State Employees.
New Haven: Health Department.
New London: U.S. Coastguard Academy.

Delaware
Delaware City: Getty Oil Co.
Wilmington: E.I. Du Pont De Nemours & Co. Inc.
Hercules Inc. Medical Department.

District of Columbia
Washington (District of Colombia): Department of State Immunization Clinic.
Freedmen's Hospital.
International Health Services Clinic, Georgetown University.
Office of Medical Affairs, Actions, International Operations/P.C.
U.S. Public Health Service Outpatient Clinic.

Florida
Bradenton: Manatee County Health Department.
Clearwater: Pinellas County Health Department.
Fort Lauderdale: Broward County Health Department.
Gainesville: Alachua County Health Department.
Jacksonville: Industrial Marine Medical Service.
U.S. Public Health Service Outpatient Clinic.
Miami: Eastern Airlines Medical Department.
Pan American World Airways, Pan Am Building.
U.S. Public Health Service Outpatient Clinic.
Orlando: Orange County Health Department.
Pensacola: Escambia County Health Department
Rockledge: Brevard County Health Department.
St Petersburg: Pinellas County Health Department.

Tallamassee: Leon County Health Department.
Tampa: U.S. Public Health Service Outpatient Clinic.
West Palm Beach: Palm Beach County Health Department.
Winter Park: Orange County Health Department.

Georgia
Atlanta: U.S. Public Health Service Outpatient Clinic.
Savannah: U.S. Public Health Service Outpatient Clinic.

Hawaii
Hilo: University of Hawaii Peace Corps Project.
Honolulu: U.S. Public Health Service Outpatient Clinic.

Idaho
Boise: Central District Health Department.
Caldwell: South West District Health Department.
Lewiston: North Central District Health Department.
Pocatello: South Eastern District Health Department.
Twin Falls: South Central District Health Department.

Illinois
Carbondale: Southern Illinois University Health Service.
Chicago: Clearing Industrial Emergency Hospital Inc.
International Health Centre, Rush-Presbyterian-St Luke's Medical Centre.
United Airlines Medical Department.
U.S. Public Health Service Outpatient Clinic.
Peoria: Caterpillar Tractor Co., Medical Department.
City Council Health Department.
Rockford: Winnesbago County Department of Public Health.
Springfield: Department of Public Health.
Urbana: University of Illinois Health Service.

Indiana
Crown Point: Lake Country Health Department.
Elkhart: County Health Unit.
Fort Wayne: Fort Wayne-Allen County Board of Public Health.
Gary: City Health Department.
Indianopolis: Indiana University.

Iowa
Desmoines: Desmoines-Polk County Health Department.
Iowa City: University Hospital Student Health Service.
Sioux City: Health Department.

Kansas
Lawrence: Watkins Memorial Hospital Student Health Service.
Leavenworth: City County Health Department.
Mission: Johnson County Health Department.

Kentucky
Lexington: Lexington-Fayette County Health Department.
Louisville: Louisville-Jefferson County Health Department.

Louisiana
Alexandria: Alexandria-Rapides Parish Health Unit.

Baton Rouge: East Baton Rouge Parish Health Unit.
Lafayette: Parish Health Unit.
Lake Charles: Calsasieu-Lake Charles Health Unit.
Maringouin: Beamon-O'Niel Clinic.
Marrero: West Bank Surgical Unit.
Monroe: Ouachita Parish Health Unit.
Morgan City: Family Medical Centre.
New Orleans: Browne-McHardy Clinic, Caroldelet Street Division.
City Health Department.
Houston, Roy, Faust and Ewen Clinic
Ochsner Clinic.
U.S. Public Health Service Hospital.
Shreveport: Caddo-Shreveport Health Unit.

Maine
Portland: U.S. Public Health Service Outpatient Clinic.

Maryland
Baltimore: Esso Shipping Co.
U.S. Public Health Service Hospital.
Bethesda: National Institutes of Health, Employee Health Service.
Cheverley: Prince George's County Health Department.
Hagerstown: Washington County Health Department.
Salisbury: Wicomico County Health Department.

Massachusetts
Amherst: University of Massachusetts Health Services.
Boston: Logan International Airport (Medical Station of the Massachusetts General Hospital).
Massachusetts Department of Public Health (Division of Communicable Diseases).
Medical Care Associates Inc.
U.S. Public Health Service Hospital.
Cambridge: Harvard University Health Services.
Woburn: Board of Health.
Worcester: Immunization Clinic, Department of Public Health, City Hospital.

Michigan:
Ann Arbor: University of Michigan Hospital.
Dearborn: Ford Motor Co. Medical Section, Central Post Office Building, Medical Section.
Detroit: Overseas Medical Centre.
Preventive Medical Clinic, Henry Ford Hospital.
U.S. Public Health Service Outpatient Clinic.
East Lansing: Olin Health Centre, Michigan State University.
Eloise: Wayne County Department of Health (Health Centre).
Kalamazoo: Upjohn Company.
Lansing: Ingham County Health Department.
Midland: City-County Health Department.
Muskegon: County Health Department.
Traverse City: Thirlby Clinic.

Minnesota
Duluth: Duluth Clinic.
Minneapolis: University of Minnesota Health Service.
Rochester: Mayo Clinic.
Olmsted County Health Department.
St Paul: St Paul-Minneapolis International Airport Medical Clinic.

Mississippi
Gulfport: Harrison County Health Department.
Jackson: State Board of Health, Division of Preventable Disease Control.
Pascagoula: Davis Clinic.

Missouri
Columbia: University of Missouri, Student Health Service.
Kansas City: City Health Department, Personal Health Service.
Trans World Airlines Medical Department.
Kirksville: Osteopath Hospital.
St Louis: U.S. Public Health Service Outpatient Department.

Montana
Billings: 1. Billings Clinic, 2. City Health Department.
Bozeman: Gallatin County Health Department.
Hamilton: U.S. Public Health Service, Rocky Mountain Laboratory.
Missoula: City-County Health Department.

Nevada
Las Vegas: Clark County District Health Department.
Reno: Washoe County District Health Department.

New Hampshire
Nashua: Sanders Associates Inc.

New Jersey
Bayonne: Maritime Medical Clinic.
Cape May: U.S. Coast Guard Training Centre.
Elizabeth: Port Medical Centre.
Englewood Cliffs: CPC International.
Florham Park: Esso Research and Engineering Co.
Hoboken: American Export Isbrandtsen Lines Inc.
Newark: Medical Dispensary.
Paulsboro: Mobil Oil Corp.
Perth Amboy: City Department of Health.
Princeton: Isabelle McCosh Infirmary, Princeton University.
Saddle Brook: Diagnostic Health Group.
Wayne: American Cyanamid Co.

New Mexico
Albuquerque: Lovelace Clinic.
Las Cruces: Student Health Service, New Mexico State University.

New York
Albany: State Department of Health, Division of Laboratories and Research.
Brooklyn: Farrell Lines Inc. Medical Department.
Seafarers Welfare Plan.

Buffalo: Erie County Department of Health.
U.S. Public Health Service Outpatient Clinic.
Ithaca: Gannett Medical Clinic, Cornell University.
Jamaica: J. F. Kennedy International Airport: American Airlines Medical Department, Eastern Airlines Medical Department, Pan American World Airways Medical Department.
New York: American International Underwriters Corp., C. V. Starr & Co.
Borden Co., Executive Health Examiners Industrial Clinic.
Broad Street Medical Centre.
Caltex Petroleum Corp., Caltex Medical Department.
Chase Manhattan Bank Medical Department.
Exxon Corporation.
International Telephone and Telegraph Corp.
Life Extension Institute.
Maritime Medical Service.
Medical Associates of Wall Street.
Mobil Oil Corporation.
Norwegian Public Health Service.
Pan Medical Associates.
Pepsi Cola Co.
Rockefeller Foundation, Medical and Natural Sciences.
Texaco Inc., Health Division.
Time Inc., Medical Department.
Tropical Disease Centre.
United Nations Health Service.
U.S. Public Health Service Outpatient Clinic.
Plain View: Nassau County Department of Health.
Poughkeepsie: Dutchess County Health Department.
Purchase: Pepsi Cola Co.
Rochester: Strong Memorial Hospital.
Diagnostic Clinic, University of Rochester.
Schenectady: Schenectady Industrial Clinic, General Electric Company.
Syracuse: A. C. Silverman Public Health Hospital.
Whiteplains: Westchester County Department of Health.
General Foods Corporation, Medical Department.

North Carolina:
Asheville: Buncumbe County Health Centre.
Charlotte: Mecklenburg County Health Department.
Durham: Duke University Medical Centre.
Fayetteville: Cumberland County Health Department.
Gastonia: Gaston County Health Department.
Rochester: University Health Department.
Wilmington: Maritime Industrial Clinic.
Winston-Salem: Forsyth County Health Department.

North Dakota
Bismarck: City Health Department.
Fargo: City Health Department.
Grand Forks: University of North Dakota, Student Health Service.

Ohio
Akron: Health Department, John D. Morley Health Centre.
Athens: Hudson Health Centre, Ohio University.
Canton: City Health Department.
Cincinnati: City Health Department, Yellow Fever Clinic.
Cleveland: U.S. Public Health Service Outpatient Clinic.
Columbus: Health Department.
University Hospital, Family Medical Clinic.
Dayton: Montgomery County Health District.
National Cash Register Co., Medical Department.
Findlay: Marathon Oil Co.
Oxford: Macmillan Hospital, Student Health Service.

Oklahoma
Bartlesville: Phillips Petroleum Co.
Enid: Garfield County Health Department.
Norman: Goddard Health Centre.
Stillwater: Oklahoma State University, Student Hospital and Clinic.
Tulsa: City-County Health Department.

Oregon
Portland: U.S. Public Health Service Outpatient Clinic.

Pennsylvania
Erie: County Health Department.
Philadelphia: Hospital of the University of Pennsylvania.
St Luke's and Children's Medical Centre, Philadelphia.
International Airport.
Temple University Hospital.
U.S. Public Health Service Outpatient Clinic.
Pittsburgh: Gulf Oil Corp. Medical Department.
U.S. Public Health Service Outpatient Department.
Reading: Reading Hospital.
University Park: Rietnour Health Centre, Pennsylvania State University.
Valley Forge: American Baptist Convention.

Rhode Island
Providence: Department of Health, Division of Epidemiology.

South Carolina
Charleston: U.S. Public Health Service Outpatient Clinic.
Clemson: Redfern Health Centre, Clemson University.
Spartanburg: County Health Department.

Tennessee
Blountville: Sullivan County Health Department.
Chattanooga: Chattanooga-Hamilton County Health Department.
Knoxville: Knox County Health Department.
Memphis: Shelby County Health Department.
U.S. Public Health Service Outpatient Clinic.
Nashville: East Nashville Public Health Centre.
Metropolitan Health Department.

Texas

Amarillo: Bi-City-County Health Unit,
Austin: Austin-Travis County Health Department.
Brownsville: U.S. Quarantine Station.
Corpus Christi: Corpus Christi-Nueces County, Department of Public Health.
Dallas: City Health Department.
Edinburg: Medical Centre.
El Paso: U.S. Quarantine Station.
Fort Worth: American Airlines Medical Department, Greater South-West International Airport.
  Department of Public Health.
Freeport: City Health Office.
Galveston: U.S. Public Health Service Hospital.
Houston: City Health Department.
  Clarke and Williamson Clinic for Magnet Cove Barium Corp.
  Diagnostic Clinic and Hospital.
  Exxon Company of U.S.A.
  Dr B. W. Grandjean, Suite 6, 9100, Westheimer.
  Drs Hamrick and Jones, 1124 Memorial Professional Building.
  Harris County Health Department.
  Houston Clinic, 1701 Crawford Street.
  Houston Clinic, 4119 Montrose Boulevard.
  Kelsey-Seybold Clinic.
  Ledbetter Clinic.
  Milby Clinic.
  Space Centre Medical Associates.
  Tenneco Oil Co.
  Texaco Inc., Health Division.
  U.S. Public Health Service Outpatient Clinic.
  Withers Medical-Surgery Clinic.
Odessa: Odessa-Ector County Health Department.
Orange: Park Avenue Medical Centre.
Port Arthur: U.S. Public Health Service Outpatient Clinic.
San Antonio: Minter Clinic.
  Petty Geophysical Engineering Co. Clinic.
  Southwest Medical Clinic.
Victoria: County Health Department.
Wichita Falls: City-County Health Centre.

Utah

Provo: Brigham Young University Student Health Centre.
Salt Lake City: University of Utah College of Medicine Student Health Services.

Virginia

Charlottesville: Albermarle-Charlottesville Health Department.
Fairfax: Joseph Willard Health Centre, County Health Department.
Herndorn: Reston-Herndorn Medical Centre.
Lynchburg: Bureau of Public Health.
Norfolk: U.S. Public Health Service Hospital.
Richmond: City Health Department.
Roanoke: City Health Department.
Yorktown: U.S. Coast Guard Reserve Training Centre.

Washington

Olympia: Thurston-Mason Health District.
Pullman: Washington State University Student Health Service.
Seattle: U.S. Public Health Service Hospital.

West Virginia

Charleston: Kanawha-Charleston Health Department, Memorial Hospital Unit.
Huntington: Cabell-Huntington Health Department.
Morgantown: West Virginia University Health Service.

Wisconsin

La Crosse: Gundersen Clinic.
Madison: University of Wisconsin Health Service.
Milwaukee: Health Department.
Racine: J. I. Case Co.
West Allis: Allis-Chalmers Corporation.

Canal Zone

Balboa: Community Health Centre, Division of Preventive Medicine.
Margarita, Christobal: Community Health Centre.

Puerto Rico

Arecibo: Peace Corps Medical Centre.
San Juan: U.S. Public Health Service Outpatient Clinic.

Virgin Islands

St Croix: Charles Harwood Memorial Hospital, Christiansted.

Department of Defence

The Surgeon General of the United States Public Health Service has delegated his authority to the Surgeons General of the Departments of the Army, Navy and Air Force for their commissioned Medical Officers to issue International Certificates of Vaccination against Yellow Fever.

Institutes manufacturing Yellow Fever Vaccines approved by W.H.O.

Australia	Melbourne	Commonwealth Serum Laboratories.
Brazil	Rio De Janeiro	Yellow Fever Laboratory, Instituto Oswaldo Cruz.
Colombia	Bogota	Instituto de Estudios Especiales Carlos Finlay.
Federal Republic of Germany	Berlin	Robert Koch Institut.
France	Paris	Institut Pasteur.
India	Kasauli	Central Research Institute.
Netherlands	Amsterdam	Koninklijk Institut Voor de Tropen.
Nigeria	Lagos	Yellow Fever Laboratory. Federal Laboratory Service, Yaba.
Senegal	Dakar	Institut Pasteur.
South Africa	Johannesburg	South African Institute for Medical Research.
United Kingdom	Beckenham, Kent	Wellcome Research Laboratories.
United States of America	Swiftwater, PA	Merell-National Laboratories, Division of Richardson-Merell Inc.

C. Admitted Malarious Areas*

Europe

Clear.

Asia

Afghanistan	
Bahrain	
Bangladesh	
Bhutan	
Burma	April-November. Not in Rangoon.
Hong Kong	Only in remote scattered areas of new territories, which can be ignored.
India	March-October. Many areas including large cities are clear.
Indonesia	Not in Djakarta.
West Irian	
Iran	
Iraq	
Jordan	Only in parts of Jordan Valley not usually visited by tourists.
Korea	May-October.
Laos	
Malaysia	
Sabah	Excluding Kota Kinabala.
Sarawak	
West Malaysia	Excluding Kuala Lumpur, Georgetown and Malacca Municipality.
Maldive Islands	Excluding Male Island and Male Atoll.
Nepal	
Oman	
Pakistan	March-October.
Philippines	Excluding Manila, Luzon and other cities.
Portuguese Timor	
Qatar	
Saudi Arabia	Excluding Jeddah, Riyadm and Mecca.
Sikkim	
Singapore	But only in small area in Northern part of Island—not in city.
Sri Lanka (Ceylon)	Excluding city of Colombo, Galle and Kalutara.
Syria	May-October. Occurs in rural areas only.
Thailand	Occurs in most rural areas. Not in Bangkok.
Turkey	July-October. Limited risk in rural areas.

*W.H.O. June 1972. All the year unless otherwise stated.

United Arab Emirates	(Abu Dhabi; Dubai; Sharjah; Ajman; Umal Gaiwayn; Fujairah; Ras al Khaymah).
Vietnam	
Yemen	September-February.

Africa

Algeria	June-October. Rural and coastal areas only.
Angola including Cabinda	
Botswana	October-March.
British Indian Ocean Territories	(Chagos Archipelago, Aldabra, Farquhar and Des Roches).
Burundi	
Cameroon	
Cape Verde Islands	
Central African Republic	
Chad	
Comores Islands	
Congo (Democratic Republic of)	
Congo	
Dahomey	
Egypt	Principally in the Nile Valley.
Equatorial Guinea	
Ethiopia	
Gabon	
Ghana	
Guinea	
Ivory Coast	
Kenya	Throughout the year, very prevalent at the coast. Up country April-June, November-December.
Liberia	
Libya	Only two small foci in the South West.
Madagascar	Scattered areas September-March.
Malawi	
Mali	
Mauritania	
Morocco	
Mozambique	
Namibia	
Niger	July-November.
Nigeria	
Portuguese Guinea	
Rhodesia	
Rwanda	
Sao Tóme and Principe	
Senegal	
Somalia	
Republic of South Africa	Walvis Bay area. Also very small risk North Eastern Transvaal and some Natal coastal areas.
Sudan	Excluding Northern Province. But not Nile Valley.

Swaziland	Some areas only.
Togo	
Tunisia	May-November. Rural and coastal areas only.
Uganda	
Tanzania	Throughout both Tanganyka and Zanzibar.
Upper Volta	
Zaire	
Zambia	November-May.

North America

British Honduras	
Cost Rica	Not in urban areas.
Dominican Republic	Only in scattered areas.
El Salvador	
Gautemala	June-November. Rural areas only.
Haiti	July-March. Scattered rural areas only.
Honduras	Rural areas only.
Mexico	Rural areas only.
Nicaragua	All rural areas.
Panama	Panama and Colon cities excluded.

South America

Argentina	September-May. Only small risk in rural Northern areas of country.
Bolivia	Rural areas.
Brazil	Rural areas.
Colombia	Rural areas.
Ecuador	Rural areas.
French Guiana	All areas.
Guyana	All areas except coastal belt which includes Georgetown.
Paraguay	September-May.
Surinam	
Venezuela	Rural areas below 600 metres.

Union of Soviet Socialist Republics

No information provided but probably in Southern States.

China

No information provided.

D. Overseas Medical Costs

Prior to January 1st 1973, when the United Kingdom joined the European Economic Community, the author strongly recommended every traveller from the U.K. to take out adequate medical insurance. Many of us thought that this added expense might be unnecessary after joining the E.E.C., but there are so many complications and variations in the rules of the E.E.C. countries that it must be very seriously considered whether it is still essential to insure against sickness. It is, anyway, essential for visitors to non-E.E.C. countries.

To consider first the problems of visiting the E.E.C. countries, and subsequently the variations in medical insurance.

The first point to remember in visiting E.E.C. countries is that self-employed and non-employed persons receive no financial cover at all. This means that no general practitioner in the N.H.S. or any practitioner in purely private practice is covered: and this goes for their wives and children as well. This is grossly unfair as all nationals of the E.E.C. countries, along with other foreigners, are covered by the N.H.S.

The next point is that those who are entitled to cover must obtain a CM1 form, from any local office of the Department of Health and Social Security or any Employment Exchange not more than six months before they intend to travel. Having completed this form and completed the fourteen questions it must be returned to the nearest Social Security office. They will then issue a form E111 which certifies that you and your dependants are entitled to benefits under the E.E.C. social security regulations. Frequent visitors, such as travelling businessmen, may obtain a special form which is valid for a longer period. The only exceptions to this need for an E111 are when visiting Denmark or the Irish Republic.

Otherwise it is absolutely essential to have your E111 readily available when you require medical attention in any E.E.C. country, else you may receive no benefits.

The final general point is that financial reimbursement, where applicable, must be obtained before the patient leaves the E.E.C. country as it is almost certain it will not be obtained later. Hence:

1. Self-employed and non-employed and their dependants have no financial cover in E.E.C. countries.
2. Within six months of travel obtain form CM1 from D.H.S.S. office, complete it and return.
3. You will be sent a E111 permit. Take this overseas with you.

Although every effort has been made to ensure accuracy of the following information, no liability can be accepted.

Belgium

Administrative authority

Auxiliary Fund for Sickness and Invalidity Insurance (La Caisse Auxiliare d'Assurance Maladie-Invalidité), 10 Boulevard Saint-Lazare, 1030 Brussels. Tel. 182300.

Addresses of the local organisation may be obtained from the head offices.

National Alliance of Christian Friendly Societies (Alliance Nationales des Mutualités Chrétiennes), 131 Rue de la Loi, 1040 Brussels. Tel. 358080.

National League of Federated Liberal Friendly Societies of Belgium (Ligue Nationale des Fédérations Mutualistés Libérales de Belgique), 19-25 Rue de Livourne, 1050 Brussels. Tel. 384154.

National Union of Federated Non-Party Friendly Societies of Belgium (Union Nationale des Fédération Mutualistés Neutres de Belgique), 145 Chaussée de Charleroi, 1060 Brussels. Tel. 388300.

National Union of Federated Professional Friendly Societies of Belgium (Union Nationale des Fédérations des Mutualités Professionelles de Belgique), 13 Rue Boduognat, 1040 Brussels. Tel. 332188.

National Union of Socialist Friendly Societies (Union Nationale des Mutualités Socialistes), 32 Rue Saint-Jean, 1000 Brussels. Tel. 136470.

The addresses of the local offices of the above organisations should be available in the local telephone directory.

If treatment from general practitioner is required

1. Go straight to doctor, showing E111.
2. Pay the doctor but obtain a receipt.
3. Take prescription to chemist. Obtain a receipt and keep copy of prescription. In some areas doctors may provide medicine, but still obtain a receipt.
4. Take receipts with E111 to local office of one of the organisations mentioned above. The refund will probably be in the neighbourhood of 75 per cent.

If hospital treatment is required

1. Go to the local office of one of the organisations with E111. They will advise where treatment can be received and authorise part payment.
2. If you have to go to hospital in an emergency show them the E111 and ask them to arrange authorisation of part payment through local offices.

N.B. If you are obtaining treatment in Belgium for an established industrial injury received in the U.K., tell the authorities this.

France

Administrative authority

Local Social Security offices (La Caisse Primaire de Sécurité Sociale). Office in most towns. Address may be obtained from the Town Hall (Hotel de Ville).

If treatment from general practitioner is required

1. First take E111 to local Social Security office, who will issue a sickness document (une feuille de maladie).
2. Take this form to a doctor or dentist. Pay for the service but see the payment is entered on the form. Similarly, at chemist see cost of medicine is entered on form and copy of prescription is given.

3. In the event of not being able to carry out (1), take E111 to doctor who should provide the sickness document.

4. Finally take E111, sickness document and copy of prescription to Social Security office. Seventy per cent repayment of doctor's fee and 70-90 per cent of prescription is usual.

If hospital treatment is required

1. Inform the local Social Security office immediately.
2. Inform hospital you are an insured worker or dependant of one.
3. At least 80 per cent of the cost will be met by the Social Security office.

N.B. For an established industrial injury follow-up treatment, carry on as above but inform Social Security office it is an industrial injury.

Germany (Federal Republic)

Administrative authority

Local sickness insurance offices (Allegemeine Ortskrankenkassen). Addresses from town hall and post offices.

If treatment from general practitioner is required

1. First take E111 to local sickness insurance office (Krankenkassen) who will provide a sickness document (Krankenschein) and a list of doctors and dentists who practise within the scheme.

2. Then take document to doctor of choice, who will treat you without charge.

3. The chemist will charge a small fixed amount for each item. This is not recoverable.

4. If you visit a doctor without a sickness document show E111. He will charge you, but if you obtain sickness document subsequently and take it to him within ten days he will repay your fee.

N.B. Not all doctors and dentists are in the insurance scheme, hence obtaining list first is best.

If hospital treatment is required

1. Obtain a certificate from a G.P., and take it and E111 to local sickness insurance office. They will issue a further certificate (Kostenübernahmeschein) to enable you to obtain free hospital treatment (third class). This is then taken to the hospital.

2. If attendance at hospital is a matter of urgency take E111 to hospital and ask them to obtain the further certificate.

N.B. It must be remembered the the free entitlement is only for 'third class' grading.

For an established industrial injury follow-up treatment, carry on as above but inform local sickness insurance office it is an industrial injury.

Italy

Administrative authority

Local offices of National Institute for Sickness Insurance (Instituto Nazionale per L'Assicurazione Contro le Malattie—I.N.A.M.). Addresses may be obtained from local post offices and town hall.

If treatment from general practitioner is required

1. First take E111 to local I.N.A.M. office and obtain certificate for free treatment plus list of doctors who practise within the scheme.
2. Take the form to the doctor, who will treat you without charge.
3. Prescription to chemist. Some medicines will be free. Some will invoke a small charge which is not refundable.

If hospital treatment is required

1. Obtain a certificate from a G.P., and take it and your E111 to the local I.N.A.M. office. They will give you a further certificate to enable you to have free treatment at one of the hospitals in the area who provide treatment under the I.N.A.M. scheme. They will also give you a list of these hospitals.
2. In an emergency if you produce your E111 you can be admitted to a public hospital. The hospital must notify I.N.A.M. within three days for you to obtain free treatment.

N.B. Not all doctors and hospitals accept patients within the I.N.A.M. scheme.

For an established industrial injury follow-up treatment can be obtained through the National Institute of Industrial Insurance (Instituto Nazionale per L'Assicurazione Contro Gli Infortuni sul Lavoro—I.N.A.I.L.). Offices are available in most towns.

Luxembourg

Administrative authority

National Sickness Insurance Office, 10 Rue de Strasbourg, Luxembourg. Local agencies at Battembourg, Clervaux, Dierkirch, Differdange, Dudelange, Echternach, Esch/Alzette, Grevenmacher, Larochette, Mersch, Pétange, Rédange-sur-Attert, Remich, Rumelange, Steinfort and Wiltz.

If treatment from general practitioner is required

1. First take form E111 to local sickness office, who will provide you with a sickness document.
2. Take the form to a doctor, who will make a charge for which you must obtain a receipt.
3. Take the prescription to the local chemist, who will again charge you, so obtain a receipt.
4. Take your receipts to the local sickness office. You will be fully refunded for the doctor's fee, but you may have to pay a small percentage of the chemist's charges.

If hospital treatment is required

1. First obtain a certificate from a doctor which you should take to the local sickness office with your E111. Hospitalisation is normally free. In an emergency you can go direct to a hospital.

N.B. For an established industrial injury follow-up treatment you must contact the Insurance Association for Accidents (L'Association d'Assurance Contre les Accidents), 1 Rue Zithe, Luxembourg. Tel. 20511.

The Netherlands

Administrative authority

Netherlands General Sickness Insurance Fund (Algemeen Nederlands Onderling Ziekenhuis — A.N.O.Z.), 56 Kromme Nieuwe Gracht, Utrecht. Tel. 030-317541.

If treatment from a general practitioner is required

1. Take your form E111 to a doctor or dentist. However, you should ask him whether he is affiliated to the A.N.O.Z. fund. There will be no charge.

2. If the drugs are not provided by the doctor, take the prescription to an approved chemist. Again there will be no charge.

If hospital treatment is required

1. It is advisable to first obtain the authority for free treatment from A.N.O.Z. in Utrecht. This is best through the doctor.

2. In an emergency, treatment can be obtained without prior authority of A.N.O.Z., but this must be cleared within two days.

N.B. For treatment for an established industrial injury the procedure is as above.

Denmark

Administrative authority

Social and health divisions of the local councils. Addresses obtained from local post offices or from the Administration of Social Security, Holmens Kanal 7, Copenhagen.

If treatment from a general practitioner is required

1. Take your passport along to your doctor of choice. E111 not required in Denmark. Names of doctors may be found in the telephone directory or from the social and health division of the local council. If the doctor charges a fee, obtain a receipt and apply for repayment at the local council. In general, the cost of specialist treatment arranged by a general practitioner will also be paid by the local council.

2. Take your prescription to a local chemist. If on the scheduled list, on production of your passport a reduced charge will be made for it. This is not refundable.

If hospital treatment is required

Free treatment normally arranged through general practitioner.

Accident and sudden illness

Ambulances can be summoned by dialling 000 in an absolute emergency. In general, contact should be made with a general practitioner first. Strict rota systems are worked by G.P.s, and the practitioners' emergency service number can be found in the telephone directory under LAEGEVAGTEN. Urgent dental treatment can be obtained on part payment on production of passport.

Irish Republic

Administrative authority

Eight local health boards. Medical care is provided free of direct charge.

An E111 is NOT necessary, and on receiving a medical service you will have to complete a form giving nationality and place of residence, also stating that you are employed in the United Kingdom.

1. On consulting a doctor it is essential you ask for treatment under the E.E.C. regulations. If you do not request this he has every right to charge a fee which is not refundable. The list of doctors participating in the scheme can be obtained from the offices of the local health boards or from the telephone directory under 'Health Boards'. Under these regulations there is no fee to pay,

the doctor is paid by the Health Board. Provided that the prescription is on the official form there will be no charge from the chemist either.

If hospital treatment is required

Normally arranged through the general practitioner. No charges in public wards at hospitals participating in the scheme. Direct charges for semi-private and private rooms when consultants charge as well, as in the U.K.

And so to summarise, there are obvious problems in relying on E.E.C. medical arrangements, which are vastly inferior to what the N.H.S. offers the visitor:

1. Self-employed and non-employed and their dependants are not covered.
2. First before travel a form CM1 must be obtained, completed and returned to a D.H.S.S. office.
3. This will provide you with an E111, which must be taken with you.
4. Children over 16 not at full time education and all children of 19 and over must obtain their own E111.
5. E111's are, however, not necessary in Denmark and Ireland.
6. In France, Germany and Italy the patient or one of his family has to visit the local social security office first to obtain a permit before seeing a doctor.
7. In Belgium, France, Luxembourg, and sometimes in Denmark, the doctor's fee must be paid, or receipt obtained and money reclaimed from the local authority, *before* leaving the country.
8. In Belgium the patient is repaid approximately 75 per cent. In France 70 per cent of the general practitioner's fees and 80 per cent of the hospital.
9. In Germany, Holland and Italy G.P. treatment is free, but only from certain panel doctors.
10. Free hospital treatment is only available in certain hospitals. In Germany this is officially described as 'third class': in Ireland as 'public'.

Needless to say, holiday resorts outside the E.E.C., such as Spain, Portugal and Greece, are not covered at all.

The author feels very strongly that with all the above-mentioned complications and variations, it is a far sounder plan to take a travel sickness insurance policy.

There is only one exception to this, and that is the elderly pensioner and his wife who are covered as above by the E.E.C. arrangements but are too old to be accepted on a sickness insurance policy.

There is a further point in favour of the insurance policy. Accident or sickness may cause delay in return home. Many policies allow for this, and cover incidental expenses and cancellation due to delays so incurred.

If it is decided to take out a medical expenses insurance policy, the first point to remember, as with all insurance, is that the sum insured must be adequate. Most inclusive tours include a medical expenses insurance. However, in general, the sum insured under this inclusive policy is too small in amount and as such may provide inadequate cover.

For any traveller to the United States and Canada it is absolutely essential to take out a policy of at least £1,000 cover for every person. A general practitioner's house call is frequently in excess of £10. When it is remembered that this £1,000 can include additional accommodation and extra travel expenses this is an absolute minimum, particularly as the patient may have to be sent home as a stretcher case by air. The cost of emergency surgery for an appendicectomy or perforated peptic ulcer can be well in excess of £500. U.K.

travellers visiting Europe may feel that £500 is enough as travel costs will be less, but here again, with soaring prices in Europe, including medical costs, it is sensible to insure for at least £1,000.

Most companies now offer medical expenses insurance policies. For many years the Avon Insurance Company has specialised in this type of policy and, several years ago, offered cover up to £1,000 while many were limiting the maximum to £250 or £500, The Commercial Union Assurance Company, C. T. Bowring & Co. Ltd. are two other large organisations who offer these policies, and any good insurance broker will advise.

One further point to remember about these various policies is that they usually cover Personal Accident, Loss of Baggage, Loss of Personal Money and Personal Liability cover. Regrettably, some companies sell these policies on a package basis. In other words, £x cover for Personal Accident, £y for Medical Fees and £z for Baggage, etc. If you wish £2y for medical insurance then you have to have £2x and £2z. Avon Insurance work on the selected benefits principle whereby the insured persons select the amount of cover they wish for each particular section, which is far better.

World-wide medical benefits and cancellation expenses to the amount of £1,000 for 17 days costs only in the neighbourhood of £1.50 while three months' insurance cover for the same amount is approximately £5. For families the premiums are halved for each person after the second. Members of British United Provident Association and Private Patients Plan have cover overseas for hospital costs as they have in the U.K., but it must be remembered that as the costs are so much higher overseas, the cover given by these schemes may not be sufficient to pay all expenses, and extra insurance may be necessary.

Most policies exclude the first part of the expenses—usually £5 or £10—incurred by children aged under five years or by persons aged over 70 or 75 years. In some companies' offices, such an exclusion applies to all insured persons.

For a policy to cover accidents due to winter sports the rate is generally about four times as much, but it is absolutely essential that adequate cover is taken out for such a holiday.

Medical Facilities for U.K. Nationals in E.E.C. Countries

	Belgium	France	Germany	Italy	Luxembourg	Netherlands	Denmark	Ireland
Administrative Authority	La Caisse Auxilaire D'Assurance Maladie—Invalidité	La Caisse Primaire de Sécurité Sociale	Allgemeine Ortskranken-kassen	I.N.A.M.	National Sickness Insurance Offices	A.N.O.Z.	Local Authorities	Local Health Boards
Is E111 necessary?	Yes	Yes	Yes	Yes	Yes	Yes	No	No
Is certificate from Admin. Auth. necessary to see doctor?	No	Yes	Yes	Yes	No	No	No	No
Is doctor free?	Pay and obtain receipt	Pay and obtain receipt	Yes	Yes	Pay and obtain receipt	Yes	Sometimes pay but obtain receipt	Yes
Is cost repaid by Admin. Auth?	75%	70% G.P. 80% Hospital	n/a	n/a	Full refund	n/a	Full repayment	n/a
Is chemist free?	Pay and obtain receipt	Pay and obtain receipt	Small fixed charge	Free or small charge	Pay and obtain receipt	No charge	Reduced charge	No charge if approved
Is cost repaid by Admin. Auth?	75%	70-90%	Not repaid	Not repaid	Partly repaid	n/a	Not repaid	Not repaid
Is certificate from Admin. Auth. necessary before going to hospital?	Yes	Inform Admin. Offices	(1) cert. from doctor, then (2) Cert. from Admin. Offices	I.N.A.M. and list of approved hospitals	(1) Cert. from doctor, then (2) Cert. from Admin. Offices	Obtain authority through G.P.	Arranged through G.P.	Arranged through G.P.
Is hospital free?	Pay and obtain receipt	Pay and obtain receipt	Yes	Yes	Yes	Yes	Yes	Yes, in public wards of certain hospitals
Is cost repaid by Admin. Auth?	Approx. 75%	80%	n/a N.B. Third class accommodation	n/a, but only certain hospitals	n/a	n/a	n/a	n/a

E. Other Useful Addresses

Hospital for Tropical Diseases, 4 St Pancras Way, London, NW1. 01-387 4411.

London School of Hygiene and Tropical Medicine, Keppel Street (Gower Street), London, WC1. 01-636 3041 and 01-580 7621.

Liverpool School of Tropical Medicine, Pembroke Place, Liverpool, 3. 051-709 7611.

Tropical Diseases Unit, East Birmingham Hospital (General Branch), Birmingham, 9. 021-772 4311.

Tropical Diseases Unit, City Hospital, Greenbank Drive, Edinburgh, 10. 031-447 1001.

Royal Society of Tropical Medicine and Hygiene, Manson House, 26 Portland Place, London, W1N 4EY. 01-580 2127.

Ross Institute, London School of Hygiene and Tropical Medicine, Keppel Street (Gower Street), London, WC1. 01-636 3041 and 01-580 7621.

Wellcome Museum of Medical Science, Wellcome Building, Euston Road, London, NW1 01-387 4477.

Wellcome Laboratories of Tropical Medicine, Langley Court, Beckenham, Kent. 01-650 3422.

Reference laboratories and reference experts

Dysentery Reference Laboratory
Enteric Reference Laboratory
Salmonella Reference Laboratory
all at: Central Public Health Laboratory, Colindale Avenue, London, NW9. 01-205 7041.

Leptospirosis Reference Laboratory
Mycological Reference Laboratory
at: London School of Hygiene and Tropical Medicine, Keppel Street (Gower Street), London, WC1. 01-636 3041 and 01-580 7621.

Brucella Identification. Dr D. J. H. Payne, Public Health Laboratory, St Mary's General Hospital (East Wing), Milton Road, Portsmouth. 0705 22331.

Cholera Identification. Mrs K. P. Carpenter, Dysentery Reference Laboratory, CPHL, Colindale Avenue, London, NW9. 01-205 7041.

Amoebic Dysentery, CFT Test. Mrs C. M. P. Bradstreet, Standards Laboratory for Serological Reagents, CPHL, Colindale Avenue, London, NW9. 01-205 7041.

Dysentery Bacilli Typing. Mrs K. P. Carpenter—see under Cholera.

Encephalitis (Acute Infectious). Dr A. D. MacRae, Virus Reference Laboratory, CPHL, Colindale Avenue, London, NW9. 01-205 7041.

Enteric Fever. Dr E. S. Anderson, Enteric Reference Laboratory, CPHL, Colindale Avenue, London, NW9. 041-205 7041.

Helminths. Prof. G. S. Nelson, London School of Hygiene and Tropical Medicine, Keppel Street (Gower Street), London, WC1. 01-636 3041 and 01-580 7621.

Hydatid Disease, CFT. Mrs Bradstreet—see under amoebic dysentery.

Leptospiral Infections. Dr L. H. Turner, London School of Hygiene and Tropical Medicine, Keppel Street (Gower Street), London, WC1. 01-636 3041 and 01-580 7621.

Malaria. Prof. P. C. C. Garnham, FRS, London School of Hygiene and Tropical Medicine, Keppel Street (Gower Street), London, WC1. 01-636 3041 and 01-580 7621.

Parasitic Infections—Serology. Dr D. S. Ridley, Hospital for Tropical Diseases, St Pancras Way, London, NW91. 01-387 6441.

Poliomyelitis. Dr A. D. MacRae, Virus Reference Laboratory, CPHL, Colindale Avenue, London, NW9. 01-205 7041.

Rabies, Diagnostic Tests. Virus Reference Laboratory, CPHL, Colindale Avenue, London, NW1. 01-205 7041.

Smallpox. Diagnostic Testing.

Dr A. D. Evans, PHL, Royal Infirmary, Cardiff. 0222-33101.

Dr J. H. Hale, PHL, General Hospital, Westgate Road, Newcastle-upon-Tyne. 0632-38811, ext. 297.

Dr M. H. Hambling, PHL, Bridle Path, York Road, Leeds, 15. 0533-645011.

Dr A. D. MacRae, Virus Reference Laboratory, CPHL, Colindale Avenue, London, NW9. 01-205 7041.

Dr K. McCarthy, Medical School, Ashton Street, Liverpool, 3. 051-709 7983, ext. 202.

Toxoplasmosis: *London:* Dr D. G. Fleck, St George's Hospital, Tooting Grove, London, SW17. 01-672 1255.

South: Dr W. K. Wates, PHL, Cockett Road, Swansea. 0792 23041/2.

North: Dr G. B. Ludlam, PHL, Bridle Path, York Road, Leeds, 15. 0533-645011.

Vaccines and other immunological materials available through the Public Health Laboratories.

Typhus vaccine

Can be obtained from the Public Health Laboratories at:

Birmingham	Leeds	Newcastle
Bristol	Liverpool	Oxford
Cambridge	London (CPHL)	Sheffield
Exeter	Manchester	Cardiff

Rabies vaccine

Can be obtained from the Public Health Laboratories at:

Liverpool	London (CPHL)	Newcastle	Cardiff

Anthrax vaccine

Can be obtained from the Public Health Laboratories at:

Bradford	Liverpool	London (CPHL)

Anti-vaccinial gamma globulin

Birmingham	Leeds	Manchester
Bristol	Leicester	Newcastle
Cambridge	Liverpool	Oxford
Cardiff	London (CPHL)	Sheffield
Gloucester		

Bibliography

Adam, J. M., Latham, F. & Wyatt, H. T. (1963). *Preliminary Observations of the Immediate Effect of Heat on Acclimatised Paratroops.* APRC Report 61/31 MRC.

Adam, J. M. (1955). *A General Review of the Physiological Problems Arising in the Army.* Report to the War Office AMD5.

Adam, J. M. (1967). Military problems of air transport and tropical service. In *The Effects of Abnormal Physical Conditions at Work.* Edited by C. N. Davies, P. R. Davies and F. H. Tyrer. Edinburgh: Livingstone.

Adam, J. M. (1967). Climate and clothing. *Practitioner,* **198,** 645.

Adams, A. R. D. & Maegraith, B. G. (1971). *Clinical Tropical Diseases.* Oxford: Blackwell.

Allen, S. D. & O'Brien, J. P. (1944). Tropical anhidrotic asthenia; preliminary report. *Med. J. Aust.,* **2,** 335.

Anderson, E. S. & Smith, M. R. (1972). Chloramphenicol resistance in typhoid bacillus. *B.M.J.,* **3,** 329.

Ashton, A. (1960). Larval granulomatosis of the retina due to toxocara. *British Journal of Ophthalmology,* **44,** 129.

Beighton, P. H. & Richards, P. R. (1968). Cardiovascular disease in air travellers. *Br. Heart Journal,* **XXX, 3,** 367.

Bentley Phillips, B. (1965). *Practitioner,* **194,** 808.

Bergen, S. S. & Roels, G. A. (1965). *Amer. Jrnl. Clinical Nutrition,* **16,** 265.

Brand, J. J. & Whittingham, P. (1970). Intramuscular hyoscine in the treatment of motion sickness. *Lancet,* **2,** 2000.

British Medical Journal (1971). Compulsory immunization procedures in Europe. *B.M.J.,* **1,** 795.

British Medical Journal (1971). **2,** 70.

British Medical Journal (1971). Clioquinol and neurological disease. *B.M.J.,* **2,** 291.

British Medical Journal (1971). **3,** 129.

Bulmer, E. (1944) Survey of tropical diseases seen in the Middle East. *Trans. Roy. Soc. Trop. Med. & Hyg.,* **37,** 3225.

Butler, T., Linm, Arnold, K. & Pollack, M. (1973). Chloramphenicol resistant typhoid fever in Vietnam associated with R. factor. *Lancet,* **2,** 7836.983.

Buxton, P. A. (1955). The Natural History of Tsetse Flies. *London School of Hygiene and Tropical Medicine, Memoir No. 10.*

Chinn, H. I. (1963). What is Motion Sickness? — *Symposium on Motion Sickness with Special Reference to Weightlessness.* Wright-Patterson, A. F. B. Ohio, 6570th Aerospace Medical Research Laboratories. Reprint No. AMRL-TDR-63-25.

Christie, A. B. (1969). *Infectious Diseases: Epidemiology and Clinical Practice.* Edinburgh: Livingstone.

Clark, I., Bassett, C. & Andrew, L. (1960). The antagonistic action of vitamin A on vitamin D toxicity. *Fed. Proc.,* **19,** 412.

Cluver, E. H. (1964). Sun trauma prevention. *South African Med. Jnl.,* **38,** 801.

Cluver, E. H. & Politzer, W. M. (1965). The pathology of sun trauma. *South African Med. Jnl.,* **39,** 1051.

Cole, L. (1953). Treatment of tetanus (Letter). *B.M.J.,* **2,** 1099.

Conroy, R. T. W. L. (1966). Mean plasma cortisol at different times of day in a group of workers in a newspaper office (unpublished data).

Cussen, D. E. (1964). Personal communication.

De Kruif, Paul. *Microbe Hunters*. London: Jonathan Cape.

Dennison, D. M., Ledwith, F. & Poulton, E. C. (1966). Computer reaction times at simulated cabin altitudes of 5,000 and 8,000 feet. *Aerospace Medicine,* **38,** 825.

Dick, G. Routine smallpox vaccination (1971). *B.M.J.,* **3,** 163.

Dorolle, P. (1972). International problems of communicable disease control. *Lancet,* **2,** 527.

Dorolle, P. (1968). Old plagues in the jet age. *B.M.J.,* **4,** 789.

Edholm, O. G., Adam, J. M., Allan, J. R., Fox, R. H., Goldsmith, R., Hampton, I. G., Underwood, C. R., Ward. E. J. & Wolff, H. S. (1964). *The effect of heat on food and water intake of acclimatised and unacclimatised men.* Army Personnel Research Committee Report No. 64/16. London: M.R.C.

El Mofty, A. M. & Nada, M. M. (1972). Vitiligo and its treatment, *Essays on Tropical Dermatology.* Edited by J. Marshall. Amsterdam: Excerpta Medica.

Endeavour Journal of Joseph Banks, F.R.S. (1768-1771). Edited by J. C. Beaglehole (1962).

Fitzpatrick, T. B. (1971). Tropical and systemic approaches to photoprotection. *Proc. R.S.M.,* **64,** 861.

Furman, K. I. (1972). Sylvasum and prevention of sun trauma. *South African Med. Jnl.,* **46,** 1670.

Furry, D. E., Reeves, E. & Beckman, E. (1967). Relationship of SCUBA diving to the development of aviators' decompression sickness. *Aerospace Medicine,* **38,** 825.

Geddes, A. M. (1973). Enteric fever, salmonellosis and food poisoning. *B.M.J.,* **1,** 98.

Goldie, E. A. G. (1942). Unpublished data quoted in *Textbook of Aviation Physiology* (1965). Edited by Gillies, J. A. Oxford: Pergamon Press.

Goldsmith, R. (1967). Temperature control and environment. *Practitioner,* **198,** 651.

Gordon, J. E. (1965). *Control of Communicable Diseases in Man.* Amer. Pub. Health Assoc.

Green, R. L., Huntsman, R. G. & Serjeant, G. R. (1971). The sickle cell and altitude. *B.M.J.,* **4,** 593.

Green, R. L. (1972). The selection of patients for air travel. *Modern Medicine.* Feb.

Gregory, M. C. & Spalding, J. M. K. (1972). Poliomyelitis in adults (Letter). *Lancet,* **7742,** 155.

Haggard, Howard W. (1941). *Devils, Drugs and Doctors.* London: Heineman.

Haneveld, D. (1960). Epidemiological aspects of traveller's diarrhoea in the Lebanon. *Tropical and Geographical Medicine,* **12,** 339.

Hauty, G. T. & Adams, J. (1966). Phase shifts of the human circadian system and performance deficit during the periods of transition. (1) East-West flight; *Aerospace Medicine,* **37,** 7. (2) West-East flight; *Aerospace Medicine,* **37,** 10. (3) North-South flight; *Aerospace Medicine,* **37,** 12.

Hellman, K. & Weiner, J. S. (1953). Antidiuretic substance in urine following exposure to high temperatures. *Journal Applied Physiology,* **6,** 194.

Hertig, B. A. & Sargent, F. (1963). Acclimatisation of women during work in hot environments. *Fed. Proc.,* **22,** 810.

Hertig, B. A. & Belding, H. A. (1963). Evaluation and contro of heat hazzards. In *Temperature: Its Measurement and Control in Science and Industry,* Vol. 3, Part 3. New York: Reinhold.

Horne, G. O. & Mole, R. H. (1949). The effect of water and salt intake in prickly heat. *Lancet,* **2,** 279.

Horne, G. O. (1950). Anhidrotic heat exhaustion. *Trans. Roy. Soc. Trop. Med. & Hyg.,* **44,** 193.

Horne, G. O. (1951). Mammillaria. *Trans. Roy. Soc. Trop. Med. & Hyg.,* **44,** 465.

Irwin, J. A. (1881). The pathology of seasickness. *Lancet,* Nov. 1881, p. 907.

James, W. (1882). The sense of dizziness in deaf mutes. *Amer. Jnl. Otol,* **4,** 239.

Johnston, J. H. & Zakon, S. J. (1958). *A.M.A. Arch. Derm.,* **71,** 267.

Kaplan, I. (1964). Motion sickness on railroads. *Ind. Med. Survey,* **33,** 648.

Kawahata, K. A. (1960). Evaluation and control of heat hazards. In *Essential Problems in Climatic Physiology*. Kyoto: Nankodo.

Kean, B. H. & Smillie, W. G. (1954). Intestinal protozoa of American travellers returning from Europe. *New Eng. J. Med.*, **251**, 471.

Kean, B. H. & Waters, S. R. (1958). Incidence of diarrhoea in travellers returning to U.S. from Mexico. *A.M.A. Archives of Industrial Health*, **18**, 148.

Kean, B. H. & Waters, S. R. (1959). Drug prophylaxis in Mexico. *New Eng. Jnl. Med.*, **261**, 71.

Kean, B. H., Schaffner, W., Brennan, R. W. & Waters, S. R. (1962). Prophylaxis with phthalylsulphathiazole and neomycin. *Jnl. A.M.A.*, **5**, 367.

Kellogg, R. S., Kennedy, R. S. & Graybiel, A. (1965). Motion sickness. Symptomatology of labyrinthine defective and normal subjects during zero gravity manoeuvres. *Aerospace Med.*, **36**, 315.

Kershaw, G. R. (1947). Acute non-specific diarrhoea and dysentery. Local chilling of the abdomen as a factor. *B.M.J.*, **1**, 717.

Kleitman, N. (1949). *Sleep and Wakefulness*. University of Chicago Press.

Kraft, E. R., Hoch, S. G., Newcomb, E. A. & Quisna, R. G. (1972). *Jnl. Soc. Cosmet Chem.*, **23**, 383.

Kuno, Y. (1956). *Human Perspiration*. Thomas: Springfield.

Ladell, W. S. S., Waterlow, J. C. & Hudson, M. F. (1944). Desert climates: physiological and clinical observations. *Lancet*, **2**, 491, 527.

Ladell, W. S. S. (1945). Thermal sweating. *Brit. Med. Bull.*, **3**, 175.

Lancet (1973). Sunburn, **2**, 30.

Lederer, L. G. & Kidera, G. J. (1954). Passenger comfort in commercial air travel with reference to motion sickness. *Inter. Record Med.*, **167**, 661.

Leithead, C. S. (1958). Natural acclimatisation to heat. *Proc. 6th Int. Cong. Trop. Med.* (Lisbon). **6**, 22.

Leithead, C. S. & Lind, A. R. (1964). *Heat Stress and Heat Disorders*. London: Cassell.

Llano, G. A. (1955). Airmen against the sea — an analysis of sea survival experiences. Maxwell AFB, Ala — Research Studies.

Lobban, M. C. (1963). Human renal diurnal rhythms in an arctic mining community. *J. Physiol.*, **165**, 75.

Lobban, M. C. & Tredre, B. E. (1964). Renal diurnal rhythms in blind subjects. *J. Physiol.*, **170**, 29.

Loewenthal, L. J. A. (1961). The pathogensis of miliaria. *Arch. Derm. (Chicago)*, **84**, 2.

Loewenthal, L. J. A. (1963). *Medical Proceedings*, **9-22**, 461.

Loewenthal, L. J. A. (1963). *Brit. Jnl. Derm.*, **75**, 254.

Loomis, W. Farnsworth (1967). Skin pigment regulation of vitamin D biosynthesis in man. *Science*, **157**, 501.

McArdle, B., Dunham, W., Holling, H. E., Ladell, W. S., Scott, J. W., Thompson, M. L. & Weiner, J. S. (1947). The prediction of the physiological effects of warm and hot environments: the P4SR index. M.R.C., R.N.P. Rep. 47/391.

McFarland, R. A. (1953). *Human Factors in Air Transport*. New York: McGraw-Hill.

McGirr, P. O. M. (1967). Circadian rhythms in flights. *Trans. Soc. Occup. Med.*, **18**, 3.

McGregor, I. (1946). *B.M.J.*, **2**, 25.

Macrae, A. D. (1973). Rabies. *B.M.J.*, **1**, 604.

Macrae, James (1973). Tetanus. *B.M.J.*, **1**, 730.

Malcolm, Napier (1972). *The Practitioner*, **208**, 268.

Manning, G. W. & Stewart, W. G. (1949). Effect of body position on the incidence of motion sickness. *J. App. Phys.*, **1**, 619.

Manson-Bahr, Sir Philip (1972). *Manson's Tropical Disease*. London: Cassell.

Marshall, J. (1972). The white skin and the sun. In *Essays on Tropical Dermatoses*. Edited by J. Marshall. Amsterdam: Excerpta Medica.

Mathews-Roth, M. M. (1970). *New Eng. Jnl. Med.*, **282**, 1231.

Millard, C. K. (1924). *Lancet*, **1**, 301.

Mills, J. N. (1964). The circadian rhythms during and after three months in solitude underground. *J. Physiol.*, **174**, 217.

Minard, D., Belding, H. S. & Kingston, J. R. (1957). Prevention of heat casualties. *Jnl. A.M.A.*, **165**, 1813.
Money, K. E. (1970). Motion sickness. *Physiologica Reviews,* V.50 No. 1.
Nakae, K., Yamamoto, S. I., Shigematsu, I. & Kono, R. (1973). Relation between subsacute myelo-optico neuropathy (SMON) and clioquinol: nationwide survey. *Lancet,* **1,** 171.
Nixon, P. G. F. (1972). *Physiotherapy,* **58,** 336.
Nixon, P. G. F. (1973). *The Practitioner,* **211,** 5.
Novy, F. G. & Ramsey, J. H. (1944). Failure of sweat mechanism in desert. *Jnl. A.M.A.*, **125,** 738.
Osterman, P. O. (1971). Myelopathy after clioquinol treatment. *Lancet,* **2,** 544.
Owen, Raymond J. (1968). Personal Communication and Medical Report on Olympic Games in Mexico 1968. British Olympic Association.
Pathak, M. A., Fitzpatrick, T. B. & Frenk, E. (1969). Evaluation of topical agents that prevent sunburn. *New Eng. J. Med.*, **280,** 1459.
Piekarski, G. (1962). *Medical Parasitology.* Farbenfabriken Bayer, A.G.
Pinkus, M. & Hunter, R. (1964). Biometric analysis of the effect of oral vitamin A on human epidermis. *Jnl. Invest. Derm.*, **42,** 131.
Pollock, T. M. & Reid, D. (1969). Immunoglobulin for the prevention of infectious hepatitis in persons working overseas. *Lancet,* **1,** 281.
Powell, J. J., Beach, A. M., Smiley, J. R. & Russell, N. C. (1962). Successful prediction of air sickness in aircrew trainees. *Aerospace Med.*, **33,** 1069.
Preston, F. S. (1970). Time zone disruption and sleep patterns in pilots. *Trans. Soc. Occup. Med.*, **20,** 77.
Preston, F. S. (1971). Motion sickness. *Practitioner,* **206,** 609.
Preston, F. S. (1972). Medical aspects of aerospace travel. *Proc. Roy. Soc. Med.*, **65,** 187.
Preston, F. S., Bateman, S. C., Short, R. V. & Wilkinson, R. T. (1973). Effects of flying and of time changes on menstrual cycle length and on performance in airline stewardesses. *Aerospace Medicine,* **44,** 438.
Reid, H. A. (1968). Snake bite in the tropics. *B.M.J.*, **3,** 359.
Richards, P. R. (1968). Modern air transport and invalids. *Jnl. Roy. Coll. Gen. Practit.*, **15,** 336.
Richards, P. R. (1973). Effects of air travel on passengers with cardiovascular and respiratory diseases. *Practitioner,* **210,** 232.
Robinson, S. (1942). The effect of body size upon energy exchange in work. *Amer. J. Physiol.*, **136,** 363.
Rowe, B., Taylor, Joan & Bettelheim, K. A. (1970). An investigation of traveller's diarrhoea. *Lancet,* **1,** 1.
Sakazaki, R., Tamura, K. & Saito, M. (1967). Enteropathogenic *Escherchia Coli* associated with diarrhoea in children and adults. *Japanese Journal Medicine, Science and Biology,* **20,** 387.
Shaw, E. W. & Nicolai, J. Z. (1953). *Annals of Internal Medicine,* **39,** 131.
Shepherd, R. D. & Barlow, J. (1962). The effects of travel fatigue and tropical conditions on the military efficiency of unacclimatised parachute troops during the first three days. A.P.R.C. Report 61/26 MRC.
Spillane, J. D. (1971). S.M.O.N. *Lancet,* **2,** 1371.
Sulzberger, M. G., Zimmerman, H. M. & Emerson, K. (1946). Tropical anhidrotic asthenia and its relationship to prickly heat. *J. Invest. Derm.*, **7,** 153.
Terry, S. I. (1973). Transient dysaesthesia and persistent leucocytosis after clioquinol therapy. *B.M.J.*, **3,** 745.
Transactions of the Royal Society of Tropical Medicine and Hygiene (1970). Discussion on imported disease. **64,** 2, 199.
Tsubaki, T., Honma, Y. & Hoshi, M. (1971). Neurological syndrome associated with clioquinol. *Lancet,* **1,** 696.
Turner, A. C. (1967). Traveller's diarrhoea. Survey of symptoms, occurrence and possible prophylaxis. *B.M.J.*, **4,** 653.

Turner, A. C. (1968). Some medical aspects of air travel. *Bull. Br. Assoc. Sport & Med.*, **3**, 3.
Turner, A. C. (1968). Athletes and air travel. *Coaching Review of Canada*, **6**, 2.2.
Turner, A. C. (1970). Keeping fit in worldwide business and holiday travel. *Trans. Soc. Occup. Med.*, **20**, 94.
Turner, A. C. (1971). Food poisoning. *Practitioner*, **206**, 615.
Turner, A. C., Barnes, R. M. & Green, R. L. (1971). The effect of a preparation of vitamin A and calcium carbonate on sunburn. *Practitioner*, **206**, 662.
Turner, A. C. (1972). Medical assessment for residence in warm climates. *Practitioner*, **210**, 519.
Varela, G., Kean, B. H., Barrett, E. L. & Keegan, C. J. (1959). Bacteriological studies of U.S. students in Mexico. *Amer. J. Trop. Med. and Hyg.*, **8**, 353.
Vedder, E. B. & Rosenberg, C. (1938). *Jnl. Nutrition*, **16**, 57.
Wang, S. C. & Chinn, M. I. (1953). Vestibular reflex pathway in experimental motion sickness in dogs. *Int. Phys. Cong. 19. Montreal.*
Weiner, J. S. & Horne, G. O. (1958). A classification of heat illness. *B.M.J.*, **1**, 1533.
Whiteside, T. C. D. (1965). *Textbook of Aviation Medicine*. Edited by Gillies. Oxford: Pergamon.
Whittingham, H. E. (1957). Impact of air travel and epidemiology. *Br. Jnl. Clin. Pract.*, **xi, 6**, 409.
Willis, Isaac (1971). Sunlight and the skin. *Jnl. A.M.A.*, **217**, 8, 1028.
Wolkin, J., Goodman, J. J. & Kelley, W. E. (1944). Failure of sweat mechanism in desert: thermogenic anhidrosis. *Jnl. A.M.A.*, **124**, 479.
Wood, C. D. (1970). Selection of an antimotion sickness drug. *J. Louisianna State Med. Soc.*, **122**, 4, 95.
Wood, C. D. & Graybiel, A. (1970). Evaluation of antimotive sickness drugs. A new effective remedy revealed. *Aerospace Med.*, **41**, 932.
Woodruff, A. W., Ashton, N. & Stott, G. J. (1961). *Toxocara canis* infection of the eye. Transactions, *Royal Society of Tropical Medicine and Hygiene*, **55**, 13.
Woodruff, A. W. & Bell, S. (1968). *Synopsis of Infections and Tropical Diseases*. Bristol: Wright.
Woodruff, A. W. (ed.) (1970). *Alimentary and Haematological Aspects of Tropical Diseases*. London: Arnold.
Woodruff, A. W. (1970). Toxocariasis. *B.M.J.*, **1**, 730.
Woodruff, A. W. (1972). Personal communication on treatment of schistosomiasis.
Woodson, R. D. & Clinton, J. J. (1969). Immunoglobulin in the prevention of infectious hepatitis. *Jnl. A.M.A.*, **209**, 1053.
Wright, H. B. (1966). Why you feel flat after flying the Atlantic. *The Director*. June, p. 458.
W.H.O. International Health Regulations.
W.H.O. Chronicle.
W.H.O. Weekly Epidemiological Review.
W.H.O. Malaria, Smallpox and Yellow Fever Maps.
W.H.O. Yellow Fever Vaccinating Centres.
DEPARTMENT OF HEALTH AND SOCIAL SECURITY LEAFLET SA 28. Medical treatment for holidaymakers and other temporary visitors to countries of the European Economic Community.

Index

Aberdeen, 111
Acclimatisation, 37-40
Acne vulgaris, 40
Actamer *see* Bithionol
Actinic dermatitis *see* Sunburn
Adam, J. M., 31, 32
Addis Ababa, 15
Aden, 54
Aedes mosquito, 61, 93, 102, 143
Afars and Issas, 173
Afghanistan, 174, 221
Africa, Central, 14, 16, 20, 59, 71, 93, 95, 97, 98, 101, 103, 104, 105, 107, 114, 123. 124, 130, 132, 138, 143, 145, 149
East, 59, 70, 71, 93, 95, 97, 98, 99, 101, 103, 104, 105, 108, 114, 116, 121, 123, 124, 129, 132, 134, 135, 138, 143, 145, 146, 149
North, 11, 101, 103, 107, 110, 114, 116, 121, 123, 134, 138, 143
South, 59, 71, 103, 104, 108, 116, 124, 128, 132, 140, 200, 206
West, 20, 59, 93, 95, 97, 98, 99, 101, 103, 105, 108, 114, 116, 121, 123, 124, 132, 134, 138, 143, 145, 147, 149
Age (in acclimatisation), 39, 45
Air sickness *see* Motion sickness
Air travel, contraindications, 157-159
medical fitness for, 153-159
Alastrim, 105
Albania, 174
Alcohol, 28, 34, 40, 153
Alcopar *see* Bephenium
Aleppo boil *see* Cutaneous leishmaniasis
Algeria, 70, 174, 222
Algid malaria, 96
Alimentary disease, 158, 165
Ambilhar *see* Niridazole
America, 100, 132, 149
Central, 14, 16, 97, 100, 108, 115, 123, 124, 128, 132, 133, 138, 149
South, 65, 78, 97, 98, 100, 103, 105, 108, 124, 128, 130, 132, 133, 135, 138, 143, 147, 149
9-aminoacridine compounds, 65
4-aminoquinoline compounds, 65
8-aminoquinoline compounds, 65
Amodiaquin, 65
Amoebiasis (amoebic dysentery), 52, 107-110
Amoebic hepatitis, 109
Amoeboma, 109
Ampicillin, 113
Anderson, E. S. and Smith, M. R., 113
Angola, 173, 174, 222
Anhidrotic heat exhaustion, 86, 87, 89
Ankles, (swelling of) in aircraft, 27, 34
Ankylostoma brasiliense *see* Larva migrans
Ankylostoma duodenale *see* Hookworm
Anopheline mosquito, 61, 62, 143
Antidiuretic hormone, 38
Antihistamines, 49
Antimony, 98, 118, 120, 133
Antiphen *see* Dichlorophen
Aperient, 32-34
Apocrine glands, 38
Arabian Gulf, 103, 114
Arabian Peninsula, 11
Aralen *see* Chloroquine
Arbovirus, 10
Argentina, 122, 174, 223
Ascaris lumbricoides, 123
Ashton, N., 148
Asia, South East, 11, 65, 114, 132
Asmara, 15
Assab, 15
Assam, 97
Atlantic, 75, 76
Atrax spiders, 78
Australia, 4, 10, 11, 17, 18, 74, 77, 78, 100, 102, 108, 122, 174, 206
Australian antigen, 102
Austria, 175
Auto-inoculation, 8

Bab el Mandeb, 11
Bacillary dysentery *see* Shigellosis
Baghdad sore *see* Cutaneous leishmaniasis
Bahamas, 175
Bahrain, 4, 176, 221
Balantidiasis *(Balantidium coli),* 110

Balboa, 15
Balkans, 11, 15, 108, 111
Bancroftian filariasis, 143-145
Bangladesh, 6, 105, 132, 173, 176, 221
Banocide *see* Diethylcarbamazine
Barbados, 176
Barracuda, 76
Barraquilla, 15
Basal cell carcinoma, 140
Bathing, freshwater, 59
Beef, 120
Belem, 15
Belgium, 6, 176, 226, 232
Belize, 176, 223
Benzophenones, 49
Bephenium hydroxynaphate, 123, 125
Berbera, 15
Bergen, S. S. and Roels, G. A., 47
Bermuda, 176
Bhutan, 177, 221
Biguanide compounds, 65
Bilharzia *see* Schistosomiasis
Birmingham, 112
Bites, 135, 136
Bithionol (Bitin), 119, 120
Blackwater fever, 96, 170
Blackwidow spider, 78
Blood, disorders, 157, 170
  slide (malaria), 96
Bogota, 15
Bolivia, 16, 173, 177, 206, 223
Botswana, 177, 222
Brain Calcification, 111
Brand, J. J. and Whittingham, P., 27
Brazil, 13, 16, 59, 105, 108, 116, 173, 177, 223
Breakbone fever *see* Dengue fever
British Airways staff, 46, 53, 56
British Honduras *see* Belize
British Indian Ocean Territories, 222
British Solomon Islands Protectorate, 177
Browne, S. G., 131
Brucella melitensis also *B. abortus* and *B. suis*, 105, 113
Brucellosis, 105
Brugia malayi, 143
Brunei, 178
Bubonic plague *see* Plague
Bulgaria, 178
Bulmer, E., 52
Burma, 16, 97, 103, 108, 114, 143, 173, 178, 227
Buruli ulcer, 134
Burundi, 178, 222
Butler, T. *et al.*, 113
Calabar swellings, 130, 145, 146
Calcium carbonate (Os sepia), 46, 48, 49
California, 78
Cameroon, 173, 178, 222
Camoquin, 67
Canada, 16, 17, 178, 209, 210
Canal Zone (Panama), 15
Canary Islands, 179
Candida albicans, 128
Cane cutters cramps *see* Heat cramps
Cantharides, 78
Cape Verde Islands, 179, 222
Carbon monoxide poisoning, 28
Cardiovascular disease, 157, 166, 167
Caribbean, 76-78, 103, 129, 138, 143
Cartagena, 15
Casoni skin test, 123
Castellani's paint, 128
Cat, 120, 148, 150
Cattle, 120
Cayman Islands, 179, 206
Centipedes, 79
Central African Republic, 179, 206, 222
Cercaria, 116, 130
Cerebral malaria, 95
Chad, 173, 179, 206, 222
Chaga's disease, 98, 100
Chancroid, 137, 138
Cheilitis, solar, 140
Chickenpox, 9
Chigoe flea, 135
Chile, 179
China, 10, 59, 103, 108, 115, 119, 143, 180, 206, 223
Chinn, H. I., 24
Chloramination (of water), 57, 58
Chloramphenicol, 104, 113
Chloroquine, 65-67, 70, 96, 97, 119, 120
Chlorproguanil, 65-67
Chlorpromazine, 27
Cholangitis, 120
Cholera, 10, 11, 113, 114
  vaccination, 10, 16
Chondrodermatitis nodularis helicis, 140, 141
Choroidoretinitis, 100, 101, 146, 147, 149
Christabal, 15
Christie, A. B., 112
Chrysops fly, 61, 145
Chyluria, 144
Cinchona alkaloids, 65
Circadian rhythms, 29-33, 153
Circulatory system (in acclimatisation), 37
Clark, I., Bassett, C. and Andrew, L., 46
Climatic bubo *see* Lymphogranuloma venereum

Clioquinol (Chlorhydroxyquinoline), 55
Clonorchis sinensis, 120
Clostridium tetani, 151
Clothing, 27, 34, 42-45, 63, 70
Cluver, E. M. and Politzer, W. M., 46
Cobras, 74
Coelenterates, 76
Cold food, 58-60
Cole, L., 151
Collagen disease, 169
Colombia, 173, 180, 223
Colombo flop *see* Heat oedema
Colon, 15
Colubridae, 74
Comores Islands, 180, 222
Concorde, 33-34
Congenital ectodermal dysplasia *see* Ectodermal dysplasia, congenital
Congo, 99, 116, 180, 222
Conroy, R. T. W. L., 29
Constipation, 32-34, 83
Cook Islands, 181, 211
Coral, 76
  dermatitis, 77, 134
  ear, 77
Cordyloba anthropophaga, 135
Corsica, 97
Corticosteroids, 9, 10, 113
Corynebacterium diphtheriae, 134
Costa Rica, 180, 206, 223
Cotton, 43
Cowpox, 6
Creeping eruption *see* Larva migrans
Creeping itch *see* Larva migrans
Crosby capsule, 115
Crotalidae (pit vipers), 74
Croydon, 111
Cuba, 180
Culecine mosquito, 61, 62
Cussen, D. J., 56
Cutaneous leishmaniasis, 133
Cyanaea group, 77
Cyclizine, 26
Cyclops water crustacean, 147
Cyprus, 122, 181
Cysticercosis *see Taenia solium*
Czechoslovakia, 181

Dahomey, 173, 181, 222
Dapsone (diamino-diphenylsulphone), 132
Daraprim *see* Pyrimethamine
Deck ankles, 34
Dehydration, 28, 38, 114, 154
Dehydroemitine hydrochloride *see* Emetine
Delhi sore *see* Cutaneous leishmaniasis
Dengue fever, 102, 103, 131
Denmark, 6, 181, 229
Dennison, D. M., 155
Dermal leishmaniasis *see* Cutaneous leishmaniasis
Dermatobia hominis, 136
Dhobie's itch *see* Tinea cruris
Diabetes mellitus, 158, 170
Diamidines, 98
Diaminopyrimidines, 65
Diathiazamine, 125, 126
Dibothriocephalus latus see *Diphyllobothrium latum*
Dichlorophen, 122
Dick, Prof. G., 6, 7
Diethylcarbamazine, 120, 145, 146, 147, 149
Diloxanide furoate (furamide), 109
Dipetanolema perstans, 130
  streptocercia, 130
Diphenhydramine, 26
Diphtheria, 18
  vaccination, 18
Diphtheritic ulcer, 134
Diphyllobothrium latum, 120, 121
Distension, 27, 28, 34, 154
Diurnal rhythms *see* Circadian rhythms
Djibouti, 11, 15
Dog, 120, 148, 149
Dominican Republic, 182, 229
Dracontiasis *see* Guinea worm
Dracunculus medinensis, 143, 147
Ducrey's bacillus, 138
Durand-Nicolas-Favre disease *see* Lymphogranuloma venereum
Dysentery, amoebic *see* Amoebiasis
  bacillary *see* Shigellosis

E.111, 231-238
East, Far, 16, 78, 100, 116, 120, 124, 128, 138, 149
  Middle, 11, 16, 18, 59, 100, 103, 108, 114, 116, 120, 123, 124, 133, 134, 143, 147, 149
East-West flight, 30, 31
Eccrine glands, 38
Ectodermal dysplasia, congenital, 40
Ecuador, 181, 223
Eczema, 8, 10
  vaccinatum, 8
Edholm, O. G. *et al.,* 39
Eels, 76
Egypt, 20, 181, 182, 222
Eire, 210, 229, 232
Elapidae (kraits, mambas, cobras), 74
Elastosis, 140

Elephantiasis, 129, 130, 143, 145
El Tor variant, 11, 114
Emetine, 109, 110, 119, 120
  bismuth iodide, 109, 110
Encephalitis, post smallpox vaccination, 8, 9, 10
  post yellow fever vaccination, 14
Encephalomyelitis, acute viral, 103, 104
Endocrine disease, 170
Entamoeba coli, 108
Entamoeba hartmanni, 108
Entamoeba histolytica, 52, 108
Entamoeba nana, 108
Enterobius (oxyuris) vermicularis, 123
Enterovioform, 55
Eosinophil count, 117, 120, 121, 123, 125, 126, 146, 148, 149
Epidermophytosis, 127
Equatorial Guinea, 182, 222
Escherichia coli, 53-56
Espundia *see* Mucocutaneous leishmaniasis
Ethiopia, 6, 11, 19, 22, 104, 146, 173, 182, 222
European Economic Community, 225-232
Europe, Northern, 22
  Western, 16
Exanthems, 9

Fantus test, 86
Fasciolopsis buski, 119
Fasciolopsis hepatica, 119
Fatigue, 23, 31, 34, 39, 44, 45, 153, 155
Fibres, man-made, 42, 43, 45
Fièvre, boutonneuse, 61, 104
  nautique du Toulon, 61
Fiji, 143, 144, 182
Filariasis, 61, 71, 129-131, 143-148
Finland, 121, 182
Fireman's cramp *see* Heat cramps
Fish, 75, 76, 120, 121
Fitness to travel by air, 153-159
Fitzpatrick, T. B., 46
Flagyl *see* Metronidazole
Flea, 61
Flies, 58-61, 71, 146
Flight, food in, 28, 154
  medical advice in, 23-35
Fluids, maintenance of, 28, 32, 34, 40, 41, 44
Folic acid, 115
Frambaesia *see* Yaws
France, 6, 97, 149, 182, 226, 227, 232
Frei intradermal test, 137
French Guiana, 183
French Guinea, 183
French Polynesia, 183
French West Indies, 183
Fruit, 58-60
Fungal infections (feet, nails, ears), 127, 128
Furamide *see* Diloxanide furoate
Furman, K. I., 49
Furry, D. E. *et al.*, 154

G-6-PD (glucose-6-phosphate dehydrogenase), 67, 70
Gabon, 183, 222
Gambia, 99, 183
Game parks, 98
Gammaglobulin, 9, 20, 21, 22
Gastrointestinal disease, 158, 165
Geddes, A. M., 112
Germany, 121, 125, 183, 227, 232
Ghana, 11, 99, 173, 184, 222
Giardiasis *(Giardia lamblia),* 110, 115
Gibraltar, 184
Gilbert and Ellice Islands, 184, 206
Gippy tummy *see* Traveller's diarrhoea
Glandular fever, 105
Gnathostoma spingerum, 120
Goldie, E. A. G., 155
Gordon, J. E., 51, 53, 54
Graupers, 76
Greece, 6, 97, 184
Greek Islands, 97
Gregory, M. G. and Spalding, J. M. K., 18
Griseofulvin, 127, 128
Ground itch, 124
Guam, 185, 206
Guatemala, 146, 185, 223
Guinea, 99, 185, 222
  Gulf of, 145
Guinea worm, 130, 143, 147, 148
Guyana, 15, 111, 185, 223
Gymnothorax, 77

Haemolytic jaundice, 95
Haiti, 185, 223
Haj pilgrimage, 11
Handicapped children, 172
Haneveld, G. T., 53
Hansen's disease *see* Leprosy
Harbours, 59
Hargeisha, 15
Hats, 43, 44
Hauty, G. T. and Adams, J., 30, 31, 33
Hawaii, 53
Heat, cramps, 83, 85, 86
  exhaustion, 84, 86
  hyperpyrexia, 83, 84, 85

oedema, 84, 90
rash *see* Prickly heat
stroke, 83, 84, 85
syncope, 84, 90, 91
Hellman, K. and Weiner, J. S., 38
Hepatitis, homologous serum, 103
infective, 20, 22, 59, 102, 103
Herpes labialis, 94
Hertig, B. A. and Belding, H. A., 42
Hertig, B. A. and Sargent, F., 40
Heterazan *see* Diethylcarbamazine
Hikojima variant, 11, 114
Hodgkin's disease, 9, 10, 14
Honduras, Republic of, 185, 223
Hong Kong, 186, 221
Hookworm, 124, 125, 129
Hungary, 6, 186
Hycanthone, 119
Hydatid (cyst) disease, 120, 122, 123
Hydrocephalus, 101
Hydroids, 76, 77
Hydrophinae, 74
Hydrophobia *see* Rabies
Hymenolepsis nana see *Taenia nana*
Hyoscine, 26, 27
Hypogammaglobulinaemia, 10
Hypothalamus, 37
Hypoxia, 28, 154, 155

Ice, 58
creams, 59, 60
Iceland, 6, 123, 186
Ilmeus, 15
Immunisation(s), medically recommended, 15, 17-22
unfitness for, 7-10
Immunoglobulin *see* Gammaglobulin
Immunosuppressive drugs, 9, 10
Inawa variant, 10, 114
India, 4, 6, 10, 11, 14-16, 18-20, 22, 75, 90, 101, 103, 108, 110, 111, 114, 115, 119, 121, 132-134, 143, 147, 149, 173, 186, 220, 221
Indian Ocean, 76, 77
Indonesia, 76, 77, 108, 115, 143, 173, 186, 221
Infancy, 9, 10
Infantile diarrhoea, 54
Infective hepatitis *see* Hepatitis, infective
Insecticides, 62
Insect repellents, 63, 70, 71, 79
Insurance (medical), 230-232
International Health Regulations, 3, 4, 15, 16
International Sanitary Convention, 3
International Sanitary Regulations, now International Health Regulations
Intestinal gases, 27
Invalid passengers, air, 153-159
sea, 34, 35
Iodamoeba butschlii, 108
Iran, 114, 116, 186, 221
Iraq, 11, 116, 187, 221
Irian, West, 221
Iritis, 146, 147
Israel, 116, 187
Itabuna, 15
Italy, 97, 108, 114, 187, 227, 232
Ivory Coast, 187, 222

Jackal, 120
Jamaica, 187
James, W., 25
Japan, 59, 116, 119, 120, 143, 188
Jaundice, haemolytic, 95
Jelly fish, 76, 77
Jenner, Edward, 4
Jigger *see* Chigoe flea
Johnston, J. H. and Zakon, S. J., 46
Jordan, 188, 221

Kala-azar, 61, 97, 98
Kean, B. H. *et al.,* 56
Kean, B. H. and Smillie, W. G., 52, 56, 109
Kean, B. H. and Waters, S. R., 53, 54, 55
Kellogg, R. S., 25
Kenya, 70, 125, 189, 222
Kerandel's sign, 99
Keratitis, 146, 147
Keratocanthoma, 140
Keratoses, solar, 140
Kershaw, G. R., 52
Khmer Republic (late Cambodia), 19, 22, 59, 116, 173, 188
Kisumu, 15
Klebsiella sp., 53
Kleitman, N., 29
Korea, 119, 188, 206, 221
Kraft, E. R. *et al.,* 49
Kraits, 74
Kuwait, 90, 189

Ladell, W. S. S., 38
Lamblia intestinalis see Giardiasis
Laos, 19, 22, 59, 116, 189, 221
Lapudrine *see* Chlorproguanil
La rage *see* Rabies
Larva migrans, 124, 126, 129
Latrodectus spiders, 78
Lebanon, 53, 189
Lederer, L. G. and Kidera, S. J., 24

Leech, 79
Leeward Islands, 189
Leishmania brasiliensis, 133
Leishmania donovani, 97
Leishmania tropica, 133
Leishmaniasis, 61, 133
Leishmanin test, 98
Leprosy, 131, 132
Leptospirosis, 102
Lesotho, 189, 206
Leucoderma, congenital, 139
Leukaemia, 9, 10, 14
Liberia, 173, 189, 222
Libyan Arab Republic, 190, 222
Lichen tropicis *see* Prickly heat
Liver abscess (amoebic), 109
Living in warm climates, medical assessment, 161-172
Lizards, 75
Llano, G. A., 24
Lobban, M. C., 29
Loewenthal, L. J. A., 89
Loiasis, 61, 130, 143, 145, 146
Louse, 61
Loxosceles spiders, 78
Luxembourg, 190, 228, 232
Lymphangitis, 144
Lymphogranuloma venereum (lymphopathia venereum), 136, 137
Lymphoma, 9, 10, 14
Lyssa *see* Rabies

McArdle, B. *et al,* 42
McGirr, O. M., 154
McGregor, J., 52
Macao, 190
Madagascar *see* Malagasy Republic
Malabsorption syndrome, 114-116, 126
Malagasy Republic, 59, 116, 190, 222
Malaria, 61-70, 85, 93-97
  prophylaxis, 61-70
Malawi, 146, 173, 190, 222
Malaysia, 76, 143, 173, 190, 221
Maldives, 221
Male fern, 121, 122
Mali, 173, 190, 222
Malignant disease, 165
Malta, 191
Malta fever *see* Brucellosis
Mambas, 74
Manaos, 15
Manchuria, 119
Mangrove flies, 145
Man-made fibres *see* Fibres, man-made
Marseilles fever, 104
Marshall, J. 140
Massawa, 15
Mathews-Roth, M. M., 46
Mauritania, 191
Mauritius, 59, 75, 116, 191
Meclozine, 26
Mediterranean, 16, 75-77, 97, 104, 110, 123, 124, 133, 143
Meladine, 139
Melanin, 45
Mel, B., 100
Melon, 58
Meloxine, 139
Meningoencephalitis, 100
Mental deficiency, 101
Mepacrine, 65, 110, 121
Metronidazole, 109, 110
Mexenone (Uvistat), 49, 50
Mexico, 53, 56, 75, 78, 108, 113, 138, 146, 191, 206, 223
Microcephaly, 101
Micrococcus melitensis, 105
Microfilaria diurna, 143
Microfilarial periodicity, 144-147
Miliaria rubra *see* Prickly heat
Milk, purity, 57, 59
Millard, C. Killick, 6
Mills, J. N., 29
Minard, D., Belding, H. S. and Kingston, J. R., 39
Mineral waters, 57, 60
Miners cramp *see* Heat cramps
Mintezol *see* Thiobendazole
Mite, 61
Mombasa, 15
Monphytol paint, 127
Montenegro test, 98
Morocco, 70, 191, 222
Mosquitoes, 61, 62, 71
Mosquito proofing, 62, 63, 70
Motion sickness, 23-27
Mozambique, 173, 191, 222
Mycelia, 127, 128
Mycobacterium leprae. 131
Mycobacterium tuberculosis, 134
Mycobacterium ulcerans, 134

Naga sore *see* Tropical ulcer
Nairobi, 15
Nakae, R. *et al,* 55
Namibia, 222
Nanometres, 45, 50
Nauru, 191, 206
Necator americanus see Hookworm
Nelmes, Sarah, 6
Neomycin, 56
Neomycin-sulphatriad, 56

Neoplastic diseases, 9, 10, 14, 165
Nepal, 18, 173, 192, 221
Netherlands, 192, 228, 232
Netherlands Antilles, 192
Neurological disease, 158, 168
New Caledonia, 18, 192
New Guinea, 76, 195
New Hebrides, 193
New Zealand, 78, 193, 206, 210
Nicaragua, 193, 206, 223
Niclosamide, 122
Niger, 173, 193, 222
  River, 116
Nigeria, 9, 173, 193, 222
Nile Valley, 7, 9, 116
Niridazole, 118, 148
Nitrazepam, 32
Niue, 193, 206
Nivaquine *see* Chloroquine
Norfolk Island, 194
North-South flight, 31
Norway, 6, 194
Nylon, 43, 45
Nystatin, 128

Obesity (in acclimatisation), 39, 45
Oestradiol, 40
Ogawa variant, 10, 114
Olympic team, British, 39, 46, 56
Oman, 194, 221
Onchocerca volvulus, 143, 146
Onchocerciasis, 61, 130, 143, 146, 147
Opisthorciases, 120
Oriental sore *see* Cutaneous leishmaniasis
Otitis, externa, 77, 128
  media, 158, 159, 170
Overlanders, 19, 101
Overseas medical costs, 225-232
Owen, Raymond, 56

Pacific Islands, 103
Pacific Ocean, 76
Pakistan, 4, 6, 10, 11, 14, 16, 19, 20, 22, 101, 103, 108, 110, 132, 194, 221
Paludrine *see* Proguanil
Pamaquin, 65, 67, 70
Panama, 14, 15, 16, 195, 223
Papua and New Guinea, 195
Paradenitis nostras *see* Lymphogranuloma venereum
Paragonimus westermanii, 119
Paraguay, 195, 223
Paratyphoid A, 15, 110, 111, 113
  vaccination, 15, 17, 22
Paratyphoid B, 15, 110, 111, 113
  vaccination, 15, 17, 22
Paratyphoid C, 110, 111, 113

Penicillin, 134, 138
Pentamidine, 98, 100
Pentaquine, 65
Peru, 195
Philippines, 59, 116, 119, 173, 195, 221
Phipps, James, 6
Phlebotomus fever *see* Sandfly fever
Phoneutra spiders, 78
Phthalylsulphathiazole, 56
Physiological rhythms *see* Circadian rhythms
Pigmentation, 45
Pinkus, M. and Hunter, R., 46
Pinta, 138
Pinworm *see* Enterobius
Piperazine salts, 123, 124
Pit vipers, 74
Pityriasis versicolor *see* Tinea versicolor
Plague, 19, 61
  vaccination, 19, 22
Plasmodium (falciparum, malariae, ovale, vivax), 61, 63-65, 67, 93-96
Poland, 195
Poliomyelitis, 18, 105
  vaccination, 14, 18, 22
Pollock, T. M. and Reid, D., 21
Pork, 120, 125
Portugal, 97, 108, 116, 196
Portuguese Guinea, 196, 222
Portuguese man o' war, 76, 77
Portuguese Timor, 196, 221
Pregnancy, 9, 10, 14, 157
Pressurisation, 27, 154
Preston, F. S. *et al,* 31, 33
Prickly heat, 84, 85
Primaquine, 65, 67, 70
Proguanil, 65, 66, 67, 70
Promethazine, 26, 27
Provitamin-7-dehydrocholesterol, 45
Psoralens, 139
Psychiatric disorders, 159, 162-165
Puerto Rico, 115, 196, 206
Pyrexia, 40, 45
Pyrimethamine, 65, 66, 67, 70

Qatar, 196, 221
Q fever, 61, 104
Quinine, 65, 96

Rabies, 19, 149, 150
  vaccination, 19, 20
Radiation, galactic and solar, 33, 34
  therapy, 9, 10
Raw fish, 120
Red Sea, 77, 114
Rehydration, 114
Reid, H. Alastair, 73

Renal calculi, 171
Residence in warm climates, medical assessment, 161-172
Resochin *see* Chloroquine
Respiratory Disease, 157, 167, 168
Restaurants, 59, 60
Reunion, 59, 116, 196
Rhodesia, 59, 99, 116, 146, 173, 197, 222
Rickettsial diseases, 61
Rift Valley fever, 61
Robinson, S., 39
Rocky Mountain fever, 61, 104
Rodents, 102, 120
Romania, 197, 206
Roundworm *see* Ascaris
Rowe, B., Taylor, Joan and Bettelheim, K. A., 54
Russia, 11, 133, 149, 204
Rwanda, 197, 222

Sahara, 133
St. Lucia, 59, 116
Sakazaki, R., 55
Salads, 58, 59
Salmonella food poisoning (salmonellosis), 108
Salmonella sp., 53, 54, 57, 59
Salmonella typhi, 110
Salt, deficiency (heat exhaustion), 86
  maintenance of, 41, 44
El Salavador, 197, 223
Samoa, 143, 198, 206
Sand fly, 61, 71, 97, 133, 138
  fever, 61, 103
Sao Tome and Principe, 198, 222
Saudi Arabia, 11, 116, 198, 221
Schick test, 18
Schistosoma haematobium, 116, 117, 118, 131
Schistosoma japonicum, 116, 118
Schistosoma mansoni, 116, 117, 118, 131
Schistosomiasis, 59, 116-119, 130
Schwann cells, 131
Scorpion fish, 75
Scorpions, 77, 78
Scuba diving, 154
Sea, anemones, 76, 77
  sickness *see* Motion sickness
  snakes, 74
  travel, 34
  urchins, 77
Seborrhoeic dermatitis, 40
Selenium sulphide, 128
Senegal, 199, 222
Septrin, 101, 113
Seven day fever *see* Dengue fever
Sewage, 57, 59
Sex (in acclimatisation), 40
Seychelles, 70, 76, 199
Shaw, E. W. and Nicolai, J. Z., 47, 48
Sheep, 120
Shellfish, 58, 59
Shepherd, R. D. and Barlow, J., 31
Shigella infection (shigellosis), 107
Shigella sp., 53, 54
Shipwrecked, 87
Sicily, 97
Sierra Leone, 99, 116, 173, 199
Sikkim, 221
Singapore, 4, 103, 199, 221
Skevos Zervos disease, 77
Skin diseases, 170, 171
Sleep, 32, 34
Sleeping sickness *see* Trypanosomiasis
Sleeplessncss (post travel), 83
Smallpox, 1, 5-8, 105
  vaccination, 4, 6-10, 14, 16
Smoking in flight, 28, 34, 154
Snail, fresh water, 116
Snakes, 73-75
Snappers, 76
Sodium thiosulphate solution, 128
Soft sore *see* Chancroid
Solar cheilitis, 140
Solar dermatitis *see* Sunburn
Solar keratoses, 140
Solomon Islands, 199
Somalia, 200, 222
South Africa, Republic of, 200, 206, 211, 212, 222
Spain, 6, 11, 108, 114, 116, 200
Spanish fly, 78
Spiders, 78, 79
Spillane, J. D., 55, 56
Spirochaetosis icterohaemorrhagica *see* Leptospirosis
Sponge fishers disease, 77
Sprue tropical *see* Malabsorption syndrome
Sri Lanka (Ceylon), 75, 128, 173, 200, 221
Staphylococcal food poisoning, 108
Steak, 58, 120
Steinfeld, J., 4
Stibamine, 98
Stingray group, 75
Stoker's cramps *see* Heat cramps
Stonefish, 76
Street hawkers, 59
Streptomycin sulphatriad (Streptotriad), 56, 60
Strongyloidiasis *(Strongyloides stercoralis)*, 125, 126, 129

Subacute myelo-optico-neuropathy, 55, 56
Sudan, 116, 146, 173, 201, 222
Sulphonamides, 137, 138
Sunburn, 34, 45-50, 84-88
lotions etc (moisturising creams), 48-50
Sunglasses, 43
Suntan vehicles *see* Sunburn lotions
Supersonic flight, 33-34
Surinam, 201, 223
Swaziland, 201, 206, 223
Sweating, 37, 38
Sweden, 201
Swimming, 59
pools, 57
Switzerland, 121, 201
Sylvasun, 46-50
Syria, 116, 202, 221

TAB, 15, 17, 19, 21, 113
TABT, 17, 22, 113
Taenia echinococcus, 120, 122, 123
Taenia nana, 120, 121, 122
Taenia saginata, 120, 121, 122
Taenia solium, 120, 121, 122
Taiwan, 119, 202
Tanzania, 8, 10, 99, 202, 223
Tapeworm, 120-122
Telmid *see* Diathiazamine
Testosterone, 40
Tetanus, 17, 150-152
vaccination, 17, 18, 22
Tetrachlorethylene, 119, 120, 125
Tetracycline, 104, 113, 114, 116, 134, 137, 138
Thailand, 103, 108, 119, 143, 173, 202, 221
Thermoregulation, 37, 38
Thiabendazole, 125, 126, 129, 148
Threadworm *see* Enterobius
Ticks, 61, 71
Time zones, 29
Tinea cruris, 128
Tinea imbricata, 128
Tinea versicolor, 128
Toad fish, 76
Togo, 202, 223
Tonga, 202, 206
Toxocara canis (and *catis*), 129, 148
Toxocariasis, 148, 149
Toxoplasma dye test, 101
Toxoplasma gondii, 100
Toxoplasma slide test, 101
Toxoplasmosis, 100-101
Traveller's diarrhoea, 51-60, 107
Travel sickness *see* Motion sickness
Trench fever *see* Typhus, louse
Treponema carateum, 138
Treponema pertenue, 138
Treponema vincentii, 133
Trichiniasis or Trichinelliasis *(Trichinella spiralis),* 125
Trichuris trichuria, 125
Trimethoprim sulphamethoxazole, 101, 113
Trinidad, 149, 203
Trisoralen, 139
Tropical bubo *see* Lymphogranuloma venereum
Tropical sore *see* Cutaneous leishmaniasis
Tropical sprue *see* Malabsorption syndrome
Tropical ulcer (tropical sloughing phagedena), 133, 134
Trypanosoma cruzi, 100
Trypanosoma gambiense, 99, 100
Trypanosoma rhodesiense, 99, 100
Trypanosomiasis, 61, 71, 96-100, 131
Tryparsamide, 100
Tsetse fly, 61, 71
Tsutsugamuchi disease *see* Typhus, scrub
Tumbu Fly, 135
Tungu penetrans, 135
Tunisia, 70, 146, 203, 223
Turkey, 116, 203, 221
Turner, A. C., 53, 54, 56, 154
Turner, A. C., Barnes, R. M. and Green, R. L., 46
Typhoid, 15, 17, 101, 107, 110-113, 131
vaccination, 15, 17, 19, 22, 113
Typhus, 19, 104, 105
louse, 61, 104
murine, 61
scrub, 61
tick, 61, 71, 104, 105, 131
vaccination, 19, 22
Tyrosine, 45

Uganda, 99, 116, 134, 203, 223
Ulcers, 133, 134
Ultra violet rays, 45
Underdone meat, 58
Undulant fever *see* Brucellosis
United Arab Emirates, 203, 222
United Kingdom, 4, 6, 17, 18, 123, 203, 207-209
Upper Volta, 173, 204, 223
Urinary tract disease, 169
Uruguay, 204
U.S.A., 11, 16, 17, 18, 109, 115, 124, 204, 206, 212-220
U.S.S.R., 204, 223
Uvistat (Mexenone), 49, 50

Vaccination, cholera *see* Cholera vaccination
smallpox *see* Smallpox vaccination
yellow fever *see* Yellow fever vaccination
Vaccinia, 8, 9
Vaccinia immune globulin *see* Gamma globulin
Varicose veins, 27
Variola *see* Smallpox
Variola minor *see* Alastrim
Vedder, E. B. and Rosenberg, C., 46
Venezuela, 59, 116, 146, 204, 223
Venous stasis, 27, 153
Venous thrombosis, 83
Vibrio cholerae, 113, 114
Vietnam, 19, 22, 113, 115, 204, 206, 222
Vincent's ulcer *see* Tropical ulcer
Viperidae (vipers), 73, 74
Viprynium (Vanquin), 124
Viral hepatitis *see* Hepatitis, infective
Virgin Islands, 205, 206
Visceral leishmaniasis *see* Kala-azar
Vitamin A, 45-50
B_{12}, 115
D, 45, 46
Vitiligo, 128, 139

Wang, S. C. and Chinn, M. I., 25
Warble fly, 135
Water deficiency heat exhaustion, 87, 88
Water purity, 57, 59
Weil-Felix test, 104
Weil's disease, 102
West-East flight, 30-33
Whipworm *see Trichuris trichuria*
Whitfield's ointment, 128
Widal test, 113
Windward Islands, 205
Winterbottom's sign, 99
Wolf, 116
Wood, C. D., 27
Wood, C. D. and Graybiel, A., 27
Woodruff, A. W., 148
Woodson, R. D. and Clinton, J. J., 20
World Health Assembly, 11
World Health Organisation, 6, 7, 20, 70, 71
Wright, H. B., 154
Wucheria bancrofti, 61, 129, 143-145

Xylose excretion test, 115

Yangtze River, 116
Yaws, 138
Yellow Fever, 11, 61, 102
vaccination, 4, 7, 10, 11, 14-16
centres, 207-220
Yemen, 146, 205, 222
Yomesan *see* Niclosamide
Yugoslavia, 97, 205

Zaire, 173, 205, 223
Zambia, 206, 223
Zanzibar (Tanzania), 59, 70, 116, 223

PRINTED IN GREAT BRITAIN BY
LOWE AND BRYDONE (PRINTERS) LTD., THETFORD, NORFOLK